CREATION AND DISCOVERY

essays in criticism and aesthetics

creation and discov

ESSAYS IN CRITICISM AND AESTHETICS

eliseo vivas

THE NOONDAY PRESS

NEW YORK

1 9 5 5

for W. A. E.

contents

Preface : ix

1 LITERARY CRITICISM

Dreiser, an inconsistent mechanist : 3
Henry and William : 17
Kafka's distorted mask : 29
the two dimensions of reality in *The Brothers Karamazov* : 47

2 PROBLEMS OF AESTHETICS

what is a poem? : 73
a definition of the aesthetic experience : 93
literature and knowledge : 101
the object of the poem : 129
naturalism and creativity : 145

3 THEORY OF CRITICISM

criticism, intrinsic and extrinsic : 161
the objective correlative of T. S. Eliot : 175
the objective basis of criticism : 191

4 AESTHETIC THEORIES

four notes on I. A. Richards' aesthetic theory : 209
a note on the emotion in Dewey's theory of art : 223
Jordan's defense of poetry : 229
aesthetics and theory of signs : 249
Allen Tate as man of letters : 267

. . . the impulse to imitation, this elemental need of man, stands outside aesthetics proper and . . . in principle, its gratification has nothing to do with art.

WILHELM WORRINGER

The artist is just as much a discoverer of the forms of nature as the scientist is a discoverer of facts and natural laws.

ERNST CASSIRER

The great question as to a poet or a novelist is, How does he feel about life? What, in the last analysis, is his philosophy? When vigorous writers have reached maturity, we are at liberty to gather from their works some expression of a total view of the world they have been so actively observing. This is the most interesting thing their works offer us. Details are interesting in proportion as they contribute to make it clear.

HENRY JAMES

preface

My interest in aesthetics originally sprang from certain convictions which thirty-five years of study have confirmed and clarified. The first of these is that art is no mere adornment of human living or an activity the end of which is pleasure, or therapy, for which a substitute could easily be found, but an indispensable factor in making the animal man, into a human person. Another is that its proper use can be discovered by an analysis of the work of art as an embodiment of objective meanings and values. A third is that we cannot grasp the work of art objectively unless we bear in mind the act that creates it and the distinctive mode of experience that apprehends it. And still another is that the test of a satisfactory aesthetics is its adequacy to all of these factors taken together.

Early in my study I came to suspect that the word "expression," which is still the predominant notion employed in the analysis of art, serves but to muddy waters already turgid enough with partial theories and with fancies masquerading as facts. Once I saw through theories of expression, it was not difficult to hit upon the role that art plays in the creation of culture. Art *creates* culture: it creates the values and meanings by which a society fulfills its destiny. But the word "creation" requires interpretation. What the artist achieves through the act of creation is not the reshuffling into an apparently novel pattern of the values and meanings already institutionalized by society; to the extent that he is a genuine artist what he does is discover new meanings and values which he informs in the work of art. Works of art reveal something new, although in each case their newness is always a matter of degree; they reveal something which cannot be traced either to the biography of the artist or to the resources with which his tradition furnishes him, or the furniture of the world in which he lives.

A satisfactory aesthetic must then face the seeming paradox that art both *creates* and *discovers* values and meanings, and the failure of both the now almost universally abandoned theory of imitation and the dominant theories of expression, consists in the oversight by each of the truth the other asserts.

But if it is true that art both discovers and creates its informed substance, theories of meaning based on the analysis of signs as these function in ordinary discourse and in the language of science are incapable of doing justice to the manner in which the artistic symbol reveals that which the artist has to say—or, in the terminology of these essays, to the manner in which the work of art reveals its object. Nor can they do justice to the problem of the ontological status of the object.

However we shall explain the manner in which art reveals its object and however we account for the status of the object thus revealed, this we must hang on to with obstinate grip: what art does is reveal *in* and *through* itself what it is about, its object. That this is the case, contemporary criticism perceived when it grasped the fact that art cannot be translated or paraphrased. This is the most valuable insight we owe to the theory of expression in its idealistic formulation. But unless I am radically mistaken, aesthetics has failed to give an adequate account of the manner in which the symbol reveals its object. Aestheticians have often referred to the way in which the symbol functions in art by locutions which the simple-minded take to be merely indices of the confusion of those who use them. And, indeed, terms like *immanent meaning, reflexive meaning, presentational symbol,* and *aesthetic icon,* leave much to be desired. But what is much worse, they merely call attention to the problem; they do not explain it. The next step in aesthetics, I suspect, will be taken by the thinker who gives us an adequate account of the aesthetic symbol. All these essays pretend to do in respect to this problem is to define it.

When the spectator apprehends the work of art properly, it reveals to him the new meanings and values it informs. Subsequently he integrates them into his culture. The proper response to the work of art, the response that constitutes the distinctive aesthetic experience, is the grasp of the work by means of an act of *intransitive attention.* So to grasp it is to grasp it as a self-sufficient object. This conception of the aesthetic experience is, in actuality, a matter of degree. This definition of the aesthetic experience is a normative construct and hence at best an ideal goal which men approach, but which perhaps they seldom or never reach. We need it, however, in order to know what we are talking about when we try to understand art as distinct from other components of living.

Because the aesthetic experience is perhaps never entirely successful and because the meanings and values revealed in and through the work of art have deeply hidden connections with the meanings and values which have previously been successfully institutionalized in extant culture, our apprehension of the art object is never entirely "pure." To see how art reveals intransitively new meanings and values, and to see how they, nevertheless, enrich extant culture, we must draw the distinction between the object of art as grasped during the aesthetic experience and the same object as it functions indirectly in culture, when we turn from its radiant reality to our tarnished actual world. During the successful aesthetic experience the *ersatz* world in which we live disappears and the poem, or the musical composition, or the picture, becomes the sole reality and its boundaries mark the limits of the universe. Any one who has, however inadequately, however fleetingly, apprehended an object in its full intransitive self-sufficiency, knows what an outrage is done to ordinary language by those who speak of art in terms of imitation or illusion. After the successful aesthetic experience the lingering memory of the object of art—the more or less clearly remembered cadenced lines of the poem, or the snatch of melody and the world of harmony it teasingly suggests, or the ordered world of color and space of the picture—these are carried into the mongrel world of actual men, the world of half-truth and half-justice and half-dignity. They enter it with royal authority and reorganize it for us. They brighten it and authenticate it by serving us as the forms of its apprehension. And thus they redeem our effort.

Our experience is "pure" to the extent that in the intensity of apprehension of the object before us it appears as self-sufficient, that it excludes all conscious external reference. If we base our judgment solely on this experience we rightfully deny all connection between art and the rest of culture. Aestheticians who assert the autonomy of art without qualification and critics who, in the same spirit, assert the validity of intrinsic criticism, have in mind an abstract picture of art as functioning in the pure aesthetic experience. On the other hand, those who without qualification emphasize its non-resident function and the exclusive validity of extrinsic criticism, whether in psychological, sociological, or historical terms, are also justified, since they base their judgment on the no less incomplete fact that during the aesthetic experience the object of art has all sorts of connections with culture, although these connections are, for the most part, during the experience, hidden from consciousness. As is so often the case, both parties to the quarrel are right in what they assert and wrong in what they deny; and the truth is, as usual, torn limb from limb by contending systems, each of which claims to be its exclusive champion.

These, then, are the central problems that make up the burden of these essays. In them I have tried to work my way to my own theory because I was not fortunate to find a ready-made one which I could fully subscribe to. But I think of it as my own, not because I claim originality for it, but because I worked my way to it in my own tortuous manner. To a great extent I find my way by means of criticism of theories that for one reason or another attract my respectful attention. This, I fear, is the only way I know how to approach what I discern to be the truth. I dare hope, in any case, that a few sympathetic readers will find in the essays a sketch of the structural lines of a consistent system. Were I to write a system of aesthetics—something I shall not do—half of the work or more is already done in these essays.

My dominant interest in the manner in which art informs culture has controlled my literary criticism. I take it for granted that we can have no grasp of a poem—as I call the work of art fashioned in language—unless we grasp it as a unique and self-sufficient presenta-·tion. So to grasp it is in some effective way to possess ourselves of the principles that determine it to be the self-sufficient object that it is. But in the essays on criticism I have attempted, I have seldom been exclusively interested in the devices by which the poet achieves his ends. Assuming in the reader the trained capacity to grasp art as art, I have tried to explore the meanings and values embodied in some poems which gave me an insight into the modern world.

These essays represent a selection from the work of nearly a quarter of a century, for the earliest of them, although not published until 1935, was drafted in 1930. I have not hesitated to revise them in order to bring them closer to what I take to be a maturer grasp of the truth than I once had. To my astonishment, however, they called for less alterations than I expected; there is in them, for me at least, a surprising degree of systematic interrelationship and a continuity of purpose that I did not suspect them to possess before I began to go over them for selection. One revision that would have improved them I did not undertake: because they were written for different occasions and with different readers in mind, I found it necessary often to state, in many of them, certain basic notions I had stated elsewhere, and the result is a certain repetitiousness when the essays are read consecutively. But to have eliminated it would have called for carpentry I would have had neither time nor taste for. I hope that the reader will forgive this defect. I have arranged the essays in terms of their systematic interconnections, rather than chronologically, except that for practical reasons I put the essays on literary criticism in Section I.

Two of the essays have not been previously published, and three of them grew out of two *Mahlon Powell Lectures* I gave at Indiana University on 22 and 24 July 1952. At last the long awaited opportunity presents itself to express publicly to the members of the Philosophy Department of Indiana University my deep gratitude for the honor of the invitation and for their warm hospitality while my wife and I were their guests at Bloomington. Thanks are due to the Editors of the following magazines for permission to reprint: *The American Bookman, Ethics, The Journal of Philosophy, The Kenyon Review, The Philosophical Review, The Review of Metaphysics, The Sewanee Review,* and *The Western Review.*

ELISEO VIVAS

Department of Philosophy
Northwestern University
13 April 1954

1

LITERARY CRITICISM

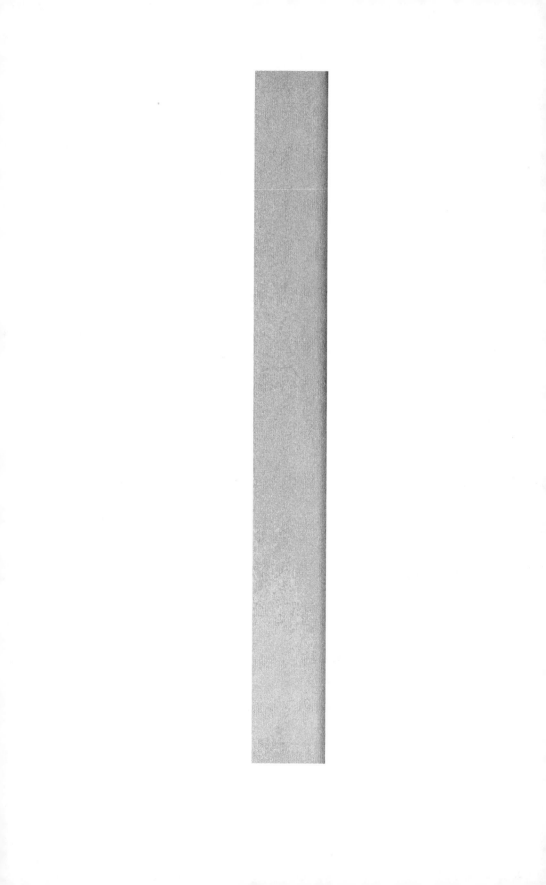

Dreiser, an inconsistent mechanist

1

It has become the fashion among the intellectuals to dismiss Dreiser in a lofty and condescending manner. The man, we are informed, is essentially confused. Hence he is not worth reading. He is passé. All the more so since, lacking style, he cannot even be superficially enjoyed. Of course if style is defined in terms of cadence and euphony, in terms of choice of the impeccable image and the inevitable word, Dreiser has no style. But if style is more than this, then he cannot be denied style. For he has architectonic genius. In his lumbering, slow, painful, clumsy way he builds up a story. And when the story is built, the manner fits the matter even to clichés and all. Again, there is no doubt that in an important sense Dreiser is a confused man. But to dismiss him without further qualification is to ignore his depth and his range.

Dreiser's philosophy may be naïve, as his critics have so often pointed out, but it should not be forgotten that "naïve" is a very relative term. In comparison with the views of professional philosophers his ideas are no doubt unacceptable. But they are not foolish or unworthy of consideration. They were held, and not in an essentially different form, by some of the best minds of the last half of the nineteenth century; and essentially in the very form in which he holds them, they are still held by a few professional philosophers. But even if we could be sure that these ideas deserve no consideration whatever as systematic philosophy, it cannot be denied that their essential contention that life has no intrinsic meaning, is still one of the basic tenets of contemporary naturalism. In any case, whether naïve or not, Dreiser's philosophy is still of interest to the reader of his novels. That he will continue to have readers, in spite of his present eclipse, we may be certain; because if he is not a philosopher he is a novelist. He has a deep sense of the dramatic movement of human life and a knowledge of its dark urges and baffled quality. He also has a wide range of vision and a deep sense of the relation of man to the cosmos. He is not only an American novelist but a universal novelist, in a very literal sense of the word. The mystery of the universe, the puzzle of destiny, haunts him; and he, more than any of his contemporaries, has responded to the need to relate the haunting sense of puzzlement and mystery to the human drama. No other American novelist of his generation has so persistently endeavored to look at men under the form of eternity. It is no love of paradox, therefore, that prompts the assertion that while Dreiser tries to demonstrate that man's efforts are vain and empty, by responding to the need to face the problem of destiny, he draws our attention to dimensions of human existence, awareness of which is not encouraged by current philosophic fashions. It is then the surest sign of critical naïvete to dismiss Dreiser on the counts of being naïve and lacking style. His prose is indeed fuzzy, his language a string of clichés; his thought is indeed naïve in many respects. But the prose is the man; his architectonic is superb; and his vision is turned towards horizons the existence of which contemporary novelists seldom suspect. But if all these claims can be asserted consistently the need arises to explain how a man guided by a naïve and unacceptable philosophy can be said to occupy the position he does—can be said to have the depth of insight he possesses.

2

Early in his youth Dreiser read and accepted the then popular materialistic mechanism. The picture of the world which he gained from
his youthful reading must have been grasped by him with a deep
sense of relief. He hated for deep personal reasons anything remotely
allied with religion. Mechanism had the sanction of science. And
the theory of evolution, with its emphasis on the ruthlessness of the
struggle for survival, was merely an extension on a larger scale of
what he himself had observed in Indiana, in Chicago, and in New
York. He was untrained in the ways of rigorous analysis; and the
materialism he accepted on affective rather than logical grounds was
reduced by him to the notion of "chemisms," a word which has
on him no doubt a strong and subtle emotive power. Through
"chemism" he thinks he explains adequately all phenomena, organic
no less than inorganic. Life is chemism, personality is chemism, the
emotions are chemisms. There can really be no difference between
the urge of the lower animals, human sexual desire, and any senti-
ment that we have agreed to call higher. The animal in the darkness
of the forest, Casanova, Dante, and Petrarch, as well as the Marquis
de Sade or an Indiana young couple on a swing under an apple
tree—they are all examples of chemism, and are fundamentally but
the same thing. On his conception of chemism Dreiser grounds an
individualistic philosophy. He tells us, not in these terms but to the
same effect, that society is a mechanical addition of atomic individuals, each an independent package of force, each a self-contained
monad, determined somehow by chemical forces, pushing or yielding, as it comes into contact with forces larger or smaller than its
own. Thus society is but an additive compounding of mechanical
forces, dynamically seeking a harmony which is constantly dis-
rupted by the addition of new forces or by the disappearance of old
ones. The individuals who additively make up society have each
their own urges and their own strength. One seeks power, one
peace, one the realization of an artist, the other security. Each encounters obstacles which baffle him or meets with helping currents
which aid him toward his goal. The strong ones forge ahead, and
the weak ones submit and are the tools of their betters. This is
Darwinism at its starkest. When powerful individuals like Cowper-

wood appear, they disrupt the previously struck balance. The giants who have already arrived, and whose power is threatened by the appearance of a new one, gang up against the newcomer, use the pigmies for their purposes, the conflict quickens, and at the end, whatever the result, a new temporary balance is struck.

In such a pitiless Darwinian world, where might is ultimate lord, he tells us that it is not morality but the appearance of it that counts. The hearty acceptance of ethical principles puts a handicap on the individual in the struggle. But pretense is a useful and invaluable aid. Society is a masked ball—that beauty, dancing so gaily with that man, is an old woman, has false teeth, suffers from arteriosclerosis, and has a bad breath in the morning; and the gallant leading her may be a beggar, or a horse thief, or a rat catcher, or a clever rogue, so cleverly disguised that he can deceive even himself. There you can see a great idealist preaching democracy and the supreme worth of each human personality; everybody wonders at his kindness and admires his gentleness. But we are all easily deceived. He is really a small man with a mean soul; he preaches equality because he hates and fears excellence; and he is a mirror of kindness because he achieves through his generosity the sense of power which big-souled men achieve directly and frankly. He hates selfishness, because it interferes with his own selfishness; and hates self-assertion, because he cannot tolerate his claims being crossed. He hates men who are arrogant, and loves modest men. But if we only look we can see he is himself the very essence of arrogance. And so with the others. Society is a masked ball. But there is one crime for which there is no forgiveness, no absolution—no man must appear in public without a mask. And a crime still greater, no man must ever tear a mask from another and leave him uncovered.

But this is not the whole picture, for Dreiser tells us that human society is made up of a number of subsocieties arranged hierarchically in terms of power and wealth, and in each one of these subdivisions the same pattern repeats itself. Within each group there are honors to be gained, privileges to be conquered, and relative ease and security to be enjoyed. And in each one, low or high, these are come by in the same way—through cunning, pitilessness, and luck.

In such a pitiless Darwinian world what can morality really mean? Morality is a technique of control, a means of keeping in check those men whose powerful and strong drives would wreck the balance struck by the group; it is in short a conspiracy of some of the masters and the slaves to keep the parvenu from running amuck. But of course truly strong men disregard the mythical sanctions which may deceive the weak but cannot deceive them. And for that reason no moral code ever fits the facts. One of his characters, obviously speaking for Dreiser himself—for he has expressed the same idea in the first person—was "always thinking in his private conscience that life was somehow bigger and subtler, and darker than any given theory or order of living." And for this reason, "life is to be learned from life, and the professional moralist is at best but the manufacturer of shoddy wares." These wares, shoddy and gratuitous for the strong, have another purpose—they are the sole consolation of the weak and the oppressed. And they may even have an aesthetic value, like the ephemeral rainbows one often catches sight of on the spray over an angry wave; but, like them, though they may be beautiful, they are utterly ineffective for controlling the danger of the sea.

In such a world, what meaning can life have? None of course. In a world which is the product of blind forces, in a world of chemic determinations and mechanical resolutions, how can one expect that life have meaning?

Privately his mind was a maelstrom of contradictions and doubts, feelings and emotions. Always of a philosophic turn of mind, this peculiar faculty of reasoning deeply and feeling emotionally was now turned upon himself and his own condition and, as in all such cases where we peer too closely into the subtleties of creation, confusion was the result . . . the world knew nothing. Neither in religion, philosophy nor science was there any answer to the riddle of existence. Above and below the little scintillating plane of man's thought was—what? Beyond the optic strength of the greatest telescope—far out upon the dim horizon of space—were clouds of stars. What were they doing out there? Who governed them? When were their sidereal motions calculated? He figured life as a grim dark mystery, a sad semi-conscious activity turning aimlessly in the dark. No one knew anything. God knew nothing—least of all himself. Malevolence, life living on death, plain violence—these were the chief characteristics of existence. If one failed in strength in any way, if life were not kind in its bestowal of gifts, if one were not born to fortune's pampering care—the rest was misery. In the days of his strength and prosperity the spectacle of existence had been sad enough: in the hours of threatened delay and defeat it seemed terrible . . . The abyss of death! When he looked into that after all of life and hope, how it shocked him, how it hurt! Here was life and happiness and love in health—there was death and nothingness—aeons and aeons of nothingness . . .

Dreiser's own life, a life of arduous labor and the most scrupulous artistic sincerity, has no more meaning than that of anyone else. And this is what he says of it in the *Bookman*, September, 1928, in a statement of his beliefs:

I can make no comment on my work or my life that holds either interest or import for me. Nor can I imagine any explanation or interpretation of any life, my own included, that would be either true—or important, if true. Life is to me too much a welter and play of inscrutable forces to permit, in my case at least, any significant comment. One may paint for one's own entertainment, and that of others —perhaps. As I see him the utterly infinitesimal individual weaves among the mysteries a floss-like and wholly meaningless course—if course it be. In short I catch no meaning from all I have seen, and pass quite as I came, confused and dismayed.

3

In its most important details this is the picture of man and the universe which Dreiser seems to believe he has discovered in his experiences and expressed in his novels. But fortunately for his greatness as a novelist, his explicit intellectual vision of the world is not point by point congruous with his vision as a novelist. And the philosophy which he has given us in essays and intercalated in the form of editorial comments in the movement of his dramas is not always true to the record. For there is more to his own concrete dramatic picture of men and society than he finds room for in his mechanistic philosophy. And if we miss this more, we miss, I am afraid, what is truly significant in Dreiser. His mechanism is indeed inadequate, but his dramatic vision of the world within the range of its discriminations is fully ripe and mature. His characters are alive and real, moving and acting and brooding with all the urge and hesitation, passion and fear, doubts and contradictions, of fully real human beings. Few contemporary novelists have built up characters as solid, as three dimensional, as fully bodied, as Dreiser. And the reason he has succeeded where others have failed is that in spite of his naïve mechanism, few novelists respond to human beings as sensitively as he does. He admires or pities all kinds of men—the forceful money-makers; the weak ones who are born to fail and suffer; the brilliant women who walk in and con-quer; the respectable men and the disreputable ones; the masters and the slaves; the happy ones and the victims of meaningless forces who are condemned to live a life of pain, frustration, and denial.

Dreiser not only responds to human beings in a very immediate and sympathetic manner, but what is more important within the limits of his vision, he understands them. And his understanding goes far beyond the chemisms through which he thinks he explains them. For what does it mean to understand a man? Does it not mean to discover some order, some underlying direction, some permanent tendency by reference to which we as observers are able to organize what we know of him, and to decide what is important or relevant and what is not? And this is the reason we read Dreiser and read him with profit, because in spite of his chemisms, and in spite of his poor taste in words and phrases, in spite of his fuzzy prose, and his addiction to unimportant realistic detail—which is never really as unimportant as we in our impatience think it is—we discover in his books insights about human beings we did not have before.

But what is most important of all, his dramatic picture of society and of morality do not corroborate the philosophic theories which he has put forth, and which have caused such violent reaction from conservative critics. His dramatic picture of men is not a picture of the hard atomic entities which his individualistic mechanism tells him they are. Nor does he really see society, when he looks at it dramatically and not editorially, as a mere collection of atomic individuals. His characters are often a-social forces, working for ends destructive of the social equilibrium. But never completely so. Nor is society a mechanical addition of forces. Cowperwood, his reckless Robber Baron, is propelled by a strong will directed to the conquest of power and reckless of the claims of society in its search for satisfaction. But even Cowperwood is not utterly destructive, and his genius, in the pursuit of its own arbitrary ends, has a constructive side to it in quite an objective social sense. Nor is his will utterly arbitrary, nor is he utterly free and a-moral. Less so is Kalvin, a powerful but respectable and conservative business man, and Wittla, the genius. We need not go any farther. The personalities and characters of his big men as well as of his small are socially determined, and this in turn means really that it is society that furnishes the shark-man with the precise mold through which his power expresses itself and sets the limits to how far that will shall express itself unchallenged. We do not need to read this into his picture of society; it is there for us to see. Some of his Titans may even be utterly devoid, as he thinks, of ordinary human ties; this is never entirely the case, but grant it. Still these Titans are what they are only in terms of the forces that shaped them, and thus it is that only in the society in which they were reared could they find the necessary outward resistance in terms of which their will can express itself. Grant this, and one has to grant that the ties one has with society are integral and internal, and the relations that exist not external to the individuals which make up society. Thus from his own picture he could have seen that society is an organic pattern and makes the individual possible as much as the individuals makes it possible. If we consider the dramatic picture and disregard the editorial bias, morality is not a club with which the individual is struck down and kept in line. It is, properly conceived, the molds in which the activities of individuals express themselves. There can be no matter without form, no activity without style. And the morality of any society is but the permissible style of activity; the manner in which individuals which are organic parts of it act.

Thus conceived, morality is always larger than the explicit codes through which men say they rule their actions, and life larger than any of its codes and rules, as Dreiser claims. But it cannot be larger than the forms and manners in which it expresses itself. "Life is larger than morality," only if morality is a set of rules, a code, which is fixed once for all and is too rigid to give way. And of course the moralist's wares are then shoddy wares. But it is co-extensive with living if it is conceived as the manner life finds in which to express itself and through which it channels its forces. The mechanistic, atomistic conception of society and the belief that the individual is prior to it in both a logical and existential sense make this notion of morality incomprehensible. But a more acceptable conception of society would urge as part of it the dependences, the interconnections, and the often deep and obscure bonds which underly many of the stresses felt by men in daily life. Even in overt conflict, interdependences exist and rules of behavior obtain. Men cannot live in utter and complete chaos. There are laws and rules of war as well as of peace. Normally men simply have to trust others and depend on them mutually to some extent at least. Nor are we free, even the least sentimental of us, from loyalties and sympathies and deep-rooted commitments to value. Factors such as these, bonds, ties, forces, deep interconnections, are always found. And they make up society as much as the will of the strong and the yielding of the weak. And they do so in Dreiser's pictures as much as they do in actuality.

4

Why does he not see this? The phenomenon is common. It is simply the common failure of readjusting theory to facts. Dreiser does not find the moral code in which he was brought up by a narrow and intense father anywhere operative in the world into which, ill equipped but sensitive, he was thrust. Therefore, he concludes, there is no morality. But why is there not? Because emotionally he has never ceased to demand that morality be what he was taught it was—a rigid code, where idealism is always unmistakably good, and selfishness always an unalloyed evil. Yet in his novels Dreiser shows that morality is actually operative in the world, even though it is the editorial philosopher who officiously undertakes to squeeze on the palette of the artist the hues with which the latter paints; or, to put it directly, Dreiser does find morality, although his philosophic prejudices succeed to some ex-

tent in controlling his artistic vision and limiting it to the lowest
and least admirable values. Yet for all his prejudices, his characters
are capable of pity, of courage, and occasionally even of idealism,
as often as they are of ruthless strength and indifference to their
fellows. And for all the successful exercise of arbitrary force with
which, with impunity, some men seek to control their fellows, in
Dreiser's pages we find that in some sense and to some degree
society is nevertheless regulated by immanent moral forces, guided
by values that control, however haltingly and weakly, the actions
of the strongest no less than of the weakest of men.

Essentially the same can be said of Dreiser's conviction that life
has no meaning. Equipped with his materialistic lenses, Dreiser reports he cannot find in the cold ranges of the universe a direction
to guide us and give our activity the assurance of transcending significance that we all so profoundly crave. Hence his perplexity, his
sense of futility, his monotonous refrain regarding the vanity of
effort in such a sorry world. But would he have been as disap-
pointed as he was, were it not for the fact that, in spite of his
philosophic commitments, he insisted on purpose, and that his
dramatic vision suggested to him, in however confused a way, that
his demand was capable of some sort of objective satisfaction? For
in spite of his futilitarian philosophy, his characters never genuinely lacked guiding purposes. One of his characters finds the meaning of his activity in success, another in power, another in love, and
another in religion. Dreiser himself found it in his uncompromising
expression of his vision of life. What other meaning can life have
for the novelist than that which is defined by the values his characters espouse? That Dreiser painted men and women as capable
of espousing values shows that he saw, although his philosophy
did not allow him to acknowledge, that life has in fact purpose.
Whether the meaning that his characters find in their lives is
anchored in the nature of Being itself or not, is no problem that
the novelist (unless he is depicting technical philosophers inquiring into the problem of axiology) need concern himself with; nor is
it a problem that as novelist he is equipped to solve. But why, if
Dreiser demanded meaning and if he found it in his novels, did
he not acknowledge it? Obviously what happened was that Dreiser
the artist was never allowed to challenge the philosophic editor.

But fortunately for us, neither did the philosophic lenses of the editor succeed in altogether obfuscating the artist's vision. Dreiser thought he knew that the universe is a purposeless affair; but fortunately for his art he never did learn the lesson his philosophy should have taught him, namely that for a consistent mechanist the very demand for meaning is nonsensical. Fortunately the sincere artist magnificently contradicted the self-taught materialist and found a purpose that, had he been consistent, he could not have found.

Thus Dreiser is a better artist than his philosophy permitted him to be. As philosophic editor, he insisted in pointing out to the reader that the picture he painted was meaningless and that the lives of his characters had no purpose. But within his novels his men and women frequently find that life has a driving significance which overpowers them. Sometimes the meaning it has is sinister; sometimes pathetic; sometimes it almost reaches tragic heights; but meaning it usually has. And if life's meaning is something sad or tragic, in Dreiser's own life, in his enormous capacity for pity, we find an example of a man who, through his work, gave the lie to his own theories.

1938

Henry and William

A radical temperamental difference seems to separate Henry James from his brother, orienting them towards opposite quarters. This difference expresses itself in many ways, but most obviously through the countries in which each chose to settle after their nomadic youth. William roots himself in Cambridge while Henry finds "a tight anchorage, a definite little downward burrow in the ancient world." And the different residences each chooses are symbols that stand for deep and complex spiritual affinities. William is an American in a special sense; he justifies certain forces and tendencies in his native culture which are widely accepted as distinctively American, and in doing so he helps to fix them, at the same time endowing them for the imagination with something of his own genial, romantic flavor. On the other hand, Henry finds his own creative needs best satisfied by a life in which the millen-

nial values of our Western culture are preeminent. There is, therefore, a temptation to view each brother in terms of the antithesis
involved in the words "European" and "American." But even if
the antithesis were itself valid, it would be useless for our purpose,
for it would grossly over-simplify the range and complexity of their
minds, overlooking similarities by focusing on differences. Thus we
shall see, in the two notes that follow, that while on the one hand,
in their moral conceptions they stand, as it were, back to back,
there is a resemblance between them, on the other, in the way in
which they conceive the mind's mode of apprehension, in which
they conceive the process, that is, through which the mind enters
into relations with its world.

1

As Henry James progressively gains in maturity of expression his
brother exhibits an increasing lack of understanding of his art.
William raises against Henry's last manner the same objections
that have often been raised since by his detractors. Henry's books
are difficult and subtle and above all lack "life." Henry's diffidence
before his brother deprives us of a complete answer to these strictures. In his reply to William's remarks on *The Golden Bowl* he
defends his work by pleading better knowledge than his critic of
his own creative needs and insisting on the right to express his own
vision of the world, such as it is. But he could have added that the
"life" that his brother thinks he lacks he abundantly possesses, for
the term need not mean, as it does for William, the satisfaction
of the largest possible number of desires. Henry expresses great admiration for the expansive, voracious life. But "life" can also legitimately refer to the thrill that comes from acuity of perception
organized by an intellect into self-contained form. Innumerable
times Henry James gives us hints that this is what life means to
him. Let us remember Millie's reflections in *The Wings of the
Dove*:

> There were immense excursions for the spirit of a young person at
> Mrs. Lowder's mere dinner party; but what was so significant and
> so admonitory as the fact of their being just possible? What could
> they have been but just part, already, of the crowded consciousness?

Life is consciousness crowded with discriminations of subtle shades of character and mood, temperament and attitudes. But the passion and the thrill are there. As in a quiet auction, where a nod of the head or a hand almost imperceptibly raised is a gesture which conceals intense anxiety and anticipates the exultation of success or the inward vacuum of defeat, so in Henry James. Thus it was with full sincerity that he answered H. G. Wells's criticism as he did: "Of course, for myself, I live intensely and am fed by life, and my value, whatever it be, is in my own expression of that."

Henry, in other words, repudiates the anti-intellectualism which underlies his brother's vision of the world, and which opposes life to thought, *real* living to theorizing, action to contemplation. He finds, as he puts it in *The Sacred Fount*, that "for real excitement there are no . . . adventures as intellectual ones." For some men at least, thinking is itself the most intense way of living. And thinking, for the artist, consists in the resolution of his "problems." These are solved, as any problem is, by the artist's use of his intellect. This, I take it, is what he means when in the letter to Wells already mentioned he says, "It is art that makes life, makes interest, makes importance . . . and I know of no substitute whatever for the force and beauty of its process. . . ."

The opposing conceptions of what constitutes life give rise, naturally, to a conflict in the ethical attitudes of Henry and William, into the examination of which, as I indicated above, I should like to put some effort. But before proceeding it is necessary to go a little out of the way in order to explain the sense in which I hold the belief that the fundamental force that fed Henry James's artistic passion and sustained his creative effort was his interest in the clarification of the ethical structure of his world. If there is a figure to be found in the carpet of his work, I suggest that this is the one. This is not to deny that he was, as Mr. Joseph Warren Beach puts it in his fine study of James, "ethically neutral." But what does ethical neutrality mean? The artistic process does not consist in lowering a bucket into the muddy current of the actual and emptying all one picks up into a book. The artist must wait till the bucket settles before he can hope to catch the elusive silvery animals that shall make his feast. It is, in plain terms, a process of

discrimination and selection. But surely this implies a bias, a principle—whether implicit or explicit—which controls the choice of
material that the artist deems worthy of treatment. Nor can this
principle be a purely aesthetic one; the man's character, such as it
may be, his preferences and aversions, exercise their control along-
side his artistic taste—or we shall have to assume a much more
complete split in the artist's personality than we have warrant for
assuming. The purely aesthetic man, like the economic man, is a
very useful scientific abstraction; but it is at best (or at worst) only
a limit which the artist can hope to approach or recede from in
varying degrees. And thus the artist's product must bear traces of a
moral attitude as well as express an aesthetic personality. These
traces we shall find, not in a moral the artist will want to preach
or a cause he will want to defend, but implicit in his treatment of
the values embodied in his drama and in the perspective from
which he reviews the relationships existing among his characters.
"Ethical neutrality" in art is nevertheless possible. But it consists
solely in submissiveness to the inner thrust of the dramatic inci-
dent which has been selected for treatment, in humility before the
object's inward dialectic, as against the arrogant and pre-intended
dominance with which the partisan violates, for his own subjective
ends, the autonomy of his material.

In order to discover Henry James' underlying ethical attitudes,
a very detailed analysis of all his work would be necessary. Here,
rather than generalize high above the data themselves, I will confine myself to one novel only, and I am taking one of his purely
English ones, in order not to get entangled in the complications
of "the international theme." I take this theme from our point of
view to be but an illustration of the underlying ethical presuppositions to be found in Henry James' most important novels throughout the whole span of his creative activity. I propose therefore to
look into The Spoils of Poynton, for it is a book which critics generally agree represents high excellence of workmanship without
exhibiting the distracting difficulties of his last manner. By no
means one of his greatest works, it ranks, however, with his best;
and I believe that it embodies clearly and fully his ethical vision.
Let me emphasize, however, that the same conception of the moral

life is to be found in his other works; or at least, so far as I know, in most of them; and that nothing that contradicts it is to be found in anything he ever wrote.

The story, it will be remembered, is about a "row" (as James himself calls it) between Mrs. Gereth and her son Owen, over the exquisite "Things" which she has collected during her husband's life-time, but which she will have to surrender to her son's future wife, Mona. Rather than let the things go to Mona, who is a woman utterly devoid of taste, and who lacks even a suspicion of the passion for beauty that has been squandered on Poynton, Mrs. Gereth audaciously moves them off to the cottage her husband left her. But she informs her friend, Fleda, that she will return them to Poynton if Fleda, for her own sake and for Mrs. Gereth's and Owen's, consents to accept Owen as a husband. For Fleda admits that she is in love with Owen. Mrs. Gereth will surrender "the spoils" to her because she genuinely appreciates them. This is the happy solution, thinks Mrs. Gereth, of the row. For Mona cannot be allowed to count—her vulgarity, aggressiveness, and even the quality of her feeling for Owen puts her outside the range of consideration. And Owen, alienated from Mona by her unyielding insistence that his mother return all the things before she will marry him, finally comes around to his mother's plan.

This is Fleda's chance. She can have Owen, whom she loves, ease and security, which she desperately needs, and Poynton, to whose beauty she responds as Mrs. Gereth does. But Fleda cannot accept Owen. She will not purchase her own happiness at the cost of a dishonorable act on Owen's part. "She could never be the girl to be drawn in, she could never lift her finger against Mona. There was something in her that would make it a shame to her to have owed her happiness to an interference. . . ." To Mrs. Gereth, Fleda's decision represents merely "systematic, idiotic perversity," and not high honor, nor respect for another's pledged word. But Fleda guided by a high ideal, regards the claims of principle as higher than those of personal convenience.

"You mustn't break faith" (Fleda said to Owen). . . . "The great thing is to keep faith. Where *is* a man if he doesn't? If he doesn't he may be so cruel. So cruel, so cruel, so cruel," Fleda repeated. "I couldn't have a hand in *that*, you know."

For Fleda has not been able to lose sight of Mona, and she is certain that Mona will never give Owen up and that Owen's anger is a passing thing. And this is precisely what Mrs. Gereth can not see—what the worldling will not see—the wounds he inflicts on his own character (One couldn't have a hand in *that*) and on another's feelings (He may be so cruel. So cruel) by his morality of expedience, his paltry felicific calculus, his Levantine haggling over what is the maximum of satisfied desires—and invariably it is his own claims, not the other's, that represent that maximum.

Now the following appears to me clear, as I ponder the details of this beautiful book: Henry James does not side with Fleda, but allows Mrs. Gereth to present her own side to the best of her ability, which is quite considerable. Yet he sees Fleda as possessed of a beauty of personality, a sensibility, which her older friend lacks. Without partiality to either, his own apprehension of the meaning of the conflict is perfectly clear from the book itself. It is a conflict between ethical principles and expedience, and the latter is not without its own rational force. But it is Fleda's character that stands out against that of the others. I am not merely guessing, for Henry James himself informs us of the fact in his preface to *The Spoils*. Fleda is a "free spirit" while her elder friend flounders "in the dusk of a disproportionate passion." But it would seem that only one who has reflected deeply on the moral problem and who has seen the cruelty that hides behind the expedience could have conceived *The Spoils*. Loyalty to the pledged word, kindness as against cruelty, honor as against expedience—these are not the only specific values with which James concerns himself in his books; but they are basic to his vision of the world; and it is in his clear apprehension of what these values mean in a world in which intelligence is usually the tool of a self-assertive or sometimes merely meddlesome, but always immoral, will, that the quick of his interest lay. James is neutral throughout; but his artistic conscience can not eliminate his own conscience as man. Without the latter the artist would obfuscate objective differences—as these appear to his sensibility and character—on which he is dependent for content.

The contrast between Henry's moral vision and William's moral theory is sharp and shocking. For the beauty of character, faithfulness to the pledged word, and scrupulous sensibility for the feelings and rights of others, which we have seen to be implicit in Henry's vision of life, we must now substitute a barely attenuated version of Darwinism in the moral life, which hardly conceals the doctrine that successful force is the right. But before we go farther let us first note that the discussion that follows refers to William James's *theory* and not to his own personal character or conduct, whose ethical rectitude furnishes the best refutation we can hope to find of his own theory. Let us also note that it was he himself who used the word "expedience" to refer to his notion of right: ". . . the right is only the expedient in the way of our behaving. Expedient in almost any fashion, and expedient in the long run and on the whole of course. . . ." *Expedient in almost any fashion and in the long run;* but in the long run the weak go under and the echo of their cries dies out and is forgotten. And yet this is the ethical flower of pragmatic wisdom.

At the basis of his ethical theory, which we find expounded in an essay entitled "The Moral Philosopher and the Moral Life," lies the belief that any claim or demand whatever carries with it a *moral obligation* of fulfillment, just because it represents a claim and for no other reason. But note that a "claim" or "demand" at this level of ethical discourse can be nothing more than a mere desire of which we happen to be aware. So that by itself my unfounded anger, or malice, or envy, constitutes a *moral* obligation in its bare psychological status, and is not immoral or even amoral. But how can we in our sorry world, in which so often one desire excludes another, satisfy them all? We can not. The moral man therefore "invents" a way of satisfying his desires "which will also satisfy the alien demands." And it is here that the Darwinism of the theory begins to show itself clearly. For by means of these inventions society "has shaken itself into one relative equilibrium after another." And he goes on, in language which distinctly recalls Darwin:

> as our present laws and customs have fought and conquered other past ones, so they will in turn be overthrown by any newly discovered order which will hush up the complaints that they still give rise to, without producing others louder still. . . . Pent in under every system of moral rules are innumerable persons whom it weighs upon,

and goods it represses; and these are always rumbling and grumbling in the background, and ready for any issue by which they may be set free.

But this is tantamount to saying that it is the successfully established force that makes right. Otherwise put, the shake-ups of history—remember the Albigensians or the Jews of Poland under the Herrenvolk—have utterly liquidated alien demands as often as they have satisfied them. When James reviewed Spencer's *Data of Ethics* he saw this clearly enough. If he forgot it eleven years later, it was perhaps because by then his 19th Century optimism and his ungrounded belief in progress had managed to convince him that force does not succeed in establishing itself firmly unless it manages to satisfy alien demands besides realizing its own objectives. But it must be said flatly that in these matters the voice of William James lacks authority. He had his troubles, this darling of fortune; but there is nothing on record to indicate that he ever ran up against one of those experiences with a psychological or physical bully that might have enabled him to look at the historical picture from the standpoint of those to whom justice has been utterly denied. His marvelous sympathy carried him far. But he was too sanguine for it to carry him far enough. In any case, I trust this much at least is clear: the *theoretical* difference between the two brothers in respect to morals is radical; as radical as is the difference between expedience instituted into principle and principle upheld against expedience.

2

There is one respect in which Henry and William are at one. I do not know exactly how to refer to it, but I seem to see between William's conception of consciousness and his philosophy of "pure experience" which is based on this conception, on the one hand, and on the other the mode of perception which became characteristically Henry's, an intimate relationship. It need not be, though it may be, a question of influence. But however it came about, each brother expresses in his own domain something which, I suspect, is somehow essential to the last half of the 19th Century, since it is not only found in pragmatism, and in the novels of Henry

James, but in Bergson and elsewhere in philosophy, in its own way in Proust, and also in the painting of the impressionists. In William it is best to be seen in his analysis of "the mind from within," while in Henry we must look for it in the way in which he apprehends his material and in the picture of the world which comes out of his way of experiencing. We might indeed say—though it can not be intended literally of course—that Henry illustrates quite aptly his brother's doctrine of the stream of consciousness and of "pure experience."

If this hunch could be made clear and plausible the results would, I am sure, amply reward the difficulties involved in presenting a topic on which, I fear, I am not adequately clear. For in Henry's case it would show that the peculiarity of his art, as it achieved fuller originality, was a personal expression of a larger movement. Otherwise his art remains an incongruous phenomenon which (as Edmund Wilson would have it) he created "in spite of everything"—of everything indeed, of his craftsmanship, of his values, and of the fact that, however restrictively he lived, he did live after all in the 19th and 20th Centuries with sensitive eyes and ears open. But relate it, as our hunch would have us do, to something larger than itself in the culture in which it flourished, and you will see that the art of Henry James is not a phenomenon floating in vacuo, the product of an isolated and ingrown "biophobiac," as we might call him, who was nevertheless, a great artist "in spite of everything."

For our purpose the most interesting feature of William James's conception of the mind, as we see it "from within," in Chapter IX of *The Principles of Psychology*, is that our thoughts are in constant change, and yet, in spite of it, there obtains among them a real and long-range continuity. There is of course, first, the continuity of our own selves, a continuity that persists in spite of breaks in our thoughts through sleep and other causes. But there is also a less obvious, and for our purposes, more important continuity, in the content of our thinking itself, which makes it resemble a stream. As James puts it,

> What must be admitted is that the definite images of traditional psychology form but the very smallest part of our minds as they actually live. The traditional psychology talks like one who should

say a river consists of nothing but pailsful, spoonsful, quartpotsful,
and other moulded forms of water. Even were the pails and the pots
actually standing in the stream, still between them the free water
would continue to flow.

Now it is true that things—the objects of our thoughts—are discon-
tinuous. But our thought of them is continuous, though the flow
is not even. "Like the bird's life," he tells us, changing images,
"it seems to be made of an alternation of flights and perchings,"
the latter being the objects and the former the relations between
them. But while the perchings are easy, the flights are difficult to
get at, since to stop them is to annihilate them. They are, nevertheless, as real as are the perchings to which they always lead. But
whether perchings or flights, the felt realities of thought "melt
into each other like dissolving views." As he tells us elsewhere, it
is "in the primitive flux of sensational life" that we must look "for
reality's true shape." For our purposes, another very important
peculiarity of the mind is that it is active, selective; it eliminates
or disregards a great deal on which it could potentially fasten itself,
grasping only a very small part. Perceiving is, thus, not merely
receiving but informing, putting the signature of our habits and
interests into what we take to be, or select, and indeed for us *is*,
the objective world.

Let us now attend to a man walking with his daughter on a
Sunday afternoon in an old English garden. They go out of a gate
and search for a bench under an oak, and sit down and talk. Our
psychological information, if we have been convinced by William
James, will make us aware that what we observe from our point
of vantage—the garden, the man and woman, their talk, the quality
of the day, its light and warmth and fragrance—comes to us en-
veloped in an affective light which fuses the elements intimately.
I take it that it is this type of experience—to which a man trained
as a painter is perhaps more prone than the rest of us—that furnished William James with one of his reasons for saying that
"the deeper features of reality are found only in perceptual experience." For perceptual experience did not consist for him of the
quick recognition of objects merely for what they were. This is
the experience of the unseeing eye. His drawings are nothing to
speak of, as art; but his training in the studio and in the galleries

of Europe seems to have left its mark on his way of perceiving. He perceives *au fond*. But who so perceives can notice, especially if he is a trained introspectionist, as William James was, that the content of awareness consists of a lucid yet affectively fused continuum, in which the elements of the various senses (with the visual obviously predominating in him, as it did in his younger brother) integrate themselves into the various objects, which, in turn, separate themselves off into the foreground without losing their ties with all that floats along with them in the stream or with the stream itself. But isn't this the world of the impressionists, of Pissarro and Monet and Sisley and Morrisot and the young Renoir? Their visual world, static of course, as the painter's world must be, is a world of flowing light and color coming together into shapes which are as fluid as is the fluid light which contains them, but all integrated by a mood. So that a cathedral or a garden can only be called the same in the morning light and towards sunset by virtue of an identity in its shape, which itself is not too fixed, not too static, since it has no intrinsic linear boundary but gains its outline by changing color merging into changing color. At any rate, it was chiefly through the aesthetic surface, in Prall's sense of the term, that William James seems to have grasped whatever meanings were available to him. These meanings came to him charged with feeling, and therefore he grasped them, without losing the sense of the objectivity of the world, always, I suspect, with a more or less conscious sense that it was he himself that was grasping them. But whether it was so for him or not, personally, it certainly was so for his theory, and that is what for us is of paramount importance.

Suppose now that we have been asked to write about the garden scene which we have just witnessed. Our psychological knowledge, if we are not artists, would not be a blessing, but a positive hindrance. For under its influence the problem that presents itself to us is not merely that of noting down faithfully what we saw and heard. If what we want is the reality of the scene, it is in its sensational flux that we must look for its true shape. Our problem then is to capture what we saw and heard in such a way as not to lose the fluid affinity that the things that make up the episode had for one another. And we would have to render it, not as it was, but as it was seen by us. Yet we can not solve our problem by the facile device of putting ourselves into the story: for it is not about our subjective feelings we are asked to write but about what we saw and heard. If we are artists, the difficulties that confront us are likely to challenge us till we have successfully disposed of them. But success could only be possible by taking liberties with the scene. The effort to remain at the literal level would be utterly falsifying, for literalness, the so called "photographic" description, misses the glowing interplay of affective light and shade which reflects mutually from the several objects before us.

While I have been suggesting how we would deal with a scene, had we read William James, I have also been generalizing on some of the things that Henry James does in the concrete, on some of the problems which he faces, and on the effects he seeks to achieve. To see how he actually managed the scene in the old garden let the reader turn to the third and fourth chapters in *The Golden Bowl*. No short quotation can give the full impression of a scene from his pen. This is to be gathered only from reading the whole of the two chapters. And of course to draw the parallel between Henry and William too closely will not do, nor is it necessary for our purposes. But at some points the parallel—if the liberty this sentence takes with Euclid be overlooked—is nevertheless very close.

Note first Henry James's repeated experimentation to discover a satisfactory way of presenting, not life, but in Mr. Blackmur's words, "someone's apprehension of the experience of it." The details of these efforts are well known—how the all-seeing eye of the traditional novelist is sacrificed, and how, in the book of which he was so justly proud, *The Ambassadors*, he brought the problem to its extremest, yet, as it seemed to him, most satisfactory, solution, by presenting the whole drama through Strether's vigilant mind. It is as if Henry James were struggling to do justice to the subjectivity of experience and yet show that we are not condemned to solipsism in spite of that subjectivity. (The charge of solipsism was leveled against William's position.) This problem intrigues Henry from various angles, and in a story like *In the Cage* or in a novel like *What Maisie Knew* he seems to be concerned chiefly with its elucidation. We need not go any farther into the matter and can drop it with one remark: The reasons that Henry James gives for his experiments are, as they should be, reasons of form, of method. I do not intend to suggest that there are "deeper" reasons. But I do mean to say that the problems with which as artist he is confronted are those which are apt to present themselves to a mind operating in the way in which William James describes the mind as doing, and not in which, let us say, Locke or the older Mill thought the mind worked.

Note next the way in which the objects in a scene of Henry James—characters and physical setting and ideas and feelings— seem to be presented. William, objecting by letter to his brother's "third manner" describes it ironically though not inexactly as follows:

> by dint of breathing and sighing all round and round [an object, you] arouse in the reader . . . the illusion of a solid object, made . . . wholly out of impalpable materials, air, and prismatic inter-ferences of light, ingeniously focused by mirrors upon empty space. But you *do* it, that's the queerness! And the complication of innu-endo and associative reference on the enormous scale to which you give way to it does so *build out* the matter for the reader that the re-sult is to solidify, by the mere bulk of the process, the like perceptions from which *he* has to start.

But this is the way in which the psychology of the stream of con-sciousness and the philosophy of pure experience would have us get at the world. Read, for proof, Chapters VI and VII of *The Pluralistic Universe* or Chapter II of *Essays in Radical Empiricism*, and you will see how Henry's breathing and sighing a world into solidity follows the pattern laid by William, who would find "real-ity's true shape" in "the primitive flux of sensational life."

Why William, with all his brotherly affection, did not see that in terms of his own theories Henry should have been his favorite novelist, we can not stop to inquire. Let us rather note the irony involved in the failure. Only once, so far as my acquaintance with the published records goes, does William seem to have shown any sympathy or understanding of what the younger brother is trying to accomplish in his "third manner" and then, as it seems to an admirer of Henry, he does not give evidence of too penetrating a grasp. Henry's earlier, less distinctive books, William genuinely and enthusiastically admires. But to the intention and success of the later work he was almost totally blind.

The relationship on which I have sought to throw light leads us to another parallel between Henry and William. For just as William heads a crucial development in philosophy, initiating strong movements of iconoclastic power, and preparing the ground for the advent of the much heralded though, I fear, doubtful bounties that our brave new world will bring us, just so Henry. His influence, too, was deeply revolutionary. For the radical innovations in literary form which are involved in the work of writers who came after him, like Mrs. Woolf, Gertrude Stein, James Joyce, follow, no doubt, the direction which he pointed in his own so magnificently successful experiments.[1]

1943

Kafka's distorted mask

1

One need not read very far into *The Kafka Problem* [1] to see how grievously Kafka has suffered at the hands of some of his critics. Mr. Flores has thrown together, unembarrassed by any controlling criterion, a large number of articles, reviews and appreciations of Kafka, of diverse value and gathered from many European languages. A few essays, like that of the French critic Miss Claude-Edmonde Magny, are penetrating studies worthy of their subject. But the problem which most of these pieces raise is as to why the editor should have wanted to rescue them from discreet obscurity. Fortunately, if you want to check for yourself the validity of the various interpretations which have been foisted on Kafka, you are no longer obstructed by the difficulty which has confronted his slowly growing public during the last four or five years. For in the last few months both his German publishers, now established in

this country, and his various American publishers, have reprinted—
although sometimes at fantastic prices—books of Kafka which it
has been hitherto impossible to find. The latest of these publica-
tions is the indispensable biography by Max Brod which has just
been translated into English.

If one may judge by Flores' volume and by a few other essays
which for some reason were left out of this democratic collection,
"the Kafka problem" arises from the confused demands made by
the readers and not from any unusual difficulty inherent in Kafka's
work. This is most clearly seen in those egregious compounds of
home-made psychoanalysis and facile sociology of art of a purely
speculative nature, which without any inductive evidence to support them find Kafka's meaning in his psychological or political
history and in so doing explain it utterly away. The sociological
critic takes Kafka's fables to be the expression of the social conditions which allegedly motivated them. For him the question is
not, What does the author say? but rather, Why does he say what
he does? The psychoanalytic critic shares with the sociological the
assumption that the content of Kafka's vision of the world is of
no importance, but differs in that what he considers of importance
is the way in which the work of art expresses an allegedly pathological condition of the author. Neither sociologist nor psycho-
analyst finds the answer by reading the objective, public content of
the work; they find it by applying to it a theory devised prior to
the reading of it, regarding the relation said to hold between either
social or psychological conditions and artistic expression. Now
even granting that this kind of genetic analysis of art is valid, and
that artistic symbols may indeed point to psychic conditions or to
social determinants, it is nevertheless at least possible that the
objective traits to which they refer are of interest to the reader as
they are without doubt to the artist (or the latter would not have
struggled as he did with the problem of choosing them and organizing them into the artistic work). This does not deny the therapist's
right to use the work of art as diagnostic evidence. Psychoanalytic
criticism is, however, seldom practised by properly trained therapists for their purposes; it is as a rule written by amateur psycho-
analysts whose insensibility to the aesthetic values and indifference

to the philosophic content of the aesthetic work is hardly camou-
flaged by their pseudo-scientific interest in it.

The reader who considers the critic's most urgent task to lead
attention to those aspects of the work which are expressed in it is
justified by passing by these highly speculative psychologistic or
pseudo-sociological constructions. He must devote his efforts to
exhibiting his subject's objective contribution and to essaying an
evaluation of it. Inadequately supported speculations about the
causes of the complicated difficulties which Kafka had with his
father or his women or his job must necessarily be relegated to a
relatively unimportant place until the work of objective criticism
is finished and a working consensus obtains as to what is to be
found in Kafka's fables. But when at last we turn our attention
to psychogenetic questions we should do so with a greater respect
than the majority of these fanciful speculations show for the demands of inductive verification. The biographical data that we
have on Kafka is inadequate because Brod, who was its chief
gatherer, interprets Kafka in his own terms and seems incapable
of distinguishing his own personal interest in his gifted friend and
his interest in the objective meaning of his friend's fables. Brod's
book does not enable us to check our fanciful psychoanalytic constructions against reliable and sufficient facts. But even if it did,
it would still leave us with the chief problems of Kafka on hand,
with the question of Kafka's aesthetic achievement and of the
objective meaning and validity of his vision of the world. We
have Freud's word, although we do not need it, for the insight
that the analysis of aesthetic values is not within the reach of his
analytic method. But psychological or sociological criticism—and
Freud's own is to be included in it—systematically rides the genetic
fallacy when it assumes that the discovery of the complete psychological or social sources of the artist's experience invalidates the
objective meaning which is expressed by his art.

Although a large number of Kafka's critics avoid the fanciful
constructions of his psychological or his sociological interpreters,
they share with these the inability simply to take Kafka seriously
as an artist at the objective level. Aware that art performs a very
important function in elucidating objective experience but not
clear as to how it does it, they have in one of two ways assumed

that the key to his work is to be found, not within it, but beyond
it. Some find it in some ready-made philosophical conception of
the world, usually in Kierkegaard, as if all the artist had to do was
to dress up in a dramatic costume a philosophic skeleton. Others,
taking Kafka to be merely an allegorical writer, consider the task
of criticism accomplished when the more or less superstructural
allegorical features of his fables are translated into that for which
they stand—or, as I shall call it, employing I. A. Richards' convenient terminology, into the "tenor" of the extended metaphor
that is the allegory. The objective of these critics becomes then
the translation of what Kafka meant by the Castle, or the Court,
or by an advocate conveniently called "Grace," or by the Chinese
emperor and his wall, or by the elaborate burrow built by the
digger obsessed with a need to seek safe refuge from a predatory
world. Although the difference in practice between these two
modes of interpretation is important enough to notice, in principle
they share the same assumption, namely, that the meaning of
Kafka's work is to be found beyond the fables themselves and can
therefore be better expressed in other terms than those which
Kafka himself used.

Sharing the same assumption, these two modes of extrinsic interpretation also share a basic error consisting of a misconception
of what the artist does and how he does it. The philosophic interpreters ignore the fact that the creative process involves a complete digestion of all the material on which the artist feeds so that
what he finally produces is essentially different from what went
into its make-up. They also ignore the fact that the poet, in the
measure in which he is indeed a maker, does not seek to "imitate"
or "represent" a reality which, independently of his poetic activity,
possesses already a formal structure which anyone can discover.
If this is true, it should be easy to see why the assumption that
Kafka's meaning is to be found in a ready-made system of philosophy such as Kierkegaard's or anyone else's even in a more or less
systematic set of abstract ideas of his own, is a disparagement of his
achievement. Artistically Kafka failed to a considerable extent.
But his was the failure of a man who was an artist of major pre-
tensions. His meaning is something not to be better stated abstractly in terms of ideas and concepts, to be found beyond the

fable, but within it, at the dramatic level, in the interrelationships thus revealed to exist among the characters and between them and the universe. The fallacy of finding his meaning in abstract ideas inverts the relationship between philosophy and art, for it is the philosopher who must go to art for the subject-matter which the poet has organized at the dramatic level, in order to abstract from it the systematic relationships which it is his business to formulate.

The allegorical interpreter fails for a similar reason. He translates the allegory into its "tenor" by supplying, not Kafka's own grasp of reality in dramatic terms, but a more or less commonplace version of it in abstract terms, and one which does not possess any of those traits which, in the fable, we discern to be the most distinctively Kafkan. But if Kafka had a contribution to make it was not to be found in the ingenuity of his allegorical "vehicle" (again in Richards' terminology) nor even in a version of a cock-eyed world whose absurdity at the human level had its source in the unqualified irrationality of transcending factors lying beyond human reach and beyond human comprehension. These conceptions of existence had already been expressed in one way or another in literature and in philosophy. What Kafka had to say was something else involving as much freshness and originality as one has a right to expect in literature. It is something which, so far as I know, he could not have borrowed from philosophy, for no thinker one hears of in standard histories of philosophy has ever viewed the world in quite the way in which Kafka viewed it. There are, undeniably, allegorical features in Kafka's vision of the world but they are obvious and relatively unimportant. What is important is the concrete dramatic world exhibited in his fables under the allegorical "vehicles" which he uses to capture it. Kafka, as Brod points out, even when trying to think conceptually, thinks in images and not in conceptual structures. But his vision has a coherence and meaningful interrelatedness the vision of the non-artistic mind lacks, since the latter is distracted by the multifarious demands made on it and it is not driven by the need to organize and unify its experience. The picture of the world as it presented itself to Kafka was a mythopoetical one and if it is our business as readers to discover its meaning for us, in our own terms, we cannot do so until we are reasonably clear as to what

was its own intrinsic meaning. Miss Magny puts the point so
effectively that it is worth transcribing her own words:

> we ought not to . . . provide dialectical constructions for the unfold-
> ing of events which should be taken as a *real* account. Otherwise
> Kafka is quickly converted into a kind of frustrated philosopher who
> needs to be explained to himself and to others for lack of sufficient
> power of analysis and abstraction. . . . That would imply a gratu-
> itous insult.

In spite of her depth and acuity, however, I believe that Miss
Magny's interpretation of Kafka's conception of existence can be
objectively shown to miss a very essential element. She says:

> the world for Kafka is essentially *turmoil*, something that is not
> *rational* and whose essence therefore only a fantastic tale can ex-
> press. . . . Only the gratuitousness of the event itself, of the *con-
> tingit*, can reveal the essential absurdity of things.

At another place Miss Magny speaks of "Kafka's predilection for
the infraconceptual, the infrarational." But Kafka's world was
not merely absurd. Indeed what constituted for him the problem
which he sought to resolve through his art—and of course the only
manner in which an artist resolves his problem is through a statement of it in mythopoetic terms—was that certain transcending
aspects of the universe envisaged through experience and seen to
be those on which normal visible existence depends, blatantly proclaimed an irrationality which, upon the most casual glimpse, appeared to be at the same time rational.

But the Magny essay has at least this value, that it poses the
Kafka problem correctly and reveals one aspect of our author without a grasp of which no understanding of him is possible. In Kafka,
as she puts it, "the irrational . . . the horrible . . . the grotesque
. . . are never induced for the sake of literary effect . . . but to
express a depth of reality." Our problem therefore is to inquire as
to what conception of existence is found in Kafka's fables. The
answer must of course be couched in abstract terms, but it is not
to be taken as a translation of Kafka's meaning but as a means
of pointing to it within the fables themselves. The validity of the
interpretation is to be judged by checking to see whether what I

claim to be found in Kafka is indeed there and whether I do not neglect important factors which are there. The allegorical features must of course be translated into their "tenors" but this goes without saying and rather than constituting a difficult task—as in fact it does for critics like Rahv when they try to translate Kafka into Kierkegaardian philosophy—it is a relatively easy one.[2] The labor of criticism however begins at that point and what it has to accomplish is a reading of Kafka. After that one may express one's own opinion as to whether Kafka's conception of existence is valid or not.

2

In order to offer inductive evidence in favor of the preceding argument we must turn to an analysis of Kafka's works in search of his conception of existence. But since an exhaustive analysis of all of his works is not here possible, I propose that we turn our attention to *The Trial* and *The Castle* which embody his most ambitious efforts to integrate his various discoveries about the world. Let us first turn to *The Trial*.

We must first remember that Joseph K.'s arrest is sudden and seems to him so unjustified that never between the period of his arrest and of his execution does he admit his guilt. But while verbally denying it, unconsciously Joseph K. betrays his sense of guilt from the very first day of his arrest in numerous small ways. Let only one instance suffice: During the preliminary examination that took place the morning of his arrest Joseph K. said to the Inspector in anger and seemingly irrelevantly, "But this is not the capital charge yet." In a more important way Joseph K. gives evidence of his sense of guilt: the outward circumstances of his life do not at first change very radically but gradually Joseph K. gets more and more absorbed in his case and finally finds out that his job is suffering from his preoccupation with it. If he truly were convinced of his innocence he would have laughed at the whole absurd business, as he tried to do the first Sunday at the preliminary investigation when he told the Magistrate that his could not be a trial unless he recognized it as such. To the reader it is quite clear that Joseph K. did not want to admit to himself when he made that statement that he had already through action eloquently yielded the recognition that his lips withheld.

Remember next that while Joseph K. realizes that the Court is a formidable organization he insists nevertheless on his belief that its purposes are absurd, and the evidence for that is to be found, as he believes, in all that he discovers about it at the lower level. Thus Joseph K. seems to be justified in his conviction, expressed angrily to the Magistrate, that the organization is interested in condemning innocent victims and doing so while keeping them in ignorance of what charges are brought against them. This belief is strengthened by the result of his efforts to gain information about the higher officials of the Court.

But is Joseph K. really justified in his belief that the Court is an utterly aimless, absurd institution? A formidable organization with a code of Law and with such a large number of employees, with traditions and equipment, an organization that will punish its employees on occasion upon the complaint of a man under arrest— such an organization is simply not aimless. Its aims may not be knowable or may not seem to be intelligible to us but the evidence, without denying Joseph K.'s conviction of its absurdity, points, at the very same time, to a rationality all its own. Joseph K. does not want to admit this to himself and insists on judging the organization and its charges against him by his own criterion of rationality. But all his actions proclaim that he is not altogether ignorant of the limitations of his own criterion. In view of his stiff-necked attitude towards the evidence, the counsel which Joseph K. gives himself on the way to the execution has a tremendous ironic force. "The only thing for me to do now . . . is to keep my intelligence calm and discriminating to the end." He therefore resigns himself. But it has been precisely the failure of his discriminating intelligence that led him to the impasse in which he found himself. For it was not resignation that the situation required of him; what it required was admission of his guilt and genuine contrition. This is precisely what the priest tried in vain to tell him in the Cathedral. But Joseph K. was too discriminatingly intelligent and too proud of the primacy of his intelligence to listen.

The Castle is a much more complex book than The Trial. Indeed it represents the most ambitious effort on Kafka's part to

gather together all the important aspects of his vision of the world
into one coherent fable. For this reason the unfinished condition
in which it was left suggests a radical criticism of the validity of
Kafka's conception of existence. In this book his preoccupations
are given a different organization from that which he gave them in
The Trial. A problem with which *The Trial* is concerned only
obliquely is here brought forward, namely the problem of man's
place in the scheme of things and, as a corollary of this more
comprehensive problem, the question as to the nature of the bond
between man and his fellow beings. In *The Trial* that bond,
after the crisis of the arrest, is somehow unhealthy; for instance,
for the normal relationship between his mistress and himself
Joseph K. substitutes the relationship with Huld's maid, Leni,
which does not involve either the fulfillment of genuine love or
even the gratification which purely sexual relations can yield. In
The Castle the emphasis seems to change but both the human and
the merely sexual relations result in the same vague frustration.
Again the question of guilt which is central in *The Trial* is subordi-
nated in *The Castle* by being presented through the episode of
Barnabas and his family. But the cause of the guilt, which in *The
Trial* is only indirectly and ambiguously suggested, is in the latter
explicitly traced to Amalia's refusal of Sortini's invitation to visit
him in his room at the Inn; the guilt is caused, that is, by the pride
of those who will not serve and is thus connected with the most
ancient of guilts, the guilt that led to the fall before man's. The
cause is brought out with sufficient clarity by the contrast between
Amalia's attitude towards Sortini and the attitude of the Landlady
and of Frieda towards Klamm. K. is himself relatively free from
a sense of guilt but he is dominated by a need to find a place for
himself in the scheme of things. The need, baffled, develops into
anxiety as his efforts lead him to discover the nature of the organization that he has to contend with.

From Olga and from the superintendent who receives K. in bed,
the Land Surveyor gains important information about the organization of the Castle. K. tries to make his informants admit that
the organization is quite absurd and leaves much to be desired.
But the superintendent does not admit that the organization lacks
order or is subject to error. The apparatus works with great pre-

cision; in the Castle nothing is done without thought and the very possibility of error on the part of the Head Bureau must be ruled out. The superintendent admits that he is convinced that in respect to K. an error has been committed. But who can tell what the first Control Officials will say and the second and third and the rest? However, if there has been one, the error is not established by the evidence K. has from Klamm, for Klamm's letter to K. is not official, and as to the telephone calls, these mean nothing. If Huld in *The Trial* is an advocate without legal standing, Klamm in *The Castle* is a protector seemingly helpless to protect his man— that is, if there is a Klamm and if it is K. and not someone else in whom Klamm is interested.

I have purposely said in a vague way that K. was trying "to find his place in the scheme of things" because I do not find that K. is anxious about obtaining a livelihood or solving any other purely secular problem but only about finding a place in the village which would give him status not only in respect to the village itself but, more importantly even, in respect to the inaccessible powers of the Castle. K. wants an unambiguous statement of his position before the authorities of the Castle. This involves documents, proofs, something to which he could refer that could not be gainsaid, like the letters from Klamm, but containing of course an official appointment and a definition of his place. He starts with large demands and ends up by offering to take anything that will be given him so long as it brings him the needed nod of recognition for which he craves. But his efforts to get into direct touch with the officials of the Castle are no less pathetically useless than those of Barnabas' father who wants his crime defined. No one can be certain of anything beyond the elementary fact that there must be a Castle which is visible above the village and from which officials and servants constantly come and go. One also suspects that it must have its method, no matter how absurd that method may seem and how deeply it may outrage the feeling of what we take to be fitness or justice or rationality. But beyond that all is doubt and incertitude.

Between *The Trial* and *The Castle* there are important differences, but to me none seems as important as the fact that Joseph K. never learns anything whatever about the invisible Judges, while

K. knows the name of the Lord of the Castle, Count West-west, and receives indications, however unsatisfactory, that between the Castle and himself there is some sort of nexus. He first tries to get into touch with the Count, then with the Castellan and, when he sees the impossibility of his ambition, he tries to reach Klamm. K.'s relations with Klamm are more baffling than those of Joseph K. with his Judges in *The Trial* because there is more teasing evidence of Klamm's existence and therefore the evidence is more unintelligible. K. thinks he once saw Klamm but it turns out later that that is very doubtful. Was it Klamm who wrote the letter to K.? The signature is illegible and Olga later tells K. that the letters that her brother Barnabas has brought him were not received from Klamm but from a clerk. Even if they were from Klamm it is doubtful whether Klamm is well enough posted on K. really to be his patron or protector as the second letter that K. receives from Klamm clearly shows. The question is even more difficult since, if you press it, it turns out that there are all kinds of contradictory reports about Klamm, and some people go so far as to say that Momus, the Secretary, is Klamm. Who then is Klamm? Some sort of fluctuating image of him has been constructed but, as Olga tells K., perhaps it does not fluctuate as much as Klamm's real appearance does. However, in *The Trial* not even such a deceptive hope ever urges Joseph K. on and he conducts his defense in a state of unrelieved and increasing enervation.

It is not necessary to demonstrate in detail that the various aspects of the conception of existence that were integrated in these two novels are separately expressed in a large number of his stories and sketches: in *Investigations of a Dog, The Great Wall of China, The Burrow* and *The Giant Mole*, for instance, as well as in some of his shorter pieces like *The Problem of Our Laws*. But it is necessary to state frankly that there are a number of more or less important stories which could not be susceptible of this interpretation, for example, *Josephine the Songstress, Blumfeld An Elderly Bachelor, The Penal Colony* and *The Judgment*. In some of these what Kafka was trying to do is not difficult to guess. He was exploring psychological reality strictly at the human level. The result of Kafka's psychological exploration, it seems to me, contradicts the purely hedonic conception of man which is found deeply

imbedded in the liberal, secularistic tradition of our western world
and which is true only of what Kierkegaard called the "aesthetic
stage" of human development. Kafka's discoveries ally him with
the tradition which Freud himself joined as a result of his meta-
psychological speculations and to which Dostoevski and Kierkegaard belong—men who repudiate the shallow optimism which
controls the conception of human destiny at the "aesthetic stage."
For Kafka's psychological conceptions we must go to stories like
Metamorphosis, The Judgment and *The Penal Colony.* With some
diffidence I venture the opinion that an analysis of his contributions to the understanding of the purely psychological problems
of contemporary men would hardly be worth the trouble it would
involve.

Amerika, begun only a few months before *The Trial,* seems to
represent, as I read it, an unsuccessful experiment of Kafka's, for
in it he views his problem as imbedded in a purely social context.
Amerika seems therefore to constitute very little more than social
criticism of his temporal world and we find in it only faint and
incomplete indications of the insights into the transcending aspects
of experience which we identify as Kafka's central focus of interest
and the elucidation of which constitutes his contribution.

3

We are now able to put together Kafka's conception of existence.
Note first that what Kafka undertook was a stubbornly empirical
exploration of experience, beyond which he discovered a constellation of factors for which evidence is found within the texture of
experience itself. For this reason allegory must be employed to
point to these factors not directly revealed. But the "tenor" of the
allegory, being itself beyond direct grasp, must be expressed in
mythopoetic terms drawn from ordinary life. Kafka, with whom
Brod read Plato in his university days, could have invoked Plato
as precedent for his use of myth, for the Greek used it to elucidate
the structure which he glimpsed as lying beyond experience
through evidence found within it. Kafka's discovery involves an
ordered process which we can more or less adequately capture in
the following formula: a crisis leads either to a sense of guilt or

to a condition of alienation. In either case the crisis generates a struggle which expresses itself, among other ways, in the arrogant demands made by the hero. As he begins to feel the effects of the crisis the hero gradually trims his demands but he never altogether ceases to press them. The reduction of demands results from the hero's gradual discovery of a transcending organization which seems beyond his power either to look into, control or understand. His discovery is based not upon unwarranted assumptions or gratuitous hypotheses but on more or less direct empirical evidence, and although what is discovered seems unintelligible to him, the evidence is ambivalent and points not only to the irrationality of the organization but to its rationality as well. The anguished doubt into which the victim of the crisis is plunged is the result of the fact that the antinomy he faces cannot be resolved since it does not occur to him to transcend his perspective or go beyond his empirical method. But what other method is there? For Kafka's heroes there seems to be no other.

It is of the utmost importance, however, to note that Kafka's "empiricism" differs radically from that which is fashionable to-day—that which constitutes the foundations of scientific natural-ism—since the latter has been devised in order to deny the evidence which experience presents of its lack of self-sufficiency, while Kafka through an empirical examination of human existence is led to assert its dependence on transcending factors.

We do not find in Kafka an assertion of a world made up of two aspects such as we find in the traditional dualism of Western philosophy; for in these the two terms, the visible and the tran-scending, are said to bear certain intelligible relations towards one another and in the major tradition the transcending term is taken as the ground of the rationality of the other. Nor do we have in Kafka a dramatized version of Schopenhauerian dualism in which a pure irrational factor is taken to be the ground of our world of experience. What we find is something quite different, something to a large degree fresh and original, expressing in challenging terms the novel conditions and predicaments of modern man. These predicaments generate anguish. But unlike Kierkegaard, who mastered his "sterile anguish" through faith, or Dostoevski, who suggested that it could be mastered through faith and love in the

way in which the Russian monk, Father Zossima, mastered it,
Kafka's man never succeeds in surpassing human anguish. Face to
face with what many of his critics recognize as a metaphysical
problem—in a vague sense of this conveniently ambiguous word—
Kafka tried to solve it empirically. But what he was up against
was the problem of theodicy and not in the Leibnizian sense but in
the fuller, in the Cartesian sense. The problem that Kafka faced
was not primarily the conventional need to find a satisfactory
human account of evil once it has been discovered that its roots
lie beyond the human level. Neither was it the problem of discovering what attitudes we may be expected to take towards an
invisible agent on which we depend and which we know to be
infinite—this was the Kierkegaardian problem. Rather it was the
problem of discovering the ground of rationality. He went so far
as to grasp clearly that that ground transcends human experience.
But he could not go beyond this relatively elementary discovery
because the stubborn empirical attitude which he assumed is helpless before questions of the magnitude he was raising.

This is not to say, however, that personally Kafka resigned
himself to the monstrous predicament into which his discoveries
plunged him. And least of all is it to say that the reader must
himself be plunged into a pessimistic attitude by contemplating
Kafka's picture of the world. Those readers who find him merely
depressing have not read him carefully. Brod quotes a trenchant
statement in his *Biography* which suggests the precise way in
which Kafka himself avoided a purely enervating pessimism and
in which the reader may also avoid it. "Our art," it reads, "consists
of being dazzled by Truth. The light which rests on the distorted
mask as it shrinks from it is true, nothing else is." The light is
Truth but the mask on which it shines, the artifact of the maker,
is "distorted"—and the rich contextual ambiguities of the statement are precisely what gives it density of suggestive meaning and
confirms the reader's hunch that in the ambiguities which Kafka
systematically exploits is to be found the comic dimension of his
picture of the world and the means of purging oneself from effects
generated by its arbitrariness and irrationality. Kafka's artistry
makes this comic feature compatible with the sense of anguish
and even of terror that is the defining quality of existence in it.

But it is not merged with or sacrificed to the latter. And in the reader its perception generates enough detachment to enable him to assimilate all the absurdity and pervasive anguish presented without surrendering to it.

The comical quality of Kafka's world is expressed in the way in which he treats the antinomous nature of existence. Generally speaking, a comic grasp of the world rests on the perception by the writer of a moral duality which elicits from the reader a "comic" response as the only means of freeing himself from the conflict towards values to which he is attached and yet towards which he cannot justify his attachment satisfactorily. It is not merely a moral duality but, if you will allow it, a cosmological duality that we find in Kafka's world, and its perception involves a disparagement of the means which reveal it, a disparagement of the mind as a rational tool of analysis. There is no gaiety in Kafka's irony as there is in Rabelais' satire; nor a deep sense of moral outrage and the bitter laughter arising from the fact that at least you know you cannot be fooled which we find in Swift. But there is nevertheless the essential element of the comic in Kafka: the transparent error involved in any statement that can be made of the world. Such a world, a world about which nothing can be said that cannot in the same breath be as plausibly contradicted, is a quintessentially comic world. You cannot of course expect its victims to find it so but you cannot, either, be expected by them to take them at their own asking value and in your mind you are ready with a discount. A world toward which one cannot develop any kind of attachment, however ideal and prospective, is a world in which the pain it creates, the terror it inspires, the cruelty it shows is not utterly crushing pain or terror or cruelty, because it crushes with its absurdity the piety it generates. The only response to it therefore is the ironic.

In the light of the foregoing it is not difficult to see in concrete terms that the differences between Kierkegaard and Kafka are essential and the affinities superficial. For the one thing one could not impute to Kierkegaard is the empirical attitude. He starts with it but he soon soars away into a region where intuition and faith, free from the demands of empirical evidence, allow him to ignore the insoluble problems which for the thorough-going empiricist

stand in the way of accepting a historical or even a personal religious view of man and the world. Kierkegaard is therefore not at
all baffled by the nature of those elements which he found to
transcend experience. He does not claim that he is able to "know"
them; but the proper response towards them is not for him that
of the pure knower, the abstract ratiocinator in search of verified
"truth." The existentialist is a man of flesh and bones—as Unamuno put it—who disregarding the artificial limitations and re-
strictions of the pure knower, makes a total human decision and
wills the act of belief; and not in the pragmatic sense of William
James, either, but in a passionate, affirmative, plenary manner. For
this reason Kierkegaard would have pooh-poohed the parallelism
which has been found to exist between himself and Kafka. A man
who tries to reach plenary conviction as to the transcending structure that subtends human experience by "cognitive" means places
himself at the very opposite pole of Kierkegaardian existentialism.
Furthermore, because for Kierkegaard the object of faith was infinite, man must be in the wrong and as a result must endure
anguish. But this is his highest condition. By contrast, the anguish
that at times almost chokes Kafka's characters—the stagnant, the
oppressive atmosphere of Barnabas' home or the claustrophobiac
closedness of Tintorelli's room, the terrifying searches, the endless
corridors—is the result of insecurity which arises from lack of
knowledge. In Kafka anguish issues from doubt, in Kierkegaard
from certitude.

There is, however, a modicum of justification for the coupling
of the Danish philosopher with the Jewish novelist, since the reading of the former does make us aware of the importance of anguish,
of the crisis and of absolute disjunctions in human experience.
Without a full appreciation of these factors as inherent in the
human situation, the effort to understand Kafka turns into a diagnostic hunt for signs of neuroses. It is important to keep in mind
however the different way in which these factors function in philosopher and poet although it is impossible to undertake here specifications of the differences.

4

There is need to make explicit some hints I have given about what
I take to be the validity of Kafka's conception of existence. Let us
disregard the fact of his failure to bring any of his major works to
completion, although such a failure may legitimately be taken as
the basis for the most devastating criticism that may be leveled
against Kafka's version of reality. Still it must be noted that Kafka's
conception of existence is defective because it is inherently unstable. It seems to me that Kafka's picture constitutes a decided
advance over that given us by contemporary naturalism, for Kafka
has no desire to deny the evidence of experience which points
to dimensions of existence which transcend it. But he could not
or would not surrender his method to the demands of rationality
and left us with a vision of the world which both artistically and
philosophically represents an impasse. The change of attitude generated by the crisis opens to the subject large ranges of hitherto
unsuspected possibilities as to the nature of existence. But these
cannot be realized unless the new attitudes brought about by the
crisis are accepted as revealing factors which experience itself cannot explore, but in which one must believe nevertheless even without a basis that those who have not gone through the crisis would
be willing to accept as adequate evidence. And this is what the
empiricist will not, cannot do. I believe it would be relatively easy
to prove from his work that Kafka saw clearly the root of the
difficulty. But his intellectual grasp of his perplexity was useless
since his difficulty arose precisely from his insistence on the use
of the intelligence beyond its legitimate range.

There is therefore a profound justification to Kafka's own remark
that he expressed the negative tendencies of his age. Note however that he does so in the sense that he grasped clearly the meaning of certain phenomena as constitutive of normal human
development in its break from what Kierkegaard called the "aesthetic" stage. But he was not able to concede what is demanded
in order to reach the "ethico-religious" stage. Having been thrust
from the aesthetic his heroes stop before they reach the next stage.
And they stop because they refuse—or are unable to bring themselves—to solve their problems by the only means that such prob-

lems can be solved: in the manner in which Plato solved his, through the recognition of the valid claims of religious intuition in certain ranges of experience, or in the manner in which Kant did, by supplying the terms required to complete a rational picture of the world as postulates made necessary by the objective demands of practical reason. It is this leap, taken by the greatest number of the major philosophers of our West, that Kafka, faithful to the limitations of his empiricism, will not take. In that refusal Kafka is at one with the negative tendencies of his age and remains impaled on the horns of a brutal antinomy.

1948

the two dimensions of reality in
The Brothers Karamazov

1

A novelist of the amplitude and depth of Dostoevski is likely to be used by his many critics each for his own special purpose. Dostoevski has been used by the founder of psychoanalysis and by innumerable amateur Freudians as an interesting pathological specimen—which of course he was. He has also been considered as forerunner of Freud in his own right, as social or political thinker, as religious prophet and as theologian. To each of these fields Dostoevski contributed interesting speculations, often original and important. But he was and always remained a novelist, although he used the newspaper article and on occasion the lecture platform as vehicle of expression.

To say, however, that Dostoevski was a novelist is not to say that his ends were "aesthetic." Dostoevski was not an artist because of the manner in which he handled his subject matter.

Henry James was unfair to him; it would be difficult, with the single exception of *The Possessed*, to suggest improvements in the architecture of his major novels, and this accords with the fact, known from external sources, that he thought long and deeply over their composition before he began them. But he never enjoyed the leisure required to bring his work to perfection. He was, nevertheless, an artist in the immediate, concrete manner in which he seized the subject matter of experience. His lack of interest in nature has often been noticed. It is as if he had an eye capable exclusively of spiritual vision and for which, therefore, the inanimate ambient world could become visible only insofar as it is helped to disclose the fluid dynamism of the psychic. He saw human beings as concrete, actual agents of action, agonists of the drama of actual life. If we contrast him with Kafka, who in some respects is not unworthy of being put on the same plane as the Russian, we see the difference between an eye which is primarily dramatic and one which is metaphysical. Kafka's world is a dynamic world, but its denizens are not genuine human beings but metaphysical hypostatizations representing certain aspects of the spiritual life. And for this reason what Kafka has to say about the soul does not refer to its concrete workings but to its dialectical tensions. As psychologist—in the sense in which the term can be used to refer to a man like Dostoevski—Kafka was negligible, for we do not learn anything from his novels which we did not already know from either Kierkegaard or Freud. We learn something else no less valuable, but we do not learn anything new about what is behind our social masks. (From Kafka himself, considered as pathological specimen, we may, using his books as diagnostic evidence, learn about a modern neurosis—but for that we do not need Kafka, and the evidence he furnishes is neither reliable nor complete.)

These remarks are not intended to deny that Dostoevski had a deep interest in social, ethical, and theological "problems." Indeed it is not difficult to isolate from his writings—or even from his novels alone—a body of doctrine to which we can be reasonably certain that he subscribed. But this doctrine, however truly espoused by him, is not representative of his total vision of the world, since it neglects the context of concrete circumstance which is an essential element in the definition of its meaning for him. It is true, of course, that Dostoevski had strong convictions. He was, for instance, a committed Christian and a political conservative. But to take his Christianity without the careful qualifications forced on us by the dramatic manner in which he conceived human destiny would be to view it falsely; his faith is not a purely intellectual, logically simple, structure; it is an extremely complex and internally heterogeneous mass of living insights—affective, moral, and intellectual—in tension, and ordered not after the manner of the philosopher but of the dramatist. When therefore one asks oneself what were Dostoevski's views on Christianity, one has to consider (simplifying for the sake of the illustration) not only what we can find out about one character or a class of characters, but what he tells us in the novels as a whole. But what he tells us is a story, in which one character acts and talks in one way and another in another, each in terms of his own convincing logic and psychology. In this picture we will have to choose the truth, as Dostoevski saw it, from the error. But this distinction cannot be made in the same sense in which one finds it made in a theological or an ethical treatise. Thus for instance, the reader, in putting Zossima and his beliefs and commitments at the center of the picture, will also have to remember that Dostoevski was able to make the predicament of Shatov perfectly convincing through his conversation with Stavrogin (*The Possessed*, Part II, Chapt. 1, vii). The latter presses Shatov for a confession, to which Shatov can only answer: "I . . . I will believe in God." But Shatov insists on his faith in "The body of Christ, in Russian Orthodoxy," and asserts, at the same time, and not unaware of his difficulty, that "the object of every national movement, in every people and at every period of its existence is only the seeking for God, who must be its own God." We cannot avoid the conviction that Shatov's predicament was something which Dostoevski had thought through passionately, and must be reckoned with in formulating his "views." But even if we reject the validity of Shatov's views, we cannot leave out of account the fact that it was in the teeth of the latter's assertions that Dostoevski held his truth. From internal evidence alone one can formulate in abstract terms the philosophy of a good many novelists and among these of

some very great ones. But the error of some of the efforts to
interpret the meaning of Dostoevski's novels lies in the assumption that there are "doctrines" or "views" to be found in them—
systematic structures of abstract thought involving major affirma-
tions and denials—when what they contain is a dramatic organization of life, which includes characters most of whom are deeply
interested in ideas.

All of this is to say that Dostoevski fulfills the primary function
of the artist, which so very few artists fulfill to the same extent.
What he does is to organize or, better, to inform experience at
the primary level and by means of animistic and dramatic categories. He does not undertake the philosopher's task, which is to
abstract from experience already dramatically informed a formal
structure in order to test its capacity to meet the exigencies of
logical coherence and clarity of the rational intellect. What he
does is to make life, insofar as man can do it, to be a poet and
to give experience the form and intelligibility required by the
whole mind, by the intellect and by the will. Without this primary
organization life would either be chaos or instinctual routine.
Men can live without philosophy, and not unsuccessfully, and
history and anthropology show that for the most part they do.
But without poetry human life is not possible.

I have labored this point because critics of Dostoevski often
undertake to give us systematic accounts of ideas and doctrines
which Dostoevski never could have entertained. Consider for
instance Berdyaev's analysis. It is certainly one of the most search-
ing, yet the total picture that we gather from it is that Dostoevski
was a theologian—which he was and was not; he was, since he
could not view the human drama except as against the far
horizon of eternity; but he was not, since a writer who sides
with a character who says that the formula that twice two make
four does not meet with his acceptance—a thinker who distrusted
the intellect as deeply as Dostoevski did—is not a man who could
have systematized his views, even if he had tried.

It has been said that Dostoevski organized his works in terms
of "an idea," but if what I have said is valid this statement
cannot stand. Nor can we say, with another of his critics, that
Dostoevski dramatized his ideas. It is closer to the truth to say

that in his books, which are pure stories, the story is the idea. However the word "idea" is not being used here in its ordinary sense, but as it is employed in musical aesthetics. His stories, however, pure drama though they are, exhibit two levels or aspects of human reality: the psychological and the metaphysical. The first we have the right to expect of any serious novelist; only, psychologically Dostoevski gives us considerably more than we are usually given by even the greatest of poets. The second very few readers demand and when they do very seldom get; indeed a number of his readers—particularly the "enlightened," "modern" ones—find it embarrassing and superfluous. When we look at the relationship between these levels we find that the philosophical informs (in the technical Aristotelian sense) the psychological and the latter in turn informs the story. The matter of the story (the object of imitation, in terms of Aristotelian aesthetics) is human experience. But Dostoevski has informed it twice through his creative activity; and we, his readers, are able with his aid to grasp the constitution of human experience at a depth inpenetrable to all but the greatest poets.

2

The fresh and profound insights which Dostoevski added to our knowledge of the human soul have been discussed thoroughly and admirably by many of his critics. All that needs to be done, therefore, is to remind the reader summarily of them; effort can be more profitably put into an analysis of the mèans through which these insights find expression. Thus, it is a commonplace that Dostoevski anticipated Freud; that he was cognizant of the fact and understood the role of the unconscious; that he had a lucid knowledge of the duality exhibited by the human psyche and of its consequences; that he understood adequately the function of dreams; that he knew how shame leads a man to frustrate the actions through which he attempts to appease it, and how pride is the expression of insecurity and shame; how cruelty constitutes self-castigation, and how injured vanity takes revenge through love. In short, all the insights that have become commonplaces since Freud were clearly his own; nor can I think

of any important phenomenological datum furnished by the
Viennese scientist which had escaped the observation of the
Russian novelist.

But no abstract catalogue of "insights" can do justice to the
breadth and depth of Dostoevski's knowledge of the man that
flourished in Europe and Russia in the Nineteenth Century and
whose descendants have merely refined his neuroses. To do justice
to his contribution we must view it not merely as the product of
his psychological acumen but as the product of his art. In the
vast canvas of his major novels—and this is particularly true of
the greatest of them, *The Brothers*—one finds a series of "studies"
of the various modalities through which certain types of human
beings express themselves. The "type" however is gathered by us
inductively from his unique specimens and it is not the former
but the latter that interest Dostoevski; nevertheless it is our
intuition of the type in the individuals that makes them intelligible,
while the individuals enable us to intuit the type, through the
interrelationships of a complex system of similarities and contrasts
which in this essay we cannot explore exhaustively but must be
content to illustrate succinctly.

For illustration let us consider a type of individual with whom
Dostoevski was profoundly preoccupied and which, for lack of a
better designation, we shall call "the liberal." In *The Brothers*
there are at least five or six fairly complete "studies" of this
type: Ivan, Smerdyakov, Miüsov, Rakitin, and Kolya. But we
could increase the number by adding some of the lesser characters.
A liberal is, in religious matters, either an unbeliever or an
agnostic; politically he is a reformist or a socialist; intellectually
a "European" or Europeanized; and morally for Christian love he
substitutes secular meliorism. Let us start with Ivan. What we
know of him directly, by listening to him talk and observing his
relation to his brothers and to his father, his feeling for Katerina
Ivanovna, his conversations with Smerdyakov, and his illness, is
far from exhausting the knowledge imparted about him, which
comes to us also indirectly through what we learn of Smerdyakov,
Rakitin, and Miüsov—to mention only these. But young Kolya,
too, throws a good deal of light on Ivan. Smerdyakov is, if you will
allow the expression, an abyss of shallowness, a pure, corrupted

rationalist whose shallow intelligence has nothing to express but his pomaded lackey's vanity and trivial, upstart ambition, while Ivan is intelligent and, in an ordinary sense, sincere. But it is impossible to claim a complete understanding of Ivan until we have seen what can happen to his ideas when they are vulgarized by his bastard stepbrother and are put to the test pragmatically. Because Ivan, an intellectual, will not find out what is "the cash value" of his ideas, the visits to the sick lackey before the latter's suicide are a revelation to him of what he himself truly is and of how he, no less than Dmitri, is as much involved in the murder as the "stinking scoundrel." But neither Ivan nor Smerdyakov are fully intelligible until we have considered Rakitin, the theological student. Here is another upstart, trying to conceal his lowly origin; he is dishonorable, egotistical, unscrupulous and evil; he is vain and clever and he is self-deceived. He says he is a liberal and looks toward Europe for the salvation of Russia, but he is a dishonorable scoundrel interested in no one but himself, lacking the greatness and depth which Ivan in a measure has while possessing advantages which Smerdyakov lacks. He is not a physical murderer, but he is much more of a murderer than the brothers Karamazov: they murdered a depraved buffoon, but he murders innocent and naïve souls with the poison of his ideas. Dmitri fears him instinctively and he has already begun to corrupt young Kolya. In the United States today he would have proclaimed himself a "scientific humanist." This is why, with a wisdom which transcends his own intellectual shortcomings, Dmitri calls him a "Bernard," intuitively grasping the evil inherent in Rakitin's trust in science. Thus Rakitin is both a contrast to and a mirror image of Ivan. The latter is honorable and his atheism is anguished. The former is a clever and shallow cad. But this is not all, for Ivan's advanced ideas must be considered by contrast with Miüsov, the Europeanized Russian liberal who liked to give the impression that he had had his turn on the barricades in Paris. Ivan is not irredeemable, because he never loses his roots in the Russian soil, while Miüsov has lost touch with his native Russia. With his wealth, family background, worldly sophistication, there is nothing inside the polished shell. He thinks of himself as a humanitarian but of course he really isn't, as his treatment of his nephew shows.

Now each of these characters throws light on the others, and
placed in order from Ivan through Miüsov, Rakitin, Smerdyakov,
and Kolya (who is a boyish Ivan who has not yet lost the lovable-
ness of childhood) they give us a complete picture of the anti-
religious, rationalistic "liberal" in his various modalities. Several
other series of contrasting modalities of the same type are
"studied," for instance that of the monks, with Zossima, Paisiv,
Ioseff, Ferapont, and the monk from Obdorsk revealing the nature
of Christian love, Christian renunciation of the world, and the
pathological manifestations to which religion can give rise.

However it is not possible to understand an individual or a
type through behavioral observation alone. We have to look into
those secret crevices of the soul which ordinarily the individual
does not suspect he has. In *The Brothers* we become acquainted
with Ivan in the ordinary manner—see him act, hear him express
his attitudes and his ideas. In the famous chapters 4 and 5 of
Book V, entitled "Rebellion" and "The Grand Inquisitor," we
see the depth of his concern for the religious problem and are
given a first look into the nature of his difficulties. But Dostoevski
goes not only beyond Ivan's observed behavior, into his intellectual
and moral structure, but into the unconscious double, which the
Freudian would call the Id. This dimension of the personality had
begun to be suspected in Dostoevski's day, but not until Dostoevski
himself clarified it does literature begin fully to explore it. Freud's
influence of course has made it the ordinary possession of literate
men. (It is merely a matter of accuracy to remember, however,
that Dostoevski has not been the only writer before Freud who
was aware of the fact that the human soul has a third, hidden
dimension. Shakespeare, to take a trite example, used a somnam-
bulistic dream to reveal a hidden sense of guilt. Nor was Freud
the first psychologist to look into unconscious motives; Nietzsche
used the method frequently and with tremendous success.) But
Dostoevski's grasp of hidden motives and of instinctual processes
which express themselves deviously differs in a very important
respect from that exhibited by contemporary novelists who go to
Freud for their knowledge of the human soul. Dostoevski conceives the soul as fluid and he presents it, so to speak, directly
for his reader's inspection. Freudians have taught us to conceive

of the soul as a stiff mechanism made up of instincts and forces and energies which constitute a lumbering and creaking machine. Again, they have made current the doctrine that the phenomena which are not directly observable can be discovered only by inference. The reading of dreams, the analysis of the true meaning of everyday errors, the discovery of our hidden desires and intentions behind our ostensible discourse and behavior, thus become a silly and rather mechanical puzzling out of facile charades. And the result is that the conception of character of the novelist who has learned his human nature from Freud and not in the world, as Dostoevski did, becomes the game of planting symbols according to a simple mechanical formula. In Freud, taken within the context of his therapeutic objectives, his analytic technique and his hypothetical constructions have a pragmatic justification. But when these constructions are used by amateurs for *their* purposes, what in the hands of the therapist is a source of insight degenerates rapidly into a shallow technique of obfuscation.

Dostoevski reveals Ivan's unconscious through the use of a Freudian device—the hallucination or delirium which Ivan undergoes when he is ill and in which he meets the Devil who, he tells us twice, is himself. Through this "visit" we find out that the man who is preoccupied with the relation between Church and State, and who clearly grasps the consequence of the denial of freedom to man in favor of happiness, is really, at bottom, a man whose soul is ripped by a contradiction of which he is perfectly aware, but which he is not able to resolve. For while Ivan cannot believe in God he believes nevertheless in evil; but he goes beyond the Manicheans, for he gives evil the primacy. The Devil says to Ivan:

> I . . . simply ask for annihilation. No, live, I am told, for there'd be nothing without you. If everything in the universe were sensible, nothing would happen. There would be no events without you, and there must be events. So against the grain I serve to produce events and do what's irrational because I am commanded to. . . .

Of course the primacy of evil is qualified by the fact that the Devil accomplishes the creative task in obedience to a command, but nevertheless it is he who is the cause of events.

In this same paragraph the "visitor" says to Ivan, "You are laughing—no, you are not laughing, you are angry again. You are forever angry, all you care about is intelligence. . . ." This is a very important remark to which we shall have to return. Let us however follow the conversation a few minutes longer. Ivan, "with a smile of hatred," asks:

> "Then even you don't believe in God?" . . . .
> "What can I say—that is, if you are in earnest. . ."
> "Is there a God or not?" Ivan cried with the same savage intensity.
> "Ah, then you are in earnest! My dear fellow, upon my word I don't know. There! I have said it now!"
> "You don't know, but you see God? No, you are not some one apart, you are myself, you are I and nothing more! You are rubbish, you are my fancy!"
> "Well, if you like, I have the same philosophy as you, that would be true. *Je pense, donc je suis,* I know that for a fact, all the rest, all these worlds, God and even Satan—all that is not proved, to my mind. . . ."

Thus it turns out that Ivan, who believes in the primacy of evil, when you press him, does not know, is an absolute solipsist, and cannot discover proof of the world, of God, or even of Satan. The reason for his plight has already been given to us by his double: all he cares about is intelligence. And intelligence by itself is the source of all evil, and ultimately of despair. This is one of the things that Dostoevski knew with the same certainty that Ivan knew that he was because he thought.

Through the delirium Dostoevski has shown us the depths of Ivan's personality, but without the need to refer us to the Freudian code-book. Other devices which Dostoevski employs in order to reveal the depths of the soul are not as easy to explain in general terms. One of the ways in which he does it is by having one character explain or reveal the meaning of another's actions; another is by having a character behave differently before each of the other characters with whom he has intercourse. Thus, Kolya, that delightfully lovable mischief-maker, is quite a different person with his fellows than he is with Alyosha or with the two children of the doctor's wife to whom his mother rented rooms.

This device gives us the complexity of a person. But usually in order to reveal the duality of the soul Dostoevski conducts the dramatic narrative on two planes, in such wise that while a character, let us say, is protesting love for another, he is revealing hatred. As illustration take the manner in which Fyodor immediately upon entering the Elder's cell reveals through his buffoonery his deep shame.

> "Precisely to our time," cried Fyodor Pavlovitch, "but no sign of my son Dmitri. I apologize for him, sacred Elder!" (Alyosha shuddered all over at 'sacred elder'.)

Before the guests have had time to take in the room, we, the readers, are plunged into the scene, shameful and comic, in which Fyodor's buffoonery discloses what it intends to cover, a sick soul consumed with the need to castigate itself. Or let us recall the chapter entitled "A Laceration in the Drawing Room," although almost any other episode chosen at random would serve as well. In this chapter Katerina Ivanovna, Mme. Hohlakov, Ivan, and Alyosha discuss Katerina's feeling for Dmitri. In this conversation Katerina tells the others that she does not know if she still loves Dmitri but that she feels pity for him and does not intend to abandon him even if he abandons her for Grushenka. She will not get in his way, she says, she will go to another town, but she will watch over him all her life. In the long run, she is certain to be able to show him that she loves him like a sister who has sacrificed her life to him. The moment that she begins to discuss Dmitri the reader begins to suspect that she is not quite sincere. The lack of sincerity is suggested by Dostoevski himself through an explanation which he makes of the word "laceration" used by Madame Hohlakov during the scene with Grushenka the preceding day. But the word "sacrifice" used by Katerina Ivanovna gives her away completely, for her statement contrasts sharply with the picture already presented of her return of the money given her by Dmitri, the way in which she declares her love to Dmitri and asks him to marry her, telling him that she will be his chattel, when we have already seen how proud she really is. Dmitri earlier had told us that she loved her own virtue, not him. Now it becomes clear that Katerina Ivanovna is really after revenge. In order to make Dmitri pay for the humiliations he has inflicted on her she is quite willing to put herself to a great deal of pain and sacrifice. This is fully confirmed by Alyosha's explosion when he tells her in a tone entirely out of harmony with his usual gentleness that she does not love Dmitri and wants to hurt him, and that she loves Ivan and wants to hurt him also. Later, at the trial, after Katerina Ivanovna has given evidence in Dmitri's favor, she becomes hysterical and gives the President of the Court the letter that convicts Dmitri, thus giving full reign to a hatred which until then she had tried to conceal from herself but which Dostoevski had already clearly revealed to the reader. But no sooner is Dmitri sentenced than she repents and seeks his love, in an oblique way again.

3

Dostoevski, of course, is not equipped to give a scientific explanation of those aspects of the personality which he discovered, nor is he interested in doing so. But he does more than give a mere phenomenological description of psychological processes. Indeed what gives his novels their depth and makes him one of the great thinkers of the modern world is that while positive science and naturalistic philosophy were straining to reduce man to purely naturalistic terms and to deny his metaphysical dimension in empirical terms, Dostoevski was rediscovering that dimension in empirical terms which gave the lie to the modernists by reinvoking ancient truths whose old formulation had ceased to be convincing. With Kierkegaard, therefore, he was one of a small number of men who helped us forge the weapons with which to fend off the onrush of a naturalism bent on stripping us of our essentially human, our metaphysical, reality.

The reason that Dostoevski is able to make these discoveries is not hard to find. It is well known that he started as a liberal and in "the house of the dead" gave up his youthful faith and turned toward orthodoxy. In Siberia he seems to have found, as many had found earlier and others have found since under adversity, that certain radical crises of the human spirit are neither intelligible nor manageable by means of any form of naturalistic philosophy.

Dostoevski's shift has frequently puzzled his readers. How was it possible for him, they have asked, to come out of prison with a heart free of resentment at the cruel mockery of the execution and the horror of the four years of prison? But no one can claim to be a serious reader of Dostoevski who does not know the answer to this question. His books are the answer—if we remember that below their psychological is to be found a metaphysical level. Dostoevski exhibits a fact that to the average Christian seems ridiculous: that the guilt of one man is the guilt of all. We see in his pages how concern with iniquity expresses itself in a liberal and in a Christian way. The former repudiates self-guilt, and this leads to cannibalism; the latter accepts it and seeks to dissolve evil in selflessness and love. This is one insight which is clear and at which Dostoevski arrived because he was a religious man and not a naturalist.

Dostoevski's turn toward political conservatism and religious orthodoxy has been taken by many of his critics as evidence that he was wrong about social and religious questions in spite of his great powers as an artist and his psychological acuity. One of his critics, Simmons, dismisses his philosophy because it implies the denial of progress. His critics pretend to admire his art but deplore the content of his philosophy, obviously blind to the organic connection between his skill as artist, his perspicacity as psychologist, and his metaphysical insight. But one has not begun to understand him until one has grasped how, as Dostoevski deepened his insight into human nature, he came more and more clearly to see that man's plight, his unhappiness, his divided soul, his need for self-laceration, his viciousness, his pride and his shame, his ills in short, flow from the same fountain-head, his unbelief. But unbelief is lack of love which in turn is hell. Dostoevski progressively gains a firmer grasp of this insight through his creative work and in his last novel he is finally able successfully to bring into a comprehensive dramatic synthesis all his views of man and of his relations to his fellows and to the universe. At the heart of all questions, he comes to see, is the question of God, which is the question of love. Early in The Brothers he tells us that if Alyosha decided that

God and immortality did not exist he would at once have become an atheist and a socialist. For socialism is not merely the labor question, it is before all things the atheistic question, the question of the form taken by atheism today, the question of the tower of Babel built without God, not to mount to Heaven from earth but to set up Heaven on earth.

This is to say that the labor question as it has been formulated since his day is the critical mode through which contemporary secularism manifests itself. For what socialism seeks is the recognition and institutionalization—achieved in Russia with the revolution—of a historical process already fully manifest in bourgeois society since the Seventeenth Century, but which the bourgeoisie has resisted acknowledging explicitly: Socialism would have man define his destiny exclusively in historical terms and denies the validity or necessity of metaphysical agencies. This process, which Dewey has called "the conclusion of natural science," would uproot as obstructive vestiges all religious institutions and beliefs and would substitute for them a conception of human destiny defined in terms of secular meliorism.

This problem poses itself in Dostoevski's mind in terms of a comprehensive metaphor possessing two conflicting terms, "Russia *versus* Europe." "Europe" promised happiness, but Dostoevski saw that the price of an exclusively secular happiness was freedom. On this side one had only the choice between the Grand Inquisitor and the nihilism of Shigalov and Pyotr Stepanovitch (in *The Possessed*), for whom is substituted the even more vicious and convincing figure of that "Bernard," Rakitin (in *The Brothers*). On the other side one had "Russia," and the term, Dostoevski believed passionately, had to be accepted, so to speak, "as was" and without bargaining. The pictures of Shigalov and Rakitin need not give us pause, however, even if we find that we cannot accept them as probable, since for these elements of the metaphor we can substitute at discretion the more up-to-date picture of the commissar with his automatic always at the back of the head of anyone who challenges his will. The truth of the insight is what matters; and at this moment history threatens to give us a complete and irrefutable demonstration of it. Confronted with such an either-or Dostoevski chose "Russia" in the belief that the Russian people would never accept atheistic socialism because they were too deeply and genuinely Christian. If we take the metaphor as intended we cannot fairly maintain that Dostoevski was wrong. Indeed he came very close to the truth. But we must add in the same breath that one element of the metaphor's tenor, "Russia," was not in his day to be found and never will be either in history or in geography.

The other element of the tenor, "Europe," includes "the state" which is force, with its instruments, mysticism, miracle, and authority; justice without love, which involves blood; equality in things; and the multiplication of desires. Those at the controls of such a society are condemned to isolation and spiritual suicide and the ruled are sentenced to envy or murder. In contrast "Russia," which in justice to Dostoevski we should remember he conceived as an ideal not yet adequately actualized, includes the church after it has absorbed the state, the denial of desires, the brotherhood of all living beings, spiritual dignity, justice in Christ and instead of pride and envy, humility and recognition of one's own sinfulness, and hence one's responsibility for the sins of all other men. The first term, "Europe," is of course exaggerated, and the second an improbable idealization. And if the reader should inquire by what means did Dostoevski identify church bureaucracy and worldliness with Europe-Rome and what permitted him to clear the Russian hierarchy of all charges, so as to make it the potential kingdom of heaven on earth, the answer, unsatisfactory to us who do not love Russia and do not hate Europe as he did, runs something like this: Dostoevski knew that the City of God is not of this world, but the route to it must be through "Russia" and not through "Europe," since the latter has been corrupted beyond redemption by the Grand Inquisitor, the Bernards and the socialists—who are three peas from the same pod. That a man who finds the ethical essence of Christianity in love could so inordinately hate Rome-Europe, or indeed could without shame exhibit the sores of his anti-Semitism, is something which no admirer of his ought to conceal or should try to apologize for. There is wisdom enough in him to make up for his ugly defects.

The question of God, however, is not a question that Dostoevski settles easily by falling back on simple faith. Dostoevski, who can

easily be convicted of blindness to the evils of his own state and
church, refuses flatly to compromise with the facts of individual
experience, untoward as he knows them to be to his religious
beliefs. Referring to *The Brothers* he is quoted as having said:

> Even in Europe there have never been atheistic expressions of such
> power. Consequently, I do not believe in Christ and His confession
> as a child, but my hosanna has come through a great furnace of
> doubt.

In his notebook, and referring to criticisms of *The Brothers*, he
writes

> The villains teased me for my ignorance and a retrograde faith in
> God. These thickheads did not dream of such a powerful negation
> of God as that put in "The (Grand) Inquisitor" and in the preced-
> ing chapter. . . . I do not believe in God like a fool (a fanatic).
> And they wished to teach me, and laughed over my backwardness!
> But their stupid natures did not dream of such a powerful negation
> as I have lived through. It is for them to teach me!

But we do not need this statement in order to discover how prolonged and anguished was his struggle with the religious question.
All we need in order to make the discovery is a hasty reading of
The Brothers. It has often been said of Milton that he did better
by his Satan than by his God; and similarly it has been argued
that Dostoevski's good and saintly characters, Prince Myshkin in
The Idiot, Father Tihon in *The Possessed*, and Father Zossima,
are far more tenuous than the human devils that abound in his
books. There is, I believe, some truth in this observation. But the
statement is partly false if it is forgotten that Dostoevski believed
that genuine goodness can only be reached by those who plunge
down to the bottom and there, in their darkest hour, somehow
find God. This was his own personal experience and it was borne
out by observation. If this is true, it is Zossima, and not Prince
Myshkin (in *The Idiot*), who is the truly good man. But it cannot be denied that none of his good or saintly characters—Sonia
in *Crime and Punishment*, Myshkin, and even Zossima—is endowed with as dense and authentic a humanity as his evil characters. Dostoevski was aware of this criticism, which is not difficult

to answer. The reason why they are not, is that genuine goodness and saintliness are harmonious, unassertive and hence undramatic, dull, affairs. But this is not a comment on them or on Dostoevski but on us, his readers.

Be that as it may, in the portraits of his great sinners and criminals Dostoevski did not merely study the effects of vice but the effects of disbelief. He traces the effect of vice, pride, and hatred on the disintegration of the personality and he is most successful in drawing men in whom vice is connected with their repudiation of their condition as creatures and with their consequent effort to set themselves up wittingly or unwittingly as gods. And he shows how men who do not believe in God end up by believing in their own omnipotence. At the root of this transposition we find pride, which would not have welled up and flooded one's consciousness had he been able to grasp clearly the fact that he is a creature, which is to say, finite and dependent. But this kind of pride is in turn traced by Dostoevski to the misuse of reason, the belief that science and the intelligence are enough for the development of human life. In the early *Notes from the Underground* he stated fully what for lack of a more adequate term we must refer to as his anti-intellectualism. From that book on, the worst evil of his characters is in one way or another connected with the belief in the self-sufficiency of the intellect. There is of course evil in the sensual animalism of Fyodor Karamazov, but there is greater evil in Rakitin. And the greatest responsibility for the crime must be assumed by Ivan, the source of whose corruption we have already looked at.

But Dostoevski is not a propagandist and much less a dogmatist. He is, in the most important sense of that word of many meanings, a genuine philosopher, for he really inquired, questioned, sought the truth, instead of seeking bad reasons for what he already believed on faith (if I may be allowed to spoil Bradley's famous epigram). It would not be inexact to say that Dostoevski was forced against his will by the facts that his experience disclosed to him into the conviction that atheism is fatal practically and false theoretically. But he would never allow any argument or any fact to involve him in the denial of an aspect of experience which presented itself to him as authentic.

But then, how can one believe in God?—How, that is, if one is not a peasant woman of simple faith but has the brains, the education, and the range of experience of an Ivan? One cannot, is Ivan's answer, so long as the evil of the world remains to give the lie to God. It is known that Dostoevski called chapters 4 and 5 of Book V of *The Brothers*—to which we have already referred—"the culminating point of the novel." The first of these chapters contains Ivan's case against God. I call it "Ivan's dossier," because he introduced his case by saying to Alyosha that he is "fond of collecting certain facts and anecdotes copied from newspapers." This is data one cannot neglect, if one is going to attempt an explanation of the ways of God to man. There is the case of Richard, the Swiss savage, burnt at the stake in Geneva; the case of the Russian peasant who beats the horse in the eyes, and then the cases of the children, culminating in the story of the child thrown to the savage dogs in front of his mother.

> The General orders the child to be undressed; the child is stripped naked. He shivers numb with terror, not daring to cry. . . . "Make him run" commands the General. "Run, run!" shout the dog-boys. The boy runs. "At him!" yells the General, and he sets the whole pack of hounds on the child. The hounds catch him and tear him to pieces before his mother's eyes.

One sentence completes the story, and it is superbly ironic in its bathos: "I believe the General was afterwards declared incapable of administering his estates." How, in view of such things, can you believe in Providence?

Dostoevski knew perfectly well that in his own terms Ivan could not be answered. The furnace of doubt through which Dostoevski said he had passed before he was able to arrive at his faith, consisted of at least two flames: the devastating knowledge he had of the criminal and depraved tendencies to be found at the bottom of the human soul and of which he gives us in *The Brothers* three superb examples, Fyodor, Rakitin, and Smerdyakov; and the knowledge he has that injustice is inherent in the structure of human living and cannot be dislodged from it. These two flames, as I may continue to call them, cannot be smothered with social reforms or mechanical improvements. This is the hope of the rationalistic liberal, a hope that springs from his shallow grasp of human nature, and which, when it is not a mere pretense, as it is with Miüsov, is a diabolical lie, as it is with Rakitin. In "The Grand Inquisitor" he finally brought to full expression the implication of the conflict between God and freedom on the one hand and the atheistic effort to bring heaven to earth by dispensing with God on the other. The point of the conflict cannot be stated abstractly without vulgarizing it, but since the long marginal commentary which would be required to do it justice is not possible here we must risk a brief statement. The conflict is between The Grand Inquisitor and Father Zossima. The alternatives are clear and exhaustive, since compromises are unstable and futile for they reproduce the undesirable features of both terms and none of the virtues of either. The villain of Ivan's poem is Jesus, who rejected the prizes offered him by The Great Spirit, Satan, and wittingly loaded man with a burden he cannot carry, freedom. It is not freedom that man wants, but miracle, mystery, and authority. He "is tormented by no greater anxiety than to find someone quickly to whom he can hand over that gift of freedom with which the ill-fated creature is born." The Roman Catholic Church has managed to correct the harm that Jesus attempted to do, and socialism but carries on from where Rome leaves off. In order to give man happiness it has been necessary for the Church to take the sword of Caesar and in taking it of course it rejected Jesus and chose Satan. For this reason Dostoevski believes that socialism and Catholicism are identical as to ends: both seek to relieve man of the burden of freedom. But happiness without God is a delusion that leads men to devour one another or leads a strong man to gain power over his fellows for their own good, and gives them happiness at the price of keeping them from realizing their full humanity.

The alternative then to the ideal of The Grand Inquisitor is to accept God, freedom, and immortality. But this alternative has somehow to dispose of Ivan's dossier. To give man freedom is not only to open to him the door of eternal salvation, it is also to open the other door, whose threshold hope cannot cross. You cannot have Heaven without Hell; Heaven entails the General and his dogs. It is a terrible choice and no one knew more clearly than

Dostoevski how terrible it was: happiness without freedom, or
freedom *and* hell. Ivan's dossier cannot be exorcised into thin air.
What is the answer? It is found in Father Zossima, and that means
in our acceptance of our condition as creatures. This calls for love
at the heart of human existence; but not the abstract and self-
deceived love of your rationalistic liberal, your Miüsov, but the
personal love of Father Zossima. The answer resolves the conflict
because it reveals that hell is life without love. And it also reveals
that Ivan's dossier is possible only through a lie. For Ivan forgets
that he is a creature, that he therefore has no right to challenge
God, nor to demand that God answer his question in a manner
satisfactory to him or he will refuse to accept His world and "return His ticket." This is, of course, to fall back on the inscrutable
designs of the Deity which Spinoza called the refuge of ignorance.
But Dostoevski is not frightened by this retort, since he is faced
clearly with an either/or: either God and love or the world
which the Rakitins, the Miüsovs, and the Smerdyakovs would
create, the world of the Grand Inquisitor. It will be retorted that
what I have said makes no sense, for freedom rejects mystery and
it is mystery Dostoevski invokes when he invokes God. The answer
is simple: what the Grand Inquisitor wants is mystification, superstition, and that is totally different from the mystery entailed by
belief in a God of love.

It should not be overlooked, besides, that what Alyosha calls
Ivan's rebellion is the challenge launched against God by a man
who claims to be concerned with human tears:

> I took the case of children only to make my case clearer. Of the
> other tears of humanity with which the earth is soaked from the
> crust to its center, I will say nothing.

But it is simply not true that Ivan loves man as he says he does.
If he did, he would follow in the steps of Father Zossima. That,
and that only, is the way of true love. The man who loves his fellows has neither time nor energy for rebellion. He realizes that
he himself is guilty, for even if his own hands are not stained with
blood, he is responsible for the blood shed by his fellows. And
instinct with love and active about the misery of others he no
longer hugs with bravado his little dossier against God. But this

Ivan was not capable of doing at this point in the novel. He first
had to be an accomplice in the murder of his father, had to be
brought by his complement, Smerdyakov, to see his complicity,
and had to peer into the depths of his soul in the form of the devil,
before there could be any hope that he might be reborn. As the
novel closes we are left with the clear indication that that hope is
a possibility. But we are also left with the insight that so long
as a man remains in the world that possibility cannot be fully realized. Ultimately Dostoevski's vision of secular life is supremely
tragic.

4

The psychological and the metaphysical make up the concrete
reality of Dostoevski's human world. But the structure of that
world and the values it embodies have only been referred to in
passing, and the reader is entitled to ask what the critic takes them
to be. Unfortunately a complete answer would require a study at
least as long as the present; in the last few pages of this essay only
a hasty sketch can be attempted.

By way of introduction let us note that Dostoevski's great novels
mirror comprehensively the bourgeois world of the Nineteenth
Century, which is to say, a world in the first stages of an illness,
which we today have the melancholy opportunity of seeing in a
more advanced phase. Dostoevski had a ground for optimism on
which we cannot fall back: his faith that Zossima's "Russia"
marked the direction toward which civilization would turn. But
Rakitin and the other "Bernards" whom Dostoevski dreaded have
won, and the process by which man will destroy himself is already
well under way. Thus the utopia of The Grand Inquisitor turns
out to be a relatively pleasant morning dream as compared with
the brave new world which our twentieth-century Bernards and
Rakitins have begun to build. We are not going back to Zossima's
"Russia," but to the world of Marx and Dewey. Shigalov was a
poet whose prophecy fell too short. Dostoevski feared Fourrier and
Claude Bernard; we face the realities of Dewey and Marx.

What Dostoevski achieves is a definition of the destiny of Western Man: he defines the alternatives and the corresponding values

of each. Against the background of nineteenth-century humanity move the heroes of his books. In his inclusive world there is only one specimen lacking, the militant industrial proletariat, and the reason is that he did not have models of this type in his industrially backward native land. Saints, murderers, debauchees, intellectuals mad with pride, virginal whores and depraved ladies are the heroes. The mediocre, who lack the energy to become heroes, are pathetic rather than tragic, self-deceived rather than hypocritical, and unhappy, although ignorant of the malaise from which they suffer. Out of this mass emerge two groups of men who are in opposition: the saintly on the one side and those I have called "liberals" and the sensualists on the other. Zossima is Dostoevski's outstanding religious character, but Dostoevski "studies" the religious type as objectively as he studies the other, and unsparingly exhibits the pathological perversions to which it can lead. This group is not exclusively made up of monks or priests, but includes also self-deceived "ladies of little faith" and "peasant women who have faith." Alyosha, who is called the hero of the book, belongs to this group of course, but his portrait is not fully enough developed for us to be able to say whether in the two volumes that were never written, his role was to mediate between the world of Zossima and the secular world. Is it possible to live according to the teachings of Zossima outside the monastery? Could a Karamazov do it? Perhaps Alyosha can, although Prince Myshkin could not. We shall never know.

Between sensualists and liberals there is a formal identity of ends, since the sensualist uses his body as instrument of pleasure and the intellectual his mind. As between these two types of men it may be hard to choose; but Dostoevski seems to reveal in a man like Rakitin a greater depth of villainy than in Fyodor, since he is the source of far-spreading corruption, while the power of evil of a man like Fyodor Karamazov is limited to himself and those he uses for his pleasure. The sensualist is consumed with self-hatred and shame, and his end is to destroy himself, but the intellectual, consumed with pride, seeks either to challenge God or to become God, and succeeds in wreaking havoc among men. Above the adult world is the world of the children, whom Dostoevski could depict with inward fidelity, without sentimentality or condescen-

sion. Most of his children are lovable but some, like Kolya, have
already begun to be corrupted, and some are full blown little
demons: Lise knows clearly that she loves evil and wants to destroy
herself.

From Dostoevski's novels, as I have insisted, one can neither
abstract an ethical imperative nor a systematic philosophy capable
of doing justice to the dramatic tensions to be found in life as he
grasped it. A Marxist or a Deweyean will find that the picture of
Zossima expresses the failure of nerve which he thinks character-
izes our society. But there is no question that the picture painted
by Dostoevski, for all its dramatic irony, reveals a vision of the
world in which the answer to Ivan is found in the love of Zossima.
In other words, Dostoevski views human destiny from the standpoint of an anti-rationalism which is more radical than that of
Kierkegaard or Schopenhauer or Nietzsche. His rejection of "reason,"—"the stone wall constituted of the laws of nature, of the
deductions of learning, and of the science of mathematics,"—is
clearly stated very early in his *Letters from the Underworld*. But
the full implications of "reason," and of his rejection of it, awaited
the explorations which are to be found in his subsequent work, and
particularly in the four major novels. It is his anti-rationalism
which is the "source and head" of all his insights and attitudes,
theological, psychological and political, and which therefore furnishes the ground on which he is often disposed of as a reactionary.
That he should be dismissed in this way is intelligible; what is
difficult to understand is how any serious reader can accept his
psychological insights and simply ignore the matrix whence they
rise and the theoretical and practical implications to which they
lead. At a time when the conflict between "life" and "reason"—
the reason of the stone wall—was not yet resolved, Dostoevski,
with full awareness of what he was doing, threw his lot on the
side of life and against the stone wall. Old Karamazov is a depraved
buffoon, shameless and corrupt; but there is a tremendous energy
in him and love of life—the energy of the Karamazovs—and there
is passion; there is something elemental in his sinfulness which
flows whence all life, whether good or evil, flows, and which therefore draws our admiration since it is true, as Lise says, that in our
secret hearts we all love evil. By contrast Rakitin is a thoroughly

depraved and contemptible reptile with nothing to his favor. Thus the meaning of human destiny which Dostoevski reveals is not difficult to formulate: a life not built on love is not human, and a world without God is a world in which a triumphant cannibal frees the mass from the burden of their freedom in exchange for happiness. What Dostoevski could not admit to himself is that the Bernards in the not too long run will win. One may sympathize with the writer of the *Letters from the Underworld* when he says, "I am not going to accept that wall merely because I have to run up against it, and have no means to knock it down." But one should not forget that the tragic alternative is ineluctable: either accept it or smash your head against it.

1951

2

PROBLEMS OF AESTHETICS

what is a poem?[1]

Our question can be succinctly answered as follows: A poem is
a linguistic artifact, whose function is to organize the primary data
of experience that can be exhibited in and through words. With
the necessary changes this can be said of all art. Put in different
terms, what poetry uniquely does is to reveal a world which is
self-sufficient. It does not communicate in the ordinary sense of the
term, nor does it imitate or designate existent or imaginary things
which can be apprehended independently of the poem. By means
of the self-sufficient world that poetry reveals we are able to grasp,
as the poem lingers in memory as a redolence, the actual world in
which we live. Without the aid of poetry our ambient world remains an inchoate, unstructured chaos.

For this doctrine I do not claim novelty. I would suspect it if
it were new. But from old truths as from old canvases, the grime

of time must occasionally be removed. All that can be claimed for
the doctrine is that it attempts to translate into contemporary
terms and to apply to aesthetics an insight inherited from Kant.
Cassirer pointed out two reasons the Kantian doctrine is unacceptable to us: Kant did not reckon with the problems which
evolution forces on us and he did not recognize that the mind
functions in other modes than the narrowly cognitive one. I would
add that Cassirer's reformulation of the Kantian doctrine, although an enrichment and an improvement of it, is still defective,
because it puts all the activities of the mind on one plane. But
knowledge, morality, and religion, presuppose and build on the
world we come to know by means of art. The world that poetry
reveals to us is usually called the common sense world. We do not
constitute it in the sense that we create it out of nothing. The
world in which we live is there, furthering or impeding our activity, independently of the mind's grasp of it; but as we come to
know it, the world is constituted by means of a symbolic process
which is the heart of the aesthetic activity. What art does is put
the world at our disposal.

It is the explication of these ideas that shall occupy us. Let us
begin with the statement that poetry is a linguistic artifact. Charles
Feidelson has recently reminded us in *Symbolism and American
Literature* that this notion is a commonplace in much of twentieth
century criticism. Immediately, however, we are confronted with a
complex difficulty. And the reason—and a good one, as it seems to
me—is that, as Feidelson puts it,

> critics and writers tend to conceive of the literary work—the *real*
> poem or novel or story—as residing primarily in language and as
> consisting primarily of word arrangements.

And he continues,

> The strategy of modern criticism is to give "language" a kind of
> autonomy by conceiving it as a realm of meaning, and the structure
> explored is discovered *in* the language, not *behind* the poem in the
> writer's mind or *in front* of the poem in the external world.

Note that it is Mr. Feidelson who employs the italics. And note also that the import of his remarks is wholly to reject the theory of imitation. Thus, it is simply not true, as has recently been claimed by a historian of philosophy, that modern critics are returning to the theory of imitation. One small flock of belated swallows does no more prevent the turning of the maples, than an overeager one speeds their budding. The present need is not for breathing old life into old corpses long ago buried, but for facing in fresh terms the problems of our age. But if Mr. Feidelson is correct, modern criticism and poetry (using the term to include both verse and prose) have given rise to a difficult problem, nor is it one whose solution can be left to the critics. For the conception of language presupposed by modern poetry runs counter to the analysis of language widely accepted by the dominant philosophy of our period. I shall refer to this analysis as "the reigning theory," and will attempt to sketch the reasons it cannot be applied to poetry. The problem is not one that a critic can overlook, since in the absence of a satisfactory conception of language he cannot fully understand what a poem is and how it fulfills its function. However, a satisfactory theory of poetic language is not sufficient to tell us what a poem is. Poetry is considerably more than language that says something in a peculiar way. It is matter informed; and an analysis of the principles of organization would have to be included in a complete answer to our question. Some of these principles, particularly the two to which I shall refer below, are generic features not only of poetry but of all art, and are therefore legitimate objects of the aesthetician's interest; in a more ambitious essay they would have to be examined with care.

The first feature to which attention must be called is one for which no satisfactory term, so far as I know, has been suggested. Sometimes one hears it said that the poem is "autonomous." But there are at least two reasons for avoiding this term. It usually refers to the power that a thing has to give the law to itself. If poetry could be made in a social vacuo, by men who never heard of other poems before they made theirs, any one poem would give the law to itself. But we knew, long before Eliot's famous essay, that the individual talent works always within a tradition by which it must in some measure be ruled, and which to some extent, if successful, it modifies.

Again, a poem means or says something for, or to, a reader. But for the poem to say something to a reader the reader must know the language in which the poem is written. The poem is not autonomous in the sense that the poet is free to employ language —words and syntax—which he creates from nothing for the purpose of writing one single poem, and which he discards after using. Not even Joyce attempted so hopeless a task. The poet employs language already in use, and a disregard of the conventions of the language exacts its price.

I prefer, therefore, to say that the poem is "self-sufficient," although I am no more satisfied with the new term than I am with the old. A poem is self-sufficient in the sense that it contains within itself all that it requires to make it intelligible to a person who has knowledge of the language in which it is written. But such a knowledge is an indeterminate factor, which may vary from the deep and broad knowledge of a man like Kittredge or Bowra to the thin hoard of hard clichés that makes up the wealth of the half-literate products of our educational factories. The poem is intelligible when we grasp what it means. Otherwise stated, a poem is a complete presentation. If it is not, it constitutes a problem, and if it does the fact can be traced to one or two factors or to both: either the poem suffers from defects of construction which deny it self-sufficiency, or we are not able to read it as the self-sufficient whole that it is.

In order for the poem to function as a self-sufficient whole, we must approach it in an aesthetic attitude. We do so when we read it with rapt, intransitive attention on its full presentational immediacy. It is not difficult to see that the self-sufficiency of the object is realized only through the intransitivity of our apprehension of it, and that the manner in which we apprehend it depends not only on the reader but also on the way in which the poem is constructed. A poem functions as a self-sufficient whole when it has, as we have long known, unity, when its discriminable elements are tied by organic interrelationships in such a manner that our attention is not led off from them but is held captive by them and is fully satisfied in its captivity.

Contemporary writers tend to substitute, for the old notion of the unity of art, the notion of its organic nature, and a recent writer on aesthetics has offered this notion as his own discovery. But that the poem is an organic whole was clearly known by critics like Bradley and philosophers like Dewey and Parker, and has been more or less clearly grasped by all those who have concerned themselves with the analysis of works of art. It may be granted, however, that the substitution of the notion of organic unity for the old notion of unity in variety enables us to emphasize the fact that those elements that criticism discriminates are such that their meanings or values depend not only on what they are taken to be when considered separately, but on what they are when conceived as interrelated to one another and as making up a complex yet somehow unified whole.

What gives the poem its unity or its organic nature is to be traced to the manner in which its substance is informed, and as regards this feature of poetry I take it that a good deal is known, nor is it the business of the aesthetician to try to do what the critic is better fitted to do. The approaches to this problem are many, the aesthetics on which these approaches are based often extremely inadequate, but the actual analysis of the features by means of which the poet achieves the information of his substance is very often enlightening. Turn to a well-known study like that of Percy Lubbock's *The Craft of Fiction,* or to Henry James' Prefaces and *Notebooks,* and you will find enlightening analyses of the means and strategies employed by the poet to give to the poem the unity it requires to become an object of aesthetic apprehension. Turn to Andrew Wright's recently published study of Jane Austen, and you will discover a painstaking and perspicuous analysis of the means employed by one of the supreme artificers of the novel to achieve her effects. Turn to the work of men like Cleanth Brooks and Arnold Stein, and you will gain a good deal of light on the means employed by writers of verse to achieve their ends. By mentioning this heterogeneous number of instances, I am trying to suggest how much is known about the means by which the poet informs his material, and how diverse are the critical assumptions that guide the analysis of these means.

This is all that it is possible to say about the two generic features
of poetry, its self-sufficiency and the unity or organic nature on
which its self-sufficiency depends. It was necessary to mention them
at least in passing because they need to be borne in mind if we are
to follow the elucidation of the question we shall turn to next:
How does the poem say what it says? But first let us note that I
shall take for granted that the poem does indeed mean or say something, although this seems to have been seriously denied by some
critics.

It is desirable, before turning to our question, to call attention to
a problem intimately related to this one but with which I shall not
here burden myself, What is the status in being of that which the
poem says? I call that which the poem says "the object of the
poem," and discuss it below (pp. 129-143).

To the question, How does the poem say or mean its object? we
answer first that it does not mean its object in the same manner in
which ordinary discourse means its referend. Nothing that a poem
says can be compared with an independent existent reality, whether
actual or imaginary. Even the so-called "probabilities" of the Aristotelians depend, not on the sense we have obtained, prior to the
reading of the poem, as to what is possible or what is absurd in
ordinary existence, but on the manner in which the poet controls
his devices in order to exclude from our consciousness just those
notions which we are apt to bring to our reading from our ordinary
experience and which make the poem appear absurd if we employ
them to judge the poem. Anyone who doubts this has not read
stories like Kafka's *Metamorphosis* or has not reflected on the fact
that what is usually called the overwhelmingly authentic reality or
the convincing authenticity of such stories has nothing to do with
what he knows about the laws of nature. But if the poem does not
mean anything that exists prior to it and independently of it, what
does it say?

It is only fair to warn the reader that a theory is to be expounded
which, if he has not come across it before, will no doubt sound
utterly absurd to him. The reason for this I have already suggested: We usually try to analyze the meaning of poetry in terms
of the reigning theory of language. But this theory has been devised
by philosophers whose dominant interest has been in science and

in practical "communication." Men preoccupied with such problems are not likely to consider seriously the question of the origin of culture. If to such indifference we add the widespread notion that the function of art is to give us pleasure or to arouse emotion, and add further the contempt for art which positivism spreads, and add besides the tendency of critics to make do with theoretical tools picked up from the pawn shops of the schools, it is not difficult to see why the problem which the language of poetry poses has not been taken seriously. What the reigning theory does is to reintroduce surreptitiously the doctrine of imitation. "Surreptitiously," because usually the disreputable old wolf is brought back under the sheep's clothes of "expression." Writers who accept the reigning theory equate Being with Existence, and define the latter in spacio-temporal terms. On that theory, if language has meaning, it must have referends and these must exist, since this is the only mode of being our dominant philosophies allow. But if referends exist, they must be open to apprehension independently of the signs through which we signify them. Thus the theory of expression which for idealists like Croce and Collingwood is an unqualified theory of creation, becomes a mere theory of discovery for those who accept the reigning theory of language, and the task of the artist is reduced to finding a way in which to refer through the medium—through sound or clay or color or language—either to emotions or to external affairs. If this is not the old theory of imitation we must revoke the principle of the identity of the indiscernibles. But since it is obvious that poetry does not refer to actual existents, and since by now we cannot forget that it cannot refer to emotions experienced by the poet prior to the writing of the poem, we save the theory by saying that it refers to "imaginary affairs," or to a realm of illusion. The Roman plays of Shakespeare are about imagined actions and characters to which historical names have been attached; and Yeats' two Byzantium poems are about valuations the poet wishes to make about the relation of youth to old age and to the ageless worth of art.

This interpretation sounds plausible until we remember that one thing contemporary criticism has made clear is that what a poem says or means is neither its paraphrase or translation nor what the paraphrase points to. The paraphrase does indeed point to part of what the poem says or means, but the best and most exhaustive paraphrase does not point to all the poem says. Somehow what the poem says cannot be conveyed by any other means than the poem itself.

If we are to account for this puzzling fact, we must look at poetry freshly and recognize that unlike the language of science and that of practical communication, what poetry says or means it says *in* and *through* its language. *Through* language it refers to an object that can also be referred to by means of a more or less carefully contrived paraphrase. *In* its language the poem says something by means of the linguistic aspect of the language as such, and not of those aspects of the language which the reigning theory recognizes as carrying the semantic and pragmatic dimension of meaning. But note that I do not claim that when poetic language says in itself something, what it does is to arouse emotion in the reader—this it often does through what scientific semioticians call its pragmatic dimension, but I am not concerned here with the question whether poetry should or should not arouse emotion. What I am saying is that poetic language does not merely refer to something through it, and hence external to it, but in it; and hence in some sense its meaning has its locus in the language itself. If what poetry refers to has status in Being, it must be a status other than that of existence. If this holds, the distinction made by the reigning theory among the semantic, the pragmatic and the syntactic dimensions of language may be adequate for the purposes of ordinary and of scientific communication. But it is not adequate for an understanding of what poetry does, whether we call it communication or, as Allen Tate calls it, communion. We must, therefore, ask what is meant by saying that language does more than enable us to exchange meanings whose referends pre-exist and are independent of the language through which we refer to them. Since it is not possible to do more than sketch an answer, I am certain that I shall have the reader's indulgence for summarizing highly controversial conclusions in a dogmatic manner. These conclusions can be epitomized in the formula: "The mind is constitutive of the world."

Consider, first, that we have at present scientific evidence that strengthens the purely speculative Kantian hypothesis that the mind is in some sense constitutive of our ambient world. I refer to the work of linguists like Whorf and those who, like Hoijer, have followed in his tracks; also to the work of psychologists (although I must confess even less familiarity with these experiments than with the work of the linguists) indicating that all perception involves a modicum of interpretation. If we accept the Kantian insight, the reigning theory of language does not fully account for the phenomena of meaning. We do not mean through language what is there independent of our signs; we constitute it as we refer to it. But the world we grasp is truly the world, for us.

Because the world we grasp is truly the world, an analysis of the symbolic process would also point out that it is the task of intelligence to break the chains of its parochialism, to universalize our grasp of the world. Some societies remain hedged around by an invisible wall of cultural isolationism. The process towards universality, as we are able to observe it in human culture, is carried along two fronts; scientific activity gives us *the real world*, in a partial and highly eulogistic sense of the word "real"—the structure of the physical world. This structure seems to be the necessary but not sufficient ground of culture, since it is presupposed in all human activity. But the world of physics—which is to say, the structure of the physical world—is a narrow or partial aspect of the total universe, and it gains its universality by narrowing its range. Universality is also achieved by a critical examination of the non-scientific symbolic structures employed in cultures, in order to make possible their grasp by alien minds. The art historian, the traveller, the anthropologist from Herodotus to the most recent graduate fieldworker, the iconographer—these men put at our disposal the cultural products of other peoples and thus extend the range of our mind's grasp of the world. Essentially what intelligence does by its critical work is to rid culture of its inveterate centripetal tendency, its inherent drift towards parochialism. Not all subjectivity, however, is sodden with error. But much of it is apt to be. And what is universally true and what false in a centripetal culture is not known until the critical intelligence does its work.

One more remark about our knowledge of the world seems desirable. The world we human beings know (not the abstract world of the physicists) is a world truly shining with the hues of value that are there to be discovered prior to interest and independently of it.

If we ask, "By what means does the mind constitute the world?" the answer is that it does so through the symbolic process, particularly through language. And if we ask, "How is the symbolic process possible?" the only answer I can give is that on this problem we are regrettably in the dark. All we can do with the question is to go to Cassirer, and all he can give us is a purely speculative theory that invokes "powers" and "faculties" of the mind. This is a procedure that any student of science would point out to us, begs the problem. It is, however, all we have, and we must be allowed to use it, on the understanding that it is only a small fig leaf to cover our theoretical shame. Among the many suggestions that we could fall back on I would like to touch on only one, because of its relevance for the problem to which I would like to return soon, the question with which we started, What is a poem?

We constitute our world because we develop the power to fix complexes of related sensory stimuli in images—chiefly aural or visual—which we somehow dislocate from the stimulus-response chain. The unphilosophical "somehow" marks the point at which our explanation breaks down. By means of the image we are able temporarily to frustrate the tendency to respond behaviorally to the stimulus. The image, when it arises, embodies values which seek our espousal. It is constitutive, in the sense that we have no grounds for saying that it is a mere mental copy of the physical stimuli for which it stands. How then do we know that the image is an image of the stimulus? In fact we know nothing of the kind, but we do take it to be in some obscure way an effect of the stimuli, and this causal relation, as regards which, as we all know, philosophers have fought long and bitterly, is the sole guarantee, if it is at all one, we have that the stimulus originally arises in a world external to the mind. I suspect that the power stimuli have of producing images and the power the mind has of calling them forth in revery or purposeful memory are closely related if not identical powers. I call the original image a "proto-image," because I assume that it antedates phylogenetically the birth of language. We need not be reminded of the fact that when man invents lan-

guage he achieves his birth into history and begins the dubious
trek which is at once his misery and his glory, the trek to realize
the values which beckon him for espousal. I assume that when
man first invented language he did not first invent separate words,
which he attached to proto-images. What he did was invent signs
that from the beginning were interrelated to one another systematically. Unless we make this assumption we are at a loss to explain,
not only the divergences of phonological structures exhibited by
the languages of the world, but the diversity of syntaxes they embody, particularly when we remember what Sapir tells us about the
resistance to change exhibited by linguistic structure. In any case,
at least in the West until positive science forces the problem to
his attention, man had no doubt that the syntax of the language
he spoke corresponded to the actual structure of things.

Let me hasten to observe that between the rudimentarily constitutive and the sophisticatedly poetic use of language lies an important difference. But it is one of degree, not of kind. An image
we concentrate in a sentence is a poem of sorts. "The maple turned
red last night." "A hawk wheels in the air." "The jump of the deer
is effortless." We who are familiar with Shakespeare, with Donne
and Milton, with Hopkins and Yeats, will insist that there is an
abyss of difference between these sentences and what we call poetry. But if we remember what the Imagists tried and often succeeded in doing only thirty-five years ago, we shall see that my
contention is not altogether absurd.

Give the animal the ability to constitute the world by means of
language and release him for a minute only from the urgency of
animal needs that demand peremptory satisfaction, and he discovers the world an object worthy of intransitive attention, even if all
he is able to look at is the maple that turned red last night or the
leaping deer whose jump is effortless. Let him next play with this
new ability of his, and he will discover that in the intrinsic resources of the language as language, in its musical quality, in its
rhythms and cadences, there is no less power of revelation than in
the language's function merely to denote, and through metaphor,
in the usual sense of this term, to enrich that which it denotes.
Let man reject the symbol and he rejects the world. This is the

reason I say that poetry gives us the world in and through its linguistic means.

I do not mean to assert that the individual mind always, in every one of its dealings with the world, and with other fellow minds, functions as a constitutive agency. We, who are born into a human society already highly organized, and who inherit a symbolic system perfected long before we were born can, and for the most part do, trade on the capital we inherit. We are not often called on to make creative contributions of our own to the world into which we were born. We are given a world whose structure comes to us already defined, which we can reject only in defiance of severe sanctions, for it is given us not to tamper with but to function practically in. Ordinary man tends to inhibit his use of language as a constitutive organon and tends to use it chiefly as an instrument of practical communication. But in the genetic sense every individual's mind is constitutive of its world, even if his world seems to be a mere copy of his neighbor's.

When we begin to constitute the world by means of language, either collectively or distributively, our practical needs, at every step in the process, successfully interrupt the constitutive activity. Our needs force us to use the world we have constituted for *their* own ends. The presentative activity is perverted, in the sense that it is used for ends extrinsic and alien to it. Man, presented with a world which is now intelligible and ordered, is able to exploit it better than he did before the poet came to his help. The poet in him presents him with the sight of a deer whose leap arrests his breath. But not for long; for the practical man in him recognizes food and stalks the animal the poet invited him to look at. But the soul has its revenge. Unsuspected by the animal when he embarks on the adventure of constituting the world, his merely physiological needs are complicated by new needs, for which there are no discernible physiological grounds, but which are excited by the power of the values he has newly discovered, and which drive him to possess those values with the same insistence that lust or hunger does. He no longer is a mere animal. The woman that would appease his lust has become his mate, the animal he hunts has a beauty that now and then holds his arm long enough to thwart the throw. And he suddenly discovers in himself strange needs for intangible things that have nothing to do with his physical survival. From this moment he is burdened with culture; he is alive to values that control his activity by demanding that he espouse them and that thus he fulfill his destiny. What I am trying to suggest is that the poet and the practical man in each of us are not as far apart in fact as we conceive them to be in our society. In each man there is a poet, and in every poet there is a practical man. The poet is needed to give the practical man the world that is his stage. The practical man is needed if the poet is not going to feed his soul and starve his body.

When first stated it may sound strange to assert that the world is given us *in* as well as *through* the language of poetry. But consider that it is precisely this thesis that we accept, after careful analysis of the manner in which music is said to express what we call "emotion." I doubt whether the term "emotion" is the best term to denote that which music is said to "express," and I strongly incline to the belief that the doctrine of expression has by now become so roiled up with inept interpretations and efforts to clarify these interpretations which further roil it, that it obstructs as much as it helps us to understand what art does. But the notion that art expresses emotion will have its run, and it is not going to be discarded at my bid. At present, indeed, the almost universal tendency among aestheticians is to patch up the dear old doctrine rather than to look for a better hypothesis. On this doctrine we must distinguish the emotion that music expresses from that which it arouses. But how can music express emotion that it does not arouse? Whether we can explain it or not, it seems that in fact it does, since we can distinguish the emotion the music expresses from the emotion it causes in us, as when we find the gayety of the music irritating because we are sad or the sadness depressing because we are gay. If music expresses emotion in this objective sense, we are confronted with two choices: We can either acknowledge that the music *in* itself expresses emotion, or we can hold that what the music does is imitate emotion. Let us look at the latter choice first. The theory of imitation assumes that, let us say, Beethoven felt in a non-musical, immediately experiential manner an emotion for which he later found an objective musical correlative in his composition. It further assumes that we, the listeners, can somehow recognize the emotion expressed because in some degree prior to the listening to the composition we ourselves felt a somewhat similar emotion. I say "somehow" because the assumption that we have experienced a similar emotion to that expressed in the music prior to our hearing it is a fatuously vain assumption for which we have no reasonable grounds. Thus put it is not difficult to see why we cannot accept the theory of imitation. It must be rejected for reasons that are by now fairly familiar among students of aesthetics, and that add up to the fact that it does not do full justice to the creative activity of the artist.

We must therefore consider the alternative. What music expresses is distinct from the emotion that it arouses, and yet it expresses it only in its specific quality as sound in its specific structural relations. That it does it, is clear enough, and we do not need the elaborate effort of analytic philosophers to tell us what we mean by it: what we mean is that the musical composition as heard is discerned to be gay or sad or martial or whatever it is. The qualities discerned in music worth hearing are, of course, far more complex than our coarse, simplistic, abstract adjectives can denote. But the fact here of importance is that it is *in* the music—in the aural patterns as heard—that the characters are discerned as residing. How such characters reside there is a question as to which, so far as my reading takes me, we are still in the dark. That they do, we do not doubt. But if the music expresses in itself these characters to which we usually refer by means of adjectives from the language of the emotions, there is no *a priori* reason the language of poetry cannot also reveal *in*, and not merely *through*, itself objective features of the world. The only ground that could be offered against the hypothesis seems to be our deeply grounded conviction—itself an hypothesis and one quite distinct from that of common-sense naïve realism—that language means by referring to things perceived independently of any mediating symbol. This is the theory we have been calling the reigning theory. We have seen why this theory fails when applied to poetry. It fails because it utterly overlooks the role of language qua phonological structure, not qua signific means, in revealing the world.

We are now ready to answer the question, "What does the poem mean or say?" What it means is not a world it reflects, or imitates, or represents in illusion, in the sense of a world as envisaged by the mind prior to the poetic activity in the manner in which it is envisaged in poetry. What the poem says or means is the world it reveals or discloses *in* and *through* itself, a new world, whose features, prior to the act of poetic revelation, were concealed from us and whose radiance and even identity will again be concealed from us the moment our intransitive attention lapses and we return to the world of affairs and of things in which we normally live. Let us recall that it was pointed out above that the moment the poet reveals to us a self-sufficient object or event the practical man in each of us, and in all of us collectively, snatches from the idler his vision, pushes him aside, and uses it practically. What the poem says or means—or, in other words, the object of the poem—is, genetically speaking, the full-bodied, value-freighted, ordered, self-sufficient world it presents to us for the first time. And even at our late date in history, the object of the poem is precisely those aspects of the familiar world—its value, its diversity in order, its structure—which we can grasp only *in* and *through* the poetic vision. As I put it elsewhere, the poet brings forth values with which history is in the pain of labor. Insofar as we lack the creative gift of the poet, we can only sense them dimly and respond to their appeal in a confused way. The values may already be there, fully actualized, or actualized in such a manner that it is possible to say of them that they already exist. But we do not notice them, because our symbolic powers are inefficient or idle. Confronted with a new situation, we see in it only an old one with which we are already familiar. The poet is the man who sees the values as they struggle to be born or who sees those that have already been born into history but that nobody notices. He is a midwife and uses the forceps of language. And while I have spoken of these values prior to their birth or apprehension by the poet as if they were identical with themselves after the poet has caught them in the constitutive means of his language, I did so merely to make things easy for myself, and must now qualify the statement at least enough to say that what they are, prior to the poet's revelation, is a question for philosophers to answer, and all I can give is but a sketchy summary of the conclusions at which I believe we should arrive were we to explore this problem exhaustively.

The statement that the mind is constitutive of the world is susceptible of several interpretations, and not only do I not accept it in its original Kantian formulation but, much less, in its unqualified idealistic sense. Again, a satisfactory analysis of the symbolic process would give us not only the universal forms employed by the mind to grasp the world everywhere and at all times—whether these be Kant's forms of intuition and his categories or others—but would also seek to discover all the diverse symbolic means through which men seek to grasp the world. It would thus warn us that Kant's forms and categories may be necessary but are not the sufficient means of grasping the world; and it would thus suggest to us why the world, as it presents itself to one mind here, does not exactly look like the world as it presents itself to another mind there. It would also point out that there are various modes of apprehension and various functions which the mind seeks to satisfy when it tries to reach towards the world. However, it would also insist, I believe, that what minds grasp is truly the world and not a mere idiosyncratic phantasmagoria that oozes spontaneously from the mind's solipsistic egocentricity. What we see, however, when we see truly is the actual material-cultural world in which we live as envisaged from a standpoint that approaches, as we improve our grasp, the generic human standpoint. Were we able to put our cognitive teeth on the aorta of Being itself, and were we able to drink the truth directly from it, were we not forced to approach Being humbly, through the mediation of symbols, we would see the world as God sees it. But the world we see, let me reiterate, is not a pure concoction of our minds but is truly "there." If I seem to be asserting a paradox let me retort that it is apparent only. For while it is the mind that knows by what means it is given to know, it is the world the mind knows when it knows truly. If, contemptuous of its object, or suspicious of its means to grasp it, the mind seeks for something which it both knows and does not know in its way and by its means, what it craves is either God's vision or something which it knows without the limitations inherent in human knowledge. God's vision is given only to God and

not to His creatures. The alternative is not given to the ordinary
mortal. What we know we know by means of symbols.

Thus, the controversy as to what is the *real* world, whether that
of the poet or that of the man of affairs, or that of the scientist, is
primarily a terminological question. If we reserve the word "real"
—as we are in the habit of doing—for the world of affairs, for the
material-cultural world in which we live, then the world of affairs
is the real world. If we reserve the word for the invariant structures discovered by the positive scientist, then they, and not the
world from which they were abstracted, are the real world. If we
reserve it for the world revealed to us in and through poetry, and
art in general, then it is the world of art that is the real world.
All three usages are legitimate, and thus there is no substantive
quarrel in this respect among Plato or Galileo, Novalis and Doctor
Johnson. The status in being of the stone the latter kicked is not
altered because only certain of its aspects interest the scientist and
because it was revealed to us through the mediation of symbols.
But whatever usage we choose we ought not to obfuscate the fact
that the world of affairs with its furniture is a world we grasp by
means of an initial creative act of the mind which is in essence
identical with the aesthetic vision, and that it remains distinct and
fresh and blushing with the hues of value because the poet in us
will not down. I do not mean to assert, let me repeat, that the
poet does what the writer of Genesis reports God did, when he
tells us that "In the beginning God created the heaven and the
earth." Rather what the poet does is more like what He is reported
to have done in the second verse. Before the poet comes along
the earth, for us, is without form and void, and darkness is upon
the face of the deep. The poet divides the light from the darkness,
and gives us an ordered world. If it were not for him, we would
never see it. How we phrase what the poet does is of no radical
importance, so long as we do not allow our language to conceal
from us, as the language of the imitation theory does, that the
poem reveals to us what the poet discerns through an act of creation.

The reader may observe that I am pushing as far as I can a difference that I seem to have trouble making clear even to myself.
Trouble I do have, nor would I conceal it if I could. But the effort

seems to me worth making; for I am convinced that the difference between a conception of poetry that in some sense reflects a world already there which is available for the mind independently of the poem, and that which I have sought to defend, is a radical difference, and has fundamental consequences for criticism and for our appreciation of poetry. If all the artist does is represent or imitate, if he does not constitute, if he does not create in the act of discovery, all he can do with his language, at best, is to add an external adornment to the object of imitation. This is the doctrine of the Aristotelians. I believe it is easy to recognize that this view fails utterly to do justice to the way in which the language of poetry functions to say or mean what it does.

Note on Method

The poetic artifact has been defined above in terms of its maker, who brings it about by an act of *creation*; of its *components*, which as the *organized* data of experience make up *the object* of self-sufficient apprehension; and of the unique role or *function* which it plays in the life of man and in culture. This analysis constitutes the field of aesthetics; nor can a responsible criticism ignore the importance of adequate foundations supplied by aesthetics. An attempt to define poetry by means of one or two of these terms, involves serious risks. To define poetry in terms of the maker alone, to go to the poet's study and nowhere else for our data, is to run almost certain risk of ignoring or misconceiving the function of art. This in turn will tend to blind us to indispensable suggestions that we can get from the effects art has on us for an understanding of its nature. To define art exclusively in terms of itself as aesthetic object, as we are advised by the phenomenologist to do, is to run the risk of failing to grasp subtle objective traits that it possesses and can be perceived only when we are made sensitive to them by a recognition of the activity that put them there and the end they are intended to serve. And to define it in terms of its effects alone is to run the risk of confusing art with other cultural agencies that perform functions somewhat similar to some of the secondary functions that art performs. A complete aesthetic may

start with any one of these factors, but it does not give the primacy
to its starting point.

I shall not here attempt to prove this contention, for I have argued it at sufficient length in *The Problems of Aesthetics*, ed. by
Eliseo Vivas and Murray Krieger (New York, 1953), pp. 10-19.
Here all I need do is illustrate the argument with one example.
Neo-Aristotelians fail to grasp truly the relation between the language of the poem, its rhythm, its rhyme, and what the poem is
about, because their doctrine does not do justice to the creative act.
One of them has written that the medium of the poem is embel-
lished by rhythm and rhyme. Poets and aestheticians know that a
poem made up by taking a medium and "embellishing" it with
rhyme and rhythm cannot be a good poem but a synthetic concoction. The statement reminds me of a graduate student—now a
sociologist of pretension—who handed me a paper with the following explanation: "This is only a rough draft. I shall add the subtleties later." I admit that he finally did embellish it with the subtleties he had promised. The trouble was that the embellishments
were like the rhythm the trainer adds to the elephant after he
teaches it the steps of what he thinks of as the elephant's dance.

Approached as I suggest, it should be evident that the problem
of the nature of poetry cannot be settled solely by means of linguistic analysis of statements made about poetry. It is a complex
empirical question, in the broad and generous sense of this term;
and to answer it we must draw heavily on whatever means of
achieving knowledge we happen to have on hand, including, of
course, linguistic analysis. The theory that this empirical approach
gives us is corrigible in terms of what art in fact does and is and
how it comes about. Nor do statements we make about poetry
depend for their validity on the ability we have to bracket dubious
essences directly intuited and as regards which much can be said
and nothing can be settled. It depends on facts that are, in principle at least, available to anyone who, endowed with the necessary
equipment of sensibility and intelligence, cares to look for himself.
Thus, as already suggested, one important assumption that controls our definition of poetry is that it plays a unique, an unsubstitutable, role in culture. It would be futile, however, to attempt
to verify this assumption by a Kinsey-like canvass of the works that

are actually read under the rubric of poetry in a given culture, and of what this poetry actually does individually and socially to the people who read it. This is no doubt a worthwhile "research project" for the social scientist, who lacking as scientist, a normative aesthetic which tells him what is poetry, has no recourse but to take for poetry anything any Tom, Dick, or Harry takes poetry to be; and who, lacking a philosophy of culture—and how many of our sociologists have such a philosophy?—has no means of evaluating his facts and is left therefore with the confusions of the cultural relativist. The conception here proposed must be tested in terms of a theory of culture which is an empirical affair, but which also involves a normative criterion. Needless to say, in this small essay only a very small part of so formidable an order has been attempted.

1954

a definition of the aesthetic experience

This paper proposes a definition of the aesthetic experience that will satisfy elementary logical requirements. Such a definition should not only distinguish the aesthetic from other modes of experience, but should be based not upon subjective data gathered solely from individual introspection, but upon as broad a factual basis as is available. And once arrived at, such a definition should throw light on the problems of aesthetics. It is unfortunate that the time at my disposal allows me only to present a very succinct and perhaps hermetic sketch of something which demands fairly extended treatment.[1]

Our first step must be to take issue with those writers who give the emotion the central role in their account of the aesthetic experience. There are in this respect two theories worth considering. One holds that the aesthetic object arouses emotion in the spectator; and the other that the content or meaning of art, objectively speaking, is emotion. Both propositions seem to be maintained by Mr. Dewey, while only the latter is maintained by Mr. Prall.[2] The first, however, is in conflict with experimental aesthetics, the results of which, I take it, indicate that the emotion is an accidental consequence of aesthetic apprehension. This being the case, it should not be included in its definition. The crucial proof that it is so lies in the fact that the same aesthetic object (or even the same object of fine art) is capable of arousing different emotional reactions in different spectators or even in the same spectator at different times. Again, competently trained persons in music and in poetry are found who deny that the adequate aesthetic experience involves the presence of the emotion. In poetry the mention of only one name should suffice—that of T. S. Eliot. In music the evidence which Vernon Lee has recently offered us is overwhelming. And her evidence is confirmed by previous empirical investigations.[3]

These observations cannot be refuted with the retort that emotion *should* be aroused by the aesthetic object, for that calls for a justification of the prescription, which an empirical definition could not furnish us with. Nor can we refute them with the retort that if there are any such differences of opinion as regards the presence of emotion, these differences point to the fact that there are at least two "varieties of the aesthetic experience" radically different from one another in one of which emotion plays the central role and another in which it does not play any role at all.[4] For this last retort would still leave us with the question as to what is common between these two types of experience, and obviously it would be this common element which alone should be included in our definition.

To the definitions of the experience grounded on the assertion that the objective meaning of art is emotion the following objections must be raised: First, as yet no adequate explanation has been given of the means by which the object expresses "emotion." In his last book Mr. Prall tries to tell us how; but his explanation, careful reading will show, does not go beyond the statement that objects do as a fact express emotion.[5] Empathy theory was, in part at least, an effort to explain this phenomenon. But empathy is not an explanation but a mystification of which Reid and Dewey have effectively disposed.[6] The second objection is much stronger: the assertion that the objective content of art—or as Mr. Prall puts it, its meaning—is emotion, fails to distinguish between objective characters in things and the objective-subjective complex which is the emotion and which has, so to speak, its center of gravity in the subjective. Objective characters of things are what they are, and when Mr. Prall maintains that they are "feeling" or that they have "a feel," so far as the careful reader is able to make out this contention can only mean that when language seeks to denote the untranslatable characters of an aesthetic object it sometimes chooses for the task terms which are often used to denote emotional states.[7]

If emotion can not be used as a defining trait of the experience, how shall the experience be defined? In our attempt to answer that question it would be advisable to bear in mind that no definition is worth considering which is not resolutely grounded on the assumption that the aesthetic experience is an experience of an aesthetic object, and that an aesthetic object is an object—any object—grasped in such a way as to give rise to an aesthetic experience.[8]

Grounded on this assumption the aesthetic experience can be defined, I submit, in terms of attention. The advantages of such definition are manifold, and the only difficulty it presents is the rather easy task of distinguishing *aesthetic* attention from that involved in other modes of experience. A brief statement of such definition would read as follows: "An aesthetic experience is an experience of rapt attention which involves the intransitive apprehension of an object's immanent meanings and values in their full presentational immediacy."

This does not mean that the experience is one of direct intuition, if "intuition" be used to signify the prehension of objective meanings by a mirror-mind. The values are objective, but the mind is to some extent constitutive of the manner in which it apprehends them. The aesthetic experience is the result of an interaction in time between a mind and an object, and "mind" includes a system of meanings in terms of which the objective presentation is apprehended for the aesthetic object that it is. This in turn must be

taken to imply that the meanings and characters of the object are
in the object for a mind, in such a way that they can be pointed
out to others of a similar equipment. The word "immanent" seeks
to signify that the meanings are immediately and directly in the
object; or in other words that the object is not a mnemonic device
or a stimulus of associative processes or a referential sign, but a
direct and immediate carrier of meanings.[9] But the important word
in our formula besides attention is the word "intransitive." By
this word I mean that attention is aesthetic when it is so controlled
by the object that it does not fly away from it to meanings and
values not present immanently in the object; or in other words that
attention is so controlled that the object specifies concretely and
immediately through reflexive cross-references its meanings and
objective characters. And thus we may contrast the aesthetic with
all other modes of attention by noting that other modes discover
in objects not immanent but referential meanings and values, which
is to say, meanings and values which carry us beyond the object to
other values or meanings not present upon it.

We ruled out emotion above on the basis of unexplained data.
But our definition now enables us to account for this data. For
rapt attention on an object excludes self-consciousness, and emotion cannot be present without the latter. True it is that experiences in which self-consciousness completely disappears must be
fairly rare, since seldom do we have the energy, interest, or training
which are their necessary conditions. But that some times we do
have them, and that we frequently are able to approach them is
a verified matter of fact.[10]

A warning is at this point necessary. Although sometimes almost
totally devoid of emotion, the aesthetic experience need never be
a cold experience. For if we distinguish, as we should, between
emotion and feeling, it will be readily seen that it is the feeling
that gives the glow to the experience and not the emotion.[11] But
the feeling is a by-product of the experience and is a concomitant
not only of aesthetic but of any other activity which is successful.
Again, our definition does not mean to suggest that exclusive emphasis is to be put upon analysis. There is no question that the aesthetic experience involves a preparation which can be achieved only
through analytic effort. But the experience proper is an experience

of adequate and full apprehension of an intransitive kind. It is a having, not a cutting up.

I should next like to suggest some of the advantages of our definition. Our definition throws light on that most important feature of the aesthetic experience which has been so loosely termed its "autonomy," and which has often served as its defining trait. The autonomy of the aesthetic experience follows from the fact that to the degree to which it is controlled fully and adequately by the object, to that degree does it seem after its enjoyment to have been thoroughly disengaged from the rest of our experience and to possess a *sui generis* character. It also throws light on a phenomenon which has been the spring board for a great deal of mysticism, namely, the deep conviction of *the superior* reality of the object in which the experience often leaves us. This conviction springs from the intransitive nature of our attention, since during the experience the object remains in complete monopolistic possession of consciousness.[12]

There are other important questions of aesthetics on which our definition also throws light. But among these there is one to which I should like to call your especial attention: our definition enables us to relate the perceiver to the object in a detailed, specific, and verifiable manner. It is not merely a question of asserting in general terms that the object controls the experience, but one of showing a more intimate and detailed relation.[13] For it can be shown that the so-called "factors of advantage," widely recognized by psychologists as controlling attention, are the very factors which under more appropriate names are discovered by analysis to be the generic traits of aesthetic objects. A list of these factors of advantage in attention usually include the following: *change, strength, striking quality,* and *definiteness of form.* Now take a representative list of the generic traits discovered by aesthetic analysis. *Unity in variety, theme, thematic variation, emphasis,* and *evolution* according to a *rhythmic pattern.* It is, of course, claimed that any other list of truly generic traits would do; but this one is a usual one. Our task is to show how the generic traits of aesthetic objects are, under different names, the very factors which psychologists discover are of advantage to attention.

Attention is described by psychologists as exploratory and restless unless somehow controlled, hence the importance of *definiteness of form* in the object which elicits it. This factor of advantage corresponds to *the unity* of the aesthetic object, without which divagation easily occurs. But attention requires *change*, or it tires and lapses. In the aesthetic object, *the variety* which is unified, carries attention from any one of its aspects reflexively to another, providing change and permitting their free apprehension, while the *unity* which relates them guides attention intransitively within the whole. Again, it is the *unity in variety* of the object which gives attention the needed rest and relief in change, which is a condition of intensity and of prolonged duration. Interpreted broadly, then, the principle of *unity in variety* corresponds to those factors of advantage which hold attention on an object. But the other generic traits of aesthetic objects mentioned above—*theme, thematic variation, emphasis,* and *evolution*—in so far as they are distinct from the widest and most generic of these, *unity in variety,* also can be shown to correspond to the factors of advantage to which reference was made. *The theme,* for instance, arrests our attention and is thus seen to correspond to the striking quality which is said by psychologists, in their own terms, to perform the same function. Again *the emphasis* with which the theme is elaborated corresponds to *the strength* demanded by the psychologists. And the need for *change,* although already referred to, is not only provided by the unified variety, but is provided in a manner which more exactly controls the attention by the way in which the artist develops his theme in *a rhythmic scheme.* The *variation* of the theme aids it in providing the striking quality required to shock attention, to surprise it, and to present it with some degree of difficulty, without which it would become lax through boredom.

These remarks do not mean to exhaust the subject. It is hoped, however, that they have enabled us to see that those traits which analysis finds in all aesthetic objects are really factors which facilitate attention while retaining it within the object.

Why, it may be asked, is it necessary to relate the object to the experience in the concrete and detailed manner here attempted? Is it not enough to assert—and this, of course, would require no proof—that the object is the stimulus to which the experience is the response? There are several reasons why it is necessary to go beyond this assertion. The first is that if the experience is controlled by the object, it is of interest to know exactly what point by point correspondence is there between the object and the experience. The second is that the correlation between object and experience in a concrete fashion enables us to approach the moot question of the aesthetic judgment in a way which will save us from subjectivism. The objectivist has always found difficulty in meeting the tendency of the subjectivist to reduce the question of the value of an aesthetic object to the question of the presence or absence of attitudes or satisfactions of a purely personal, private kind. But it can be shown that the subjective state is not a purely arbitrary affair, but depends on two factors, the structure of the object which determines the state, and the values and meanings which this structure subtends. The latter, the informed substance of the object, cannot be conveyed to the mind in any other way than by pointing to it. Either the mind grasps it or it does not. But if it does not, the critic frequently can point to the structure that subtends the informed substance, in the hope that with its help the perceiver will grasp the values and meanings that are there to be grasped, and which are subtended by the structure. Since the structure is an objective affair, to the extent to which the object determines the state, to that extent have we grounds on which to base judgments of aesthetic values which are truly objective.

It is time to come to a conclusion, and in view of the variety of related subjects discussed in the brief compass of this paper, a summary of the high points of these notes would be perhaps advisable. The aesthetic experience was defined as an experience of intransitive attention, to which, if the empirical evidence is examined, the emotion will be found to be a widely variable concomitant and therefore unavailable as its defining term. Indeed when the self disappears in an intense experience of attention, the emotion is hardly present. In the light of our definition a good number of the problems of aesthetics are elucidated which otherwise remain opaque and stubborn. But among these, the problem of correlating object and experience was given especial attention, on account of the importance such correlation would have for the problem of the aesthetic judgment.

1937

literature and knowledge [1]

The claim that art gives us knowledge is as old as Western aesthetics, and in our own age it has been made for all the arts by both aestheticians and critics. Thus, while distinguishing aesthetic knowledge or expression from other kinds of knowledge, Croce, Collingwood and T. M. Greene assert that art is a vehicle of knowledge. Recently Morris Weitz has made a similar claim. Among critics we find Allen Tate asserting that "literature is the complete knowledge of man's experience," Van Ogden Vogt tells us that from a little brass tray typical of Saracenic art you could "describe almost off hand the main characteristics of the life from which it came, as a scientist reconstructs some old dinosaur from one of the fossil bones. You could conjure, for instance, the whole structure of fatalism in philosophy, despotism in government, the abstract decoration, the polygamy, and everything else from beggar to caliph that belonged in the same world with the little piece of brass." And Cecil Gray quotes Schweitzer with approval, to the effect that the dogma of the Trinity "can be expressed much more clearly and satisfactorily in music than in verbal formula." When we consider the multiplicity of the claims and the complexity of the problem they pose, it becomes evident that it would be hopeless to try to discuss it in the compass of a short essay. We would have to examine critically the typical claims and order them in some sort of fashion, and we would have to consider them in reference to the different arts. For it is obvious that literature seems to give us something that at least looks as well as feels like knowledge, but only a top-flight musicologist like Schweitzer can read off the dogma of the Trinity from Bach. Let us therefore turn to the easiest of the questions that can be asked under the general problem: "Does literature give us knowledge?" This is not a small question; but it is not altogether beyond the possibility of a sketchy answer in a short essay. Nor is it quite as restrictive as it may at first blush seem; the generic traits shared by the arts ought to make it possible to learn from one of them about the others, when appropriate modifications and allowances are made.

Since the argument rests on a few key distinctions, it is essential to grasp firmly the terms by means of which they are conveyed. I have adopted, with a minor modification, the terminology that A. C. Bradley used in his inaugural dissertation, and with it I have accepted, of course, his substantive analysis.[2] Within the experiential resources that are brought by the writer to the creative act, I mark off those resources that are distinctly aesthetic, because they have functioned as such in the creation of other aesthetic objects or in the training of the artist, from those resources to which we may refer as experiential in a wide sense of the term. The term "form" (employed usually in the plural) and the term "subject matter" mark this distinction. The term "the informed substance" of the work of literature, is used to point to the non-aesthetic aspect of the subject matter after it has been elaborated in the creative process and to indicate the intimate nature of the relationship in which the forms, as transformed by the act of creation, stand to the substance, as transubstantiated by the same act. Thus it is assumed that the informing forms can be distinguished from the informed substance by a critic, for his purposes; but that they cannot be separated.

The validity of this distinction is denied on organicist grounds by some aestheticians like Weitz. Consistently with the denial it can be argued by organicists that no resource which the writer brings to the creative act can properly be called aesthetic until it is used in the creation of the aesthetic object; and that all resources so used are aesthetic. These assertions are unobjectionable if they are taken to refer to the object within the aesthetic transaction. But the distinction between informing forms and informed substance is essential for criticism and for the resolution of our problem, although to argue this claim would require an essay of the length of the one I propose to write. Here I can only say that the distinction will justify itself pragmatically in what follows. Note finally that the knowledge which is in question in this paper is that which can be tested by positive methods because the thing known is in some sense independent of the formulated knowledge and is referred to by the latter. But we cannot forbid anyone the right to use the term "knowledge" in any sense he chooses, so long as its meaning is exhibited with satisfactory clarity.[3]

1

If the function of literature were to imitate something which exists prior to the act of imitation and independently of it, as was generally believed until about the end of the eighteenth century, our problem would not be difficult. Our only question would be that which is argued between Plato and Aristotle as to the quality of the knowledge that art gives. But contemporary aesthetics almost universally rejects or simply ignores the classical theory. According to a contemporary interpreter of Aristotle, Richard McKeon, artistic imitation is "the presentation of an aspect of things in matter other than its natural matter." And this is possible because "the form joined to matter in the physical world is the same form that is expressed in the matter of art." Contemporary aesthetics does not deny that the writer does indeed take from the world both forms and subject matter and that the creative process turns these into the informed substance of his work; he is not God and cannot create out of nothing. But it argues that the Aristotelian account does not do justice to the creative process. For the writer does not gather up a form waiting to be picked up; his is an activity which for good reasons men have agreed to call "creative."

The creative process consists of a wrenching by the artist of a form (or complex of forms) from the heart of nature or of the human actions which constitute his subject matter. But the form is not fully realized in the subject matter from which the artist pries it loose; nor is it partially realized in the exact manner in which the artist would have it. The artist must divine the form that is potential in the matter of his experience, where ordinary men who lack his gift do not even suspect it to be hiding. But his guess is *creative*, because he does not take some of his forms from here and some from there and put them together like a jig-saw puzzle. He does this. But he also adds to the forms that he takes, and subtracts from them, by activities for the most part unconscious, which are conditioned by factors which neither the artist, the psychologist, nor the aesthetician seems to be able to get at. The subject matter also has to be added to and whittled off, and it has its own stubborn way against which the artist must work. Artists, of course, vary widely in all respects, but it simply does not seem possible that they compose good poetry in the manner in which Poe tells us that he wrote *The Raven*. The genuine work of art comes from the unknown depths of the soul, where its growth is even more mysterious than the development of a foetus. The artist, moved by forces over which he exercises only limited conscious control, does not know clearly what he wants to say till the labor of the file is finished and he can discover his intention in his composition. Imitation assumes a conscious clarity about the end that the artist seeks to accomplish that does not square with the facts as we know them. Note, however, that the language I have used in speaking of the creative activity is not intended as explanatory. All it is intended to do is to catch impressionistically some of the important aspects of the creative act which can be observed or which must be posited, in terms that are frankly animistic and metaphorical. The analysis of these phenomena in scientific terms is something which, so far as I can discover, is a long way off yet. Nor do I intend by what I have said to relegate the labor of creation exclusively to any particular level of the mind. So far as we know, artists vary considerably in respect to where the gestation and the finishing of their work takes place.[4]

But why, the puzzled reader may ask, beat a dead horse? The answer is that aestheticians have been sending to the press notices of the demise of the imitation theory which are indelicately premature. It is true that outside of the "Chicago School of Criticism" the imitation theory has very few open defenders today. But the idea of imitation is frequently employed even by those who repudiate it explicitly, and the interest in the problem of art and knowledge which at the moment seems to engage the energy of our up-and-coming young aestheticians almost exclusively has brought it back with renewed vigor, although more often than not under a new alias and with false face. Nor can we ever expect to eliminate it altogether as a theory to contend with in aesthetics, since it points with a modicum of adequacy to a fact which cannot be overlooked by the aesthetician and the critic. It seems therefore necessary to review the grounds on which it has been repudiated, lest the indispensable gain made by aesthetics in the last one hundred and fifty years be lost sight of, and lest the solution of our problem be speciously and too easily achieved.

If we are asked what evidence we have for the belief that the mind adds to what it takes from experience, we can answer that a thorough examination of an artistic tradition, or of a single work, which discriminates all discoverable influences, reveals novelty which cannot be traced to these influences; or, otherwise stated, that with the knowledge we possess we are far from being able to predict in its full specificity, the composition which a writer will achieve when he sets out to write. The late Alfred Einstein, discussing this very point, speaks of Mozart's creative listening. This phrase applies to all genuine artists and serves to distinguish them from the mere imitator of life or art. The artist perceives creatively; nor will an indefinite extension of the work done by John Livingston Lowes on "Kubla Khan" exhaust what any sensitive reader of the poem is able to find in it.

Clearly, even when this argument is looked at sympathetically it cannot be claimed for it that it adduces evidence that can be expected to convince an embattled mechanist. I accept it with the proviso that it requires the reinterpretation I shall offer below. Anyone who asserts or denies the spontaneity of the mind can do so only on grounds that go beyond our limited positive knowledge of what goes on beyond the range of direct observation, as the writer busies himself with the labor of composition; the assertion or denial is therefore purely speculative or philosophical. But within the area of aesthetics proper it ought to be remembered that those who have first-hand acquaintance with an artistic tradition, or with the work of any one artist, have felt that their experience favors the hypothesis of creativity. A thinker who approaches experience with humility cannot disregard this fact, nor will he be taken in by the coarse and altogether unphilosophical analogies between the human mind and calculating machines. But if it is positive evidence of the sort found in physics that is required to settle the issue, those who reject the notion of creativity ought to admit that in respect to such tests as they demand the problem remains an open one—until they are able to furnish us with an exhaustive analysis of the genesis of a genuine poem in which it is actually shown how the poem is to be traced to psychological or sociological factors that are causally related to it. In the absence of such data, at the phenomenal level at least, and from the standpoint of both critic and writer, a genuine work of literature contains novelty. It is essential for criticism to emphasize this fact, until it is positively disproved, since it constitutes the indispensable basis for part of its work. Without assuming novelty the critic could not attribute excellence to the work of art. To sacrifice the practical role of criticism to a general philosophical theory, particularly one the coarseness of which ought by now to be so patent as is that of mechanism, is not wisdom and is not empiricism.

A more complete analysis of the aesthetic transaction adds another factor that widens the distance that we find between literature and the actual world. The literary work is not merely endowed with novelty; it is generally recognized by aestheticians today that in the aesthetic transaction it also appears as self-sufficient or autonomous, in the sense that, as I am wont to put it, it is able to capture attention *intransitively* upon itself, and is thus able to prevent the mind from seeking comparisons between it and the actual world. Because this is one of the points on which aes-

theticians are almost unanimous today, it is not necessary here to
do more than to refer to it. As readers, we go to the poem with
minds stocked with knowledge, and the better stocked our minds
are the better readers we make. But what we focus attention on is
what we have before our mind's eye, a unique, self-evident and
self-contained presentation which inhibits philosophic or scientific
inquiries, inhibits the practical need to resolve moral perplexities
as well as the need to respond to any objects within the work in an
explicitly religious mode. This is the phenomenon towards which
the phrase "suspension of disbelief" points without explaining
how the work of art enables the reader to do it.

How to explain the sense in which art embodies meanings which
are not referential and are yet in some sense meaningful, and how
to account for the mechanism by means of which it performs this
feat, is a difficult problem which it is easy to overlook or to brush
aside. It has been said by an analytic philosopher that Mrs.
Langer's "presentational symbol" is a contradiction in terms because for her the symbol does not represent or stand for anything
beyond itself. This is hacking at a problem with a verbal meat-
cleaver. On the other hand, the fact is not explained by pointing
to it with a fancy label, and neither the expression "presentational
symbol" nor the notion of "icon" does more than refer to the fact.
But it is essential to point to the fact of intransitivity, for it is
determinative of the aesthetic transaction. The diversity of theoretical contexts with which we can approach aesthetics enables us
to envisage the fact in a multiplicity of ways. From the standpoint
of the reader, the phrase "the captive mind" conveys the fact, since
the reader's attention is imprisoned and utterly engrossed. Sometimes it is so thoroughly captured that the word "ecstasy" is quite
an appropriate designation of the state, since the basic and ever-
present sense that we carry with us of ourselves as distinct from the
world tends to vanish, and on rare and fortunate occasions it disappears entirely.

If the facts of creativity and intransivity are accepted, it follows
that literature cannot give us knowledge about the world. But
serious intercourse with literature, which is not controlled by doctrinaire presuppositions, will reveal to us that this is not the end
of the matter; for literature does seem to have in some sense or

other a resemblance to life or to the world. Nor is the novelty imported by the creative mind into the literary work an obstacle to its conveying knowledge. Indeed, the better the work, the greater its originality, and the more capable it is of capturing our mind, the deeper the knowledge it seems to be able to give us.

2

The strategies used by those who deny that literature is a vehicle of knowledge are many, nor could we examine them all. But at least two of these ought to be referred to in passing, since they have been profoundly influential not only in contemporary aesthetics but in contemporary criticism. One of these is perhaps best represented by John Dewey. He tells us that "no genuine work of art has ever been a repetition of anything that previously existed." Therefore, art cannot give us knowledge about our world. But Dewey cannot deny that in our intercourse with literature we get something which feels very similar to what we experience when we acquire knowledge. These experiences, he tells us, can be translated naturally as meaning that art enriches immediate experience.[5]

The expression theory has had to share dominance in the last twenty-five years with the doctrine of I. A. Richards, whose aesthetics constitutes the most systematic defense of poetry that we can find in the English language. But Richards also denies the cognitive claims of art. The function of art is not to give us knowledge, but to organize our attitudes. What we find in literature are not genuine statements, but pseudo-statements. In this manner, Richards attempted to prove that literature, and especially poetry, in which he is primarily interested, is "worth the devotion of the keenest hours of the best minds." [6]

It is a question of great interest, although not one precisely pertinent to our main subject, whether Richards's defense of literature does not, in fact, end up by digging a deeper grave for it than would have been dug by the forces from which he tried to rescue it. For he defended it on what we may call "therapeutic grounds." Religion, he tells us, was able, once upon a time, to organize our attitudes; but science has made it impossible for us today to take its claims seriously. But since religion performed an essential task, we must let literature do what religion no longer is able to do. Before we yield to the impulse to dismiss this doctrine as both psychologically and sociologically naïve, it is only fair to remember that *The Principles of Literary Criticism* was written at a time when it was much more difficult than it is today to grasp how false was the shallow positivistic notion that religion can be dispensed with or substituted for. But aside from this it is difficult to understand how lovers of poetry failed to see through Richards's defense.

It constitutes an unanswerable indictment of our confusions that critics and amateurs of art accepted so readily Richards's doctrine as a defense of art, when at its heart the doctrine showed no awareness of the fact that art has a function all its own. According to Richards, the basic function of poetry is to organize our attitudes. But if this is its justification, it must and should give way to any agency which can perform it more efficiently. With the development of psychiatry, or with the development within us of a viable faith capable of engrossing and orienting our energies, the need for poetry disappears. But poetry can at best organize the attitudes of the small minority that can read it and it can do it only in an unstable and accidental manner. For obviously whether Milton or Calderon can organize a man's attitudes depends not merely on the poet but on the man, and obviously the organization it is able to achieve cannot last long. An effective faith or a developed psychiatry should be able to organize anyone's attitudes and should do it in a stable fashion. The faith need not be one that is universal and capable of pragmatic verification because it is creative of stable culture. Any faith will do, so long as it awakens our energies and orients us towards an end. For that purpose, the faith of a Schweitzer cannot be called more effective than the faith of a Goebbels. If Richards is right, then, his defense of literature can at best only give us a stay of execution for poetry. It cannot expect to save it from ultimate elimination. And this is true of any defense of literature that fails to realize the fact that art has a function to perform in the human economy for which there can be no substitution.

Be that as it may, those who maintain that literature is a vehicle of knowledge reply to the defenders of the expression and the organization theories that more than the subjective organization of attitudes or more than something that merely feels like knowledge is involved in the reading of literature. And they base their claim on the resemblance between literature and the world. That the imitation theory ignores the novelty of the work of literature is true. That in the aesthetic transaction the resemblance between the work of literature and the world is irrelevant and does not obtrude itself for consideration is also true. It is also true that a work of literature gives us a rich experience. That the richness of the experience has its source in the fact that literature creates order where chaos reigned, by organizing our attitudes, may be true. But literature does more. Literature gives us a grasp of the world which is in some sense reflected in it.

Richards tells us that *The Waste Land* is merely music of ideas, and that the ideas in the poem are arranged "not that they may tell us something, but that their effects in us may combine into a coherent whole of feeling and attitude and produce a peculiar liberation of the will." [7] Let us assume that we know what we mean by the pretty phrase, "the music of ideas." Is this all that we can get from *The Waste Land*? Can we prevent the ideas of the poem from telling us something of the quality of contemporary life? Collingwood finds that in *The Waste Land*, Eliot "has expressed his idea (not his alone) of the decay of our civilization, manifested outwardly as a breakdown of social structures and inwardly as a drying-up of the emotional springs of life." Whether this is what the poem expressed or not can be easily ascertained by anyone who reads it; and whether Eliot is right or wrong about our civilization is susceptible of confirmation. If the reader had already made up his mind, before reading *The Waste Land*, that the condition of the world was such as was expressed by Eliot in his poem, he might be able to add a depth to his insight that he did not possess before he read it, and not merely an emotional but a cognitive depth.

At this point the defender of Dewey will want to interpose a remark. Whatever is true of Richards, for whose ideas he is not responsible, he will submit, it is precisely the failure to notice the special way in which the work of literature functions in the aesthetic experience that Dewey objects to. For Dewey, the work of art exists only in the aesthetic experience, and the work out of the experience is not the same as the work in it. Out of the experience what there is is paper with marks on it, or perhaps, if it is being read in a non-aesthetic mode, sociological data, or perhaps phrases and incidents that have been disjoined and cannot any longer be considered parts of the work of art, since they are not functioning aesthetically to make up a self-sufficient whole. But for anyone who knows how to read poetry, *The Waste Land* is not a sociological document or a more or less incoherent jumble of phrase and images, but a complete aesthetic experience. This is indeed the case on Dewey's objective relativism; and I cannot here argue against it. What needs to be shown is that, even if we grant the truth of Dewey's observation, both Richards and the expression theory misinterpret the relation between the work-in-the-transaction and the work-out-of-it. It is true that the artist makes something new out of the stuff of his experience, both in respect to matter and form; and it may also be true that the work of art exists only in the aesthetic transaction. But from these facts it does not follow that the reader cannot carry out of the transaction and into the world of affairs the informed substance of the work to use it for his own non-aesthetic purposes. That he does it is a fact. How he manages to carry it out and to what uses he puts it is what must be explained.

3

It is, then, these seemingly contradictory considerations that set our problem. On the one hand, we have seen that the writer is creative and that in the aesthetic transaction the work of literature appears to the reader as self-sufficient; on the other, that literature is or seems to be a vehicle of knowledge. But if the former is true, the latter cannot be true. Yet neither the former nor the latter can be denied. There are similarities between the work of literature and the world by means of which the work can tell us something about the world. But in spite of them the work obeys its own laws, so to speak, and does not refer to the world. That a work of literature is not like life is as irrelevant as is the fact that a painting of Pollock is unlike anything we have ever seen in nature. To criticize

Kafka because in actual life little balls do not follow a man upstairs to his flat when he returns from his job is as irrelevant as it would be to reject Shakespeare because we know that ghosts cannot appear to their sons and ask them to revenge them.

But if this is the case, what criterion of confirmation can be offered by those who assert that literature gives us knowledge? And what kind of knowledge does it give us, if the knowledge it gives is not about the world? It would seem, therefore, that if we claim that literature gives us knowledge, we have to deny its self-sufficiency and its novelty; and if we assert its self-sufficiency and its novelty, we have to deny that it is a vehicle of knowledge. In order to resolve this seeming difficulty we must investigate what the literary artist does in the work and what kind of continuity exists between literature and the world. For these are the bases for asserting that the work of literature has a distinctive function to perform in the human economy. If we define this function properly, the question as to whether we classify it under knowledge or not, and what is its relation to positive knowledge (or knowledge in the narrow sense of the term) is one that answers itself.

Our solution of this problem will be most easily grasped if we first turn to a concrete illustration and attempt on its basis to arrive at an abstract formulation of what the writer does and of the use to which his product can be put.

For our illustration let us take Céline's novel, *Journey to the End of the Night*. There are several reasons for selecting this disagreeable novel, which should become clear as our examination of it proceeds. The novel tells about the adventures of its narrator-hero, named Ferdinand. He joins up early in 1914 as the Germans advance on Paris and is discharged after a period in a psychiatric hospital. He goes to Africa, gets shanghaied and shipped off in a boat going to the United States. In New York he jumps ship and finally goes to Detroit in search of work. He returns to France and studies medicine and practices in the environs of Paris. The novel consists of a number of characters and a succession of dramatic episodes which constitute a fictional world of deserters, cowards, stupid officers, murderers, lechers, heartless exploiters, the whole unsavory mess drenched in hatred, distrust, ill-will—in a word, the novel presents us with a thoroughly evil fictional world.

Let us assume that we have read it carefully. Is to grasp by careful reading what the author offers us for our apprehension all we can do? We have not finished with the book until we have digested our experience. This act of digesting the reading of a work of literature may or may not be chronologically continuous with the aesthetic experience. In some cases it may take place considerably later than the reading, after other experiences enable us to grasp the meaning of what we read; in others it may even happen during the reading, in those periods of oscillation away from intransitive attention upon the object. In any case, the act of digesting is distinguishable and often separable from the aesthetic transaction. In the reading of a long work, the normal mind, incapable of sustained intransitive attention for a long period of time, will find itself oscillating between the aesthetic transaction and the critical activity. But whether we do it as we read it or afterwards, having grasped intransitively what is presented to our attention, we must try to master its powerful impact. In order to do so we seek to determine what it will do or has done to our convictions about men and the world.

To claim that what *Journey* does is not done to our intellect but to our attitudes exclusively—to distinguish between our cognitive and our emotive response and to claim that our reading of *Journey* elicits a purely emotive response—is to take an analytic distinction which is perfectly valid at the conceptual level as if it referred to phenomena that actually existed in us in separate compartments, and to command us to keep it separate; and this is a patently arbitrary imperative. All that we need consider here is that the imperative is not an aesthetic one but a moral one and that its effect, if obeyed, would be to compartmentalize life even more than it already is, and to foster schizophrenia. *Journey* undoubtedly affects us emotively. But this is not its exclusive effect on us. For a picture of man has been presented to us which does not jibe with what we know precisely because at least one of the factors constituting its novelty consists in excluding almost absolutely from the work itself those aspects which in actual life modify and disguise the malice of which men are capable. And the failure of the picture to jibe with what we previously knew about men instigates the need to digest the picture.

This is the critical task, or, at least, an essential part of it. We
do not undertake it for extrinsic reasons. We undertake it because
it is a necessity, since the novel has left us disturbed and even confused, dissatisfied, perhaps irritated; and the need to compose our
mind, to look at our conception of the world and to see what has
happened to it, is both urgent and reasonable. The urgency is felt
directly and cannot be argued against. That it is reasonable may
seem to require some sort of justification. I take it that it is because it is urgent and because its urgency expresses a basic human
need which shares generic traits with the need towards integration
that we see operative in philosophy, in science, and in practical life.
There will, of course, be men who will read *Journey* with absorbing
attention and who, reaching the last line, will go about their business undisturbed. But to take this kind of men as exemplars of the
ideal reader does not seem reasonable. If, then, the normal reader
feels the need to undertake the critical task, the question now con-
fronts us as aestheticians as to whether aesthetics has been justified
in dismissing the theory of imitation as it has done.

4

How do we go about the task of criticism? Here we can only consider its most superficial traits. Having read the novel intransitively,
we can ask what the presuppositions are which must be posited as
required to bring about and to sustain in the aesthetic transaction
the work we have read. Let me dwell for a moment on the term
that I have just introduced. It is not a felicitous term, but it will do.
The term "presuppositions" is intended to cover all the factors,
both of a purely aesthetic nature and others, which control the
selection of subject matter and the elaboration which the artist
gives to it in order to inform it into the substance of his work. Since
most of the activity takes place beyond the reach of observation,
we are almost entirely in the dark as to how it happens. But in
spite of our ignorance, it is possible to assert with a modicum of
confidence that the process is not one which is guided exclusively
by purely aesthetic considerations. The artist's total personality, including the whole complex of his espoused and his recognized
values—and this constitutes a major part of himself—is involved

in the choice.[8] In making this assertion I am not moralizing the process of artistic creation. What is usually called morality becomes operative when we have to resolve practical perplexities as regards which we notice differences of value. Note also that although what I mean by the term "presuppositions" covers all the operative principles controlling the selections, whether aesthetic, intellectual, moral, or religious, which make the work of literature possible, what we are interested in here almost exclusively are the presuppositions that control the selection of the subject matter of the work.

In actual practice the critic will meet with varying degrees of success when he seeks in the finished object for its presuppositions. And in his search it will be easy for him to fall into a trap, because the tendency—particularly in an age debauched by the facile techniques of parlor psychoanalysis—is to abandon the objective search and to enter into a search for the subjective intentions that guided the writer in the completion of his work. About these subjective motivations we seldom know enough, but what we know is sufficient to assert that they need not be identical with the actual operative principles that control the production of the work. The principles to which I refer, the presuppositions of the work, are inferred from the work itself. The reason for this is obvious: Consciousness proposes and the id disposes.

I cannot enter into the details of the process by which I arrived at the results I am about to state as regards *Journey*, but it is hardly necessary to do so, since one of the reasons for choosing it was that I could not think of a serious novel that presents so easy a critical task as it does. Should there be disagreement about my results, it is not necessary to resolve it, since the analysis is not given here for its own sake, but solely for the sake of the illustration that it furnishes.

Succinctly stated, *Journey* was made possible by a systematic selection of subject matter such that nothing in it contradicts the hatred that constitutes one of the informing factors of the novel. The actual journeys of the narrator-hero and the moral voyage of discovery which constitutes his quest run parallel and both finally take him to the end of the night, not to the dawn of the new day. No subject matter is accepted for information into the substance of the book whose affective tone can be characterized by words like "love," in any but its most animal sense, "joy," "gratitude," "piety." When pitiful incidents are introduced, what is contemptible or weak or mean in them is brought forward. Virtues are shown up as fronts for self-interest and malice, and only one of the minor characters of the novel, the whore in Detroit, is capable of decency. The dominant attitude of the narrator-hero is fully explicit; to cite only one of the innumerable examples that could be given, he tells us, "One human being can only tolerate another human being and rather like him, if he plays the part of an admiring doormat." But it is not merely Ferdinand who is instinct with impotent hatred and resentment. The world must also be, if it is to justify Ferdinand's attitude. The novel is thoroughly consistent, and its contrivance gives evidence of superb creative power. To enter its world is to have an immediate fictional experience of a world created by a paranoid at an advanced stage in the development of his psychosis. But only a magnificently gifted paranoid, of course, can create the world in which Ferdinand lives.

From what I have said, it follows that although the aesthetic object appears in the aesthetic transaction as involving uniqueness and as being self-sufficient, its uniqueness and self-sufficiency are not absolute, for the object is dependent on the presuppositions that make it possible, and not all of these are purely aesthetic. If, then, the self-sufficiency of a work of literature in the intransitive experience gives it a sort of congressional immunity from moral and cognitive jurisdiction, it does so only within the transaction. Outside it, it is open to criticism. The work is open to criticism not only in the obvious sense that we must consider the practical effects that it has on us, but also in the sense that we must criticize the presuppositions that make it possible in moral and cognitive terms. The criticism to which *Journey* is open, succinctly stated, is that the presuppositions that control it are perverse and have produced a work which, while perhaps not open to serious criticism from a purely aesthetic standpoint, is open to condemnation because the subject matter it has organized into its informed substance has been selected by a perverted mind and is valid only for that type of mind.

But why is this objectionable? This question can be answered both at the aesthetic level and at the non-aesthetic. A complete answer must include, of course, both, with a clear exhibition of the intimate way in which each answer affects the answer we give the other. Aesthetically it would have to be shown that in the case of *Journey* the intransitivity of the transaction is blocked by the informed substance of the novel. While it would be a relatively easy task, and a radically important one, to demonstrate this fact, we must ignore it, in order to turn to the second and give reasons why the perverse informed substance of the novel is objectionable. However, I shall not attempt to answer this question as stated. Instead, I shall consider the broader problem, what is it that the artist does to his subject matter when he creates a work of literature and how does the created work function in human experience? If this can be made clear, any one ought to be able to see for himself why perversity must be objected to in a work of art.

5

One thing we know about the artist, and that is that he has a passion for order, in response to which he shapes or informs experiential subject matter into a self-sufficient and relatively novel object. The subject matter of his work lies heaped pellmell in his mind as it is dumped in it by the accidents of experience, and he has what almost amounts to a compulsion to inform it. The "Prefaces" of the New York Edition and *The Note Books* of Henry James, to cite familiar examples, are full of instances of the way in which a chance suggestion germinates in the writer's mind, grows, and forces him, so to speak, to master it by ordering it into a work of art. It is the recognition of this primary need that gives formalist aesthetics its undefeatable strength; but the process involves more than struggle to achieve order, and this the formalist misses. However, the act of creation does not take place if it does not seek order, which is achieved when an object is constructed which can be apprehended intransitively as self-sufficient in the aesthetic transaction. This process I call "the organization of the primary subject matter of experience."

By the phrase, "the organization of the primary subject matter (or the data) of experience," I would refer to the fact that the writer organizes into a literary work the subject matter or data gathered by him in his practical living. What experience presents him with is a mass of stuff which is usually too disorderly for his mind to be able to comprehend. I am not referring to the "data" of experience of the epistemologist, which is the stuff of experience analyzed down to its elemental components. I mean the stuff of life as lived, as it comes to the artist in its own terms, in its presentational or dramatic concreteness, with its dynamism and fuzziness, involving action and passion, value freighted, and already exhibiting a discernible modicum of order. The writer eats, loves, hates; he plays and works and quarrels. He is a father and a citizen. He may have a more or less articulate abstract theory about the life of man. He is curious about men and the way they go about their business. His whole life is a constant gathering of stuff which he later uses as subject matter for his art. When we consider the relation of the artist's life to his work it appears that no simple theory will account for the resources that he brings to the creative act. Yet in spite of the bewildering variety of types which we find among writers, this we can say, that if a man is an artist the subject matter that he brings to the creative act is made up, for the most part, not of a heap of abstract formula, but of concrete presentational or dramatic subject matter. I call it "dramatic" in order to emphasize the fact that it consists of the actions and passions of men and is not an articulated system of abstractions such as we may find in even the most concrete descriptions of the anthropologist or the social scientist. In this sense, the subject matter of the writer is dramatic even if it consists of mere yearning and not of action. And it is concrete, even if the writer is concerned with the moral structure of experience or with the metaphysical values which sustain human existence. In this connection the first chapter of Berdyaev's study of Dostoevski makes rewarding reading, for in it is suggested the manner in which the great Russian novelist fused "ideas" and used them along with the actions and passions of men, as constituents of his novels.

We must not forget, however, that the subject matter out of which he makes his art he also gathers from art itself. His love of art is something that occupies a unique place in his scale of espoused values. Malraux tells us that "every artist's career begins

with the pastiche." This is true. But it is not the whole truth.
For to the love of art we must add a selective yet voracious hunger
for certain aspects of the primary data of experience. It is well
known that Henry James was as finicky, when he listened to a
story, as a spoilt child before his food tray. The dinner companion
who told him, for instance, the story that led to *The Spoils of
Poynton*, told him more than he needed to hear. "Life being all
inclusion and confusion, and art being all discrimination and
selection," the writer has to know when to close his mind's ear
to the person who is giving him more than he cares to take. But
for all his choosiness, James nevertheless pounced on the morsel
he selected from the offered tray with the wolfish relish of a
starved man. The data that the artist picks—James's "germs"—are
not, as he stumbles upon them, in a state of absolute chaos. The
artist is not a Hebrew God; he does not find, as Jahveh did, that
his subject matter is utterly without form, and void, and that
darkness is upon its face. I take it that there is no need to dwell on
the fact that the artist, as artist, is not interested in organizing the
actual data of experience but in its symbolic elaboration—he is not
a Solon, intent on rearing a state; he is a fictioner working with
symbols.

Note that the organization to which I refer is not that of which
Richards spoke. What I have in mind is the symbolic organization
of the primary data of experience achieved by the artist in the
literary work. For its proper aesthetic perception, it *is to be found
in the object*, whatever philosophy may decide about its real locus
later on. The organization is achieved with reference to principles
of order which it is the business of criticism to discover. In our
novel the formal unity of the tale is achieved by the participation
of the narrator-hero in the episodes he tells about. Through the
variety of his experience the hero first discovers and then confirms
what he gradually learns about the evil nature of the world. Thus
the presuppositions that control the selection of the subject matter
of the novel are in "harmony," as critics say, with those which
selected the form in which the subject matter was informed.

6

It is the fact that the artist orders and defines the elements of
primary experience that gives Bergson's theory of art the irrefragable content of truth it has. Bergson lays it down that art reveals
the reality of things. He is working with a contrast between the
practical grasp of things and this other grasp, the aesthetic, which
tears the veil behind which things hide from our urgency and
resolution. We need not accept the theoretical wrappings in order
to discover a valid truth in this claim. There is no question here
of a reality superior to the reality to which the physicist's formulas
refer. There is a superior reality symbolized in the work of art—
but it is superior, not to the reality of the world of physics, but to
the alleged reality of our physical world, that is, of the cliché-
cluttered, hastily grasped, by-passion-blurred world in which we
daily live. It is the reality of this world that the artist seeks, through
his activity, which we now have to call, not an act of *creation,* but
of *discovery.* The resolution of this apparent contradiction I must
postpone for a while. Here I would indicate that Bergson is right
when he argues that practical perception has no need to discriminate the full presentational, concrete-structured reality of what it
seeks to grasp only to use. But that only the gaze of the artist
descries the real seems to me to be an unwarranted assertion. The
physicist also reveals a deep-seated reality, namely the mathematical structure of nature, which is an aspect of the complex
structure of reality, and one in which the artist is only superficially
interested, just as the physicist is not interested in the deep-seated
reality which the artist reveals.

Since this assertion may seem to blur the distinction between
art and science it is necessary to draw it explicitly. For all practical
purposes, we can distinguish between art and science in terms of
the subject matter and of the levels of abstraction in which physicist and artist are respectively interested as well as of the purposes
they seek to realize. But this is not where the radical seat of the
distinction lies, for only arbitrarily can we declare that a man
cannot look intransitively upon the physical reality to which his
formula points or the interrelated pattern of implicative relations
which constitutes a mathematical demonstration. When I re-

member my old chemistry teacher I must maintain that a laboratory experiment, even reeking of hydrogen sulphide, can to some
men be a thing of beauty, just as a clean job of decapitation must
have seemed a thing of beauty to so accomplished a craftsman as
the late M. de Paris. Where, then, does the distinction radically
lie? Not in the substance apprehended, but in the manner and
in the purpose for which it is apprehended. And this is the reason
why it is so difficult actually to separate and even to distinguish
the cognitive from the aesthetic mode of experience. As contrasted
with the religious and the moral, the cognitive and the aesthetic
modes share in the fact that the direction of attention is not reflective but outwards on an object (even if it be the self) with
which the attending self is not identified during the act of cognition or of aesthetic apprehension. This is the truth of Kant's
famous disinterested interest, but it ought to be noted that it
holds for the object of knowledge as well as for the object of
aesthetic apprehension.

There is a distinction, however, between the aesthetic and the
cognitive modes of experience, since the knower does not center
his attention intransitively on a self-sufficient object, but on relations, implicative or causal, that branch out indefinitely from it
backwards and forwards, towards the hypothesis his inquiry confirms or towards the consequences and the new problems it opens
up. And this is true of the mathematician who, having enjoyed
the elegant self-sufficiency of a demonstration, soon takes up from
where he left off merely to gaze on the beauty of the relations he
has disclosed, and seeks new relations suggested by those already
explored. The artist presents an object for contemplation which
during the act of contemplation elicits rapt attention, sustains it,
and feeds it intransitively. Spinoza, fascinated by a spider capturing
a fly—was he a naturalist or an amateur of the drama? The answer
depends on what went on in his mind as he looked.

The artist orders experience at what we usually call the commonsense level, but what I prefer to call the dramatic level. This is
the level at which we all live when we return from the cells where
we carry on our specialized professional activities. It is a world
which does not seem ever to succeed in assimilating in an operative
manner the viable knowledge which at any stage in the develop-

ment of a civilization the creative mind in science or philosophy, in morality and in religion, puts at its disposal. It is the world in which men actually live whether they are civilized technosophists or preliterate Australian aborigines. This world derives the order which it possesses inherently from many sources, but, back of all of them, finally from the creative activity of men who rear institutions and discover values and establish a hierarchy among them and create "myths" which are expressive of the relations that they discern to obtain among themselves and between themselves and the universe.

To claim that it is the artist that brings about this order would be to turn him into a statesman, prophet, theologian, scientist, and engineer all in one. But the order the world inherently has is never satisfactory, since it is always threatened by chaos and is at best—whether we are speaking of the sociological or the cosmological dimension—a generic order, structured in institutions and conceptions which must serve the members of a society indifferently in their several roles and statuses. Nor is it easy to grasp, for all the seeming familiarity with it that members of a society seem to possess. Particularly in historically dynamic, complex societies, it requires constant redefinition in concrete viable terms. To discover in its specificity the nature and structure of experience as lived, and to present it in terms that men can grasp, is the creative task of the artist. And it is an essential task. He is engaged in giving us a refurbished picture of our world in concrete terms. He teaches us to discern what we in our purblindness cannot see for ourselves; he tells us what is the dramatic pattern of human life and thus defines for us its sense. It is this fact, as has often been noticed, that gives Oscar Wilde's shopworn epigram its validity; for life imitates art in the sense that we discover in it what the artist through his work tells us is there. For this reason, without his aid our comprehension of our culture coarsens, we get confused, our sensibilities harden; and because, as a result, our imaginative grasp falters, our daily living insensibly relapses to the level of instinct, automatism and animal brutality.

In one of Van Wyck Brooks's earliest essays, "America's Coming-of-Age," referring to Whitman, he speaks of the function of the poet in the most radical and primitive sense of the word, as a

man who first gives to a nation a certain focal center in the consciousness of its own character. To do this is to exhibit to a people
in dramatic terms the structure of its life and the order of rank
of its values. This is what the literary artist does in the degree to
which he is creative. He presents us with a symbolic fiction of a
world charged with value; he defines that value in dramatic terms
within the grasp of men; he shows the hierarchy that structures
it; and he thus gives us the means to give vivid individual content
to the generalizations on which we fall back when we take stock of
our experience. Thus the reader of *Journey* comes face to face with a
symbolic world which reveals precisely what quality life can have
when men are as here depicted. And it is a sad comment on the
quality of our life that many prominent critics saw our world
faithfully reflected in *Journey*. Hatred, distrust, malice, selfishness,
and murder never rise to grandeur in *Journey* as they do in *Mac-
beth* or *Othello*. *Journey* gives us a world in which no defeat of
heroic proportions is possible. Neither audacity nor love nor malice
are creative of epic destruction; they are impotent. Resentment
and self-hatred trims all size to its own scale, and perceives nothing
but what is emotionally and morally congruous with it.

7

But how shall we resolve the contradiction involved in the claim
that the artist *creates* novel objects and that he *discovers* the
hidden reality of our practical, commonsense world? The contradiction is only apparent, not real, since the two assertions were
made from different points of view. From an external point of view,
there is novelty in his product and spontaneity is involved in the
process. From the standpoint of the artist, however, we grasp a
different aspect of the creative process, since what the artist does
is not to invent something new but to extricate out of the subject
matter at hand its own proper structure or order.

If this is what the theory of imitation intends—and there are
some passages in the *Poetics* which, with the usual tucking and
pulling that constitute the art of learned exegesis, could be used
to justify this interpretation—it is a valid theory, and in this respect
at least is not necessarily in conflict with expression theories that

emphasize the novelty or uniqueness of the work of art. If this is true, McKeon's statement in the article referred to above is justified when he tells us that "it is possible for the doctrine of imitation to persist in all essentials even when the term has disappeared." What the artist does, as we have already seen, is to wrench from his subject matter something that is not fully realized in it, or that, life being the bungling thing it is, is realized in a different manner than it would be if it were designed to meet the demands of aesthetic order exclusively. In talking of the creative activity, above, we emphasized the fact that *he* did the wrenching. Now we must emphasize that he wrenches *something*. The artist *creates* then, in the sense that he makes a dramatic structure out of subject matter in which the ordinary ungifted mind would not think of looking for it. But the structure is no more invented by him than it is by the physicist when the latter discovers the laws of the physical world and expresses them in the tools he has at hand. The writer *discovers* this structure, in the sense that the forms and the substance of his work are found by him in the data of experience which is the subject matter of his art.

In James' *Notebooks* we find numerous examples of the way in which a story takes the bit in its mouth in spite of the writer's editorial commitments as to length and general development, and in spite of the intentions that he formulated as he began to explore the possibilities involved in the initial "germ" from which his creative activity took off. In successive entries we see James gradually discovering the story, and we are able to follow the way in which, as it reveals itself to him, it forces him to alter his plans.

In view of these facts, an author's relation to his theme is poorly described as an effort to say what he wants. We come closer to the facts if we speak of it as an effort to tease out the potentialities of the story, an effort to discover how to do them justice, by so treating them as to meet their objective requiredness. The writer who says what he wants, or what the editor, or the Commissar in charge of artistic production, wants him to say is not an artist, however useful his product may be for political or for moral reasons. This is what critics mean when they speak of the "sincerity" of the writer. It is very easy for the writer to push his subject matter around with the bulldozer of a lucid will, so as to come out where he wants to come out and not where the story wants to come out. This is the reason why there is such a profound truth in the Platonic myth of poetic inspiration. What the writer does is to accept or to reject what is offered to his consciousness from the depths of his mind. His responsibility as artist is to decide whether what is offered to him now belongs with what he has already accepted or has a greater right to survive than what he has already put down on paper. This is a great responsibility, and calls for acuity of superior power; but it is one which is controlled by his ability to discern the requiredness of the potentialities of the object as this gradually reveals itself to him, and not by what he wants.

When we, as readers, look upon the object that the artist has made, we find it to be a symbol embodying the order towards which, in terms of presuppositions we seldom do more than sense in a confused way, the subject matter of experience tends. True that the constructions of the writer are those of a unique man at a given time working within a given artistic tradition in a specific culture at a specific stage in its history; nor can they be reduplicated by anyone else nor can they be confirmed in any sense in which the scientist confirms his hypotheses. But to the extent to which the literary object approaches perfection, the order which informs it is not arbitrary, since it is inherent in it. It is to the extent that it is able to exhibit order that is inherent in it that it is able to become a public object.

There is a kind of congruence, or pre-established harmony, between the work of literature and actual life. But it is not one in which literature imitates life. Rather the relation is, so to speak, "normative," in the sense that it tells us, not what actual life is like, but what it would be like if it had the wisdom or the good fortune to possess the economical interrelatedness that art possesses for attention. What literature, therefore, gives us is a symbolic construct of what life ought to be like in order to answer the demands of aesthetic apprehension of it. What it gives us we can, if we desire, call "knowledge" in an extended and vague sense of the word, since it is a product of the mind and it is an object of perception, and since it has undeniable similarities with the symbolic constructions which we call knowledge in the narrow sense. But while we cannot deny anyone the right to use words as he chooses, we have a right to demand that his use does not confuse him and mislead us.

8

It is desirable to emphasize the fact that the "ought" of which I have been speaking is neither a cognitive, religious, nor moral, but a purely aesthetic "ought." The aesthetic ought is satisfied when the analytically discernible components of the object are so related as to elicit and sustain intransitive attention on the object. To speak of the organization which elicits such a response as a "logical affair," as is done by James K. Feibleman, is misleading, since no one has discovered the implicative relations which allow the innumerable components of a work of literature to go together in order to constitute an object so organized as to elicit and sustain intransitive attention. And it is at least as misleading to argue that the work of literature ought to be plausible in the sense that it must be satisfying in the light of the reader's inductive knowledge about the world. Non-aesthetic demands, cognitive, moral or religious, intrude on the aesthetic experience when for any reason the aesthetic object fails to capture attention in an intransitive manner, or when for abnormal reasons we fail to yield attention to it. To argue that literature refers to the world because it must be plausible is to deny to the creative artist his autonomy and to the object created its self-sufficiency. Thus our knowledge of the world tells us that men do not change in their sleep into "monstrous beetles." But the writer of *Metamorphosis* transports us without effort, it would seem, into a world of his own creation, by devices which the acuity of a good critic can disclose, although seldom exhaustively, and the purpose of which is to exclude from our conscious response our non-aesthetic demands in such a way that they do not become the basis of a criticism of his symbolic construction.

Man, among the other things which make him unique, is a culture building animal. And he has never been known to create a culture which did not include a more or less well defined hierarchy of values: dramatic conceptions about himself and about the nature on which he depends to survive, and animistic conceptions of the forces which define and control his destiny.[9] These, the girders of culture, are seldom formulated by him in the abstract way in which theologians, philosophers and scientists discuss them. They are expressed in mythopoetic terms, essentially dramatic and anthropomorphic. And they are created or discovered—depending on our point of view—by the artist at a given juncture in history, in terms of the factors of a culture which, when he starts his work, is already a going affair, but which would not survive for long if it did not have the benefit of his renovating ministrations. In the narrow sense of the word, literature does not give us knowledge, since it does not give us a picture of which we may demand correspondence with the actual world as we actually grasp it. It gives us an aesthetically ordered picture. But life seldom achieves the order that a work of literature possesses; and when it does, it does so only by happy accident. But if literature does not give us knowledge, it ought to be recognized that it is prior in the order of logic to all knowledge, since it is constitutive of culture, which is one of the conditions of knowledge.

1952

the object of the poem [1]

1

Let us ask what status in being can be assigned (in A. C. Bradley's usage of the term) to the poem's "substance," or to that which the poem is about or, as I shall call it in this essay, to its object. What we are asking is whether the object of the poem can be said to "exist" or has to be assigned some other status in being. But let us note first that the question we are asking falls within the field of poetics, or the aesthetics of poetry, which is a sub-division of aesthetic inquiry. Limited as it is, however, it is not unreasonable to suppose that most of its conclusions may be applicable, with appropriate changes, to the other arts.

In order to answer our question, "What is the object of the poem?" we must consider two stages of the coming to be of the poem. This is what unqualified organicists forget. The first stage discloses what is called by A. C. Bradley the "subject matter of the poem." It shows the subject matter to consist of the objects of non-aesthetic experience, with whatever structure they may inherently possess as appropriate to their natures, which the poet employs in the making of his poem. These objects can be classified by the philosopher of culture into four main categories: the cognitive, the aesthetic, the moral, and the religious. The reason for including aesthetic objects as possible stuff which makes up the subject matter of the poem is the fact that the artist sometimes uses finished poems in the same way in which he uses the rest of his experience, as when a Shakespeare, a Goethe, or a Marlowe employs old poetry to make new.

The second stage in the coming to be of a poem discloses the finished poem. Bradley designates what the poem is about at this stage as "the substance of the poem," and I often refer to it as "the informed substance" to mark by means of pleonastic emphasis the fact that the subject matter has been transubstantiated in the creative act. "The substance" of the poem is not rendered directly but symbolically; when a poem is about love or grief or the evil or the glory of men it does not point to actual value but to symbolized value. But what the symbols refer to, the informed substance of the poem, and the subject matter employed in its elaboration, both possess, or at least so I assume in this inquiry, some sort of status in being. The question to which we seek an answer is, "What is the status in being of the informed substance of the poem?"

Back of these assumptions there stand a few methodological principles and a number of substantive commitments suggested by the exigencies of a philosophy of culture, one or two of which it is desirable to sketch succinctly. It is assumed, first, that the purposes for which we discriminate things or events and their inter-relations are many, and the objects which we thus select to focus awareness on, and the psychological processes of discrimination, differ with these purposes. Thus, a phenomenological analysis of the modes of experience (without which, of course, there can be no rational grasp of the structure of experience as it is embodied in culture) carried on with a view to an exploration of the components of culture, distinguishes three other modes besides the aesthetic—the cognitive, the moral, and the religious. Each one of these modes grasps an object which is appropriate to it and which can be defined independently of the mode that grasps it, since it embodies traits peculiar to the object that determines that mode. Since, however, we may assume that there is, generically speaking, a fixed relationship between object and mode, it is possible, and there are occasions when it is desirable, to define the object in terms of the mode. Thus approached, those objects that are the end of any other than the aesthetic mode are, in Dewey's convenient terminology, merely *recognized*, not *perceived*.[2]

On this usage, "perception" and "aesthetic perception," are synonymous terms. And it follows that ordinary objects, which is to say, objects recognized as what they are for non-aesthetic purposes, are not grasped in their full individuality and uniqueness, and that if we are to grasp them in their individuality we must grasp them aesthetically. While, however, it is desirable to mark off various modes of experience, the analytic discrimination of these modes ought not to prejudice two independent questions: whether, or to what extent, we can actually undergo pure modes of experience; and whether, if we can actually undergo such pure modes, they are as valuable as mixed modes. These are not questions that can be answered on this occasion. But we should not forget that it is essential to answer them if we are to gain a complete understanding of the role that art plays in the creation of culture.[3]

Whatever the answers that we give to these two questions, it is assumed that the aesthetic object is grasped intransitively as a unique individuated object which is, for perception, self-sufficient.[4] It is also assumed that the aesthetic response is possible because the object of art as a public object—or, what is the same thing, as one of the components of culture—is a contrived whole, which embodies symbolically meanings and values in a fully integrated and structured manner, and is thus so ordered as to constitute a self-sufficient, coherent, and congruous complex datum, available through a distinctive mode of apprehension, which exhibits it as the unique object that it is.[5] What most obviously distinguishes other kinds of aesthetic objects from poems is of course the linguistic medium. But the medium limits the meanings and the values which can be embodied in the poem. Structure, or form, or order, or organic interrelatedness, then, of diverse component meanings and values conveyed by means of linguistic symbols, which criticism can discover in the poem, and self-sufficiency and intransitivity, which have their ground in that order, are the factors which make the poem possible. There are, of course, others; but these are, for our purposes, the only ones that need be mentioned.

It is finally assumed that the question we are interested in cannot be answered in psychological terms. Aestheticians have frequently recorded the fact that intercourse with art sometimes produces an overwhelming feeling of reality. Our soul, to use an expressive phrase of William James, "sweats with [the] conviction" that in the object of our aesthetic attention we have at last come upon the really real. Different men seem to get this kind of feeling from different arts. Some obtain it from music and others from poetry, while still others may derive it from painting or sculpture. But if we compare what they say about their experiences, we conclude that it is very much the same in any art. L. A. Reid puts it very clearly:

> And often it will happen that in this harmonious satisfaction of our profoundest impulses we feel a tremendous conviction of knowledge, which is accompanied sometimes by a sense of the superiority of such knowledge to other forms of it. Our conviction is closely akin to the conviction of the mystic. . . . In such moments the riddle of existence seems to be solved; we experience the perfect moment; we "*feel*" intensely "real"; and, feeling so, we feel also that we are intuiting objective reality, as it were, from the inside.[6]

We need not question, of course, that the feeling occurs. But whether art gives us knowledge, whether that knowledge is about reality or about phenomena, and whether it is a superior kind of knowledge to that which we have of familiar objects, or to that which the physicist has of the structure of the physical world— these are not questions the philosopher would decide by appealing to the feeling of the amateur as evidence. If the intensity of the amateur's conviction of the objective reality of art were acceptable as evidential, hallucinations and apparitions that are the effects of drugs would be more real than the objects of our workaday world.

In an obscure paper published over fifteen years ago I analyzed in psychological terms how the amateur arrives at the intense conviction he derives from art.[7] The conviction or feeling of reality, I argued, following close on the steps of William James, is a by-product of the manner in which an object of art excludes from consciousness everything else but itself. The exclusion is made possible by the unification achieved by the artist of all discriminable aspects of the object which he offers to us for intransitive apprehension. The amateur's intense feeling, then, is no ground on which to argue that we are here presented with a superior reality. The psychological explanation of the amateur's feeling, therefore, fails to throw light on the question to which we want to turn.

2

Since there are today many thinkers who hold that the question we have posed need not legitimately arise, let us review the grounds on which we must assert that there is a distinction between the poem, its linguistic vehicle, and its object. A poem is a special kind of linguistic thing. Language is able to point to actual things in the world and to purely intelligible or ideal things and to fictions, all of which have some sort of status in being independently of the language by means of which we point to them. Let us call this function of language its "ostensive function." What the locution means is that the object to which the language refers is external to the language and independent of it. It follows that the object of ostensive language can be referred to in various synonymous expressions in the same language and in several tongues without loss, although not necessarily with the same economy and elegance. The objects to which ostensive language refers may be real, or ideal, or fictitious, but whatever they are, they are external to the language by which I point to them and in a sense can be exhibited independently of it, since they can be exhibited in a large number of different languages. And this holds irrespective of what status in being we may finally assign to them at the conclusion of our ontological inquiries. I may not be able to tell you exactly what status in being they have, but that they have some I know. It may be retorted that fictions of any kind, including poetic ones, have no status in being whatever, since contemporary philosophy has devised techniques that enable it to make a clean sweep of all such pseudo-entities. But this criticism would miss the point we are seeking light on, namely, that whether we call them pseudo-entities or imaginary, or ideal entities, or anything else we choose, the fact remains that the object of poetry differs in an important respect from other objects to which language refers.

The language of poetry is not ostensive; the object it reveals has no discoverable existential status independent of the language that reveals it—it has no status in space and time. What reason have we, then, to say that poetry reveals an object and that this object has some sort of status in being? What grounds have we for asserting that the language of the poem is not identical with its object? Unless good grounds are produced, there is a justified suspicion that we may be asserting a distinction without a difference. This is what those who fear, as they put it, the proliferation of metaphysical entities and of realms of being, or of ontological levels or modes of reality, would assert. They argue that the assumption that the content of poetry, or as we are calling it, its object, can have any other than the existential status, is metaphysical nonsense. What are the reasons for asserting that poetry has an object and that this object has some sort of status in being distinct from the language of the poem? The first of these questions is not difficult and I shall try to answer it below. But the question as to what is the status in being of that object is indeed one of the most difficult questions that a philosopher could ask. I shall answer it here in a dogmatic manner. I hope that the edge of the dogmatism will be blunted by the fact that I have already discussed it elsewhere, where I have tried to adduce what arguments I was able to muster in favor of my position.[8]

The reason we must distinguish the language of the poem from the object it reveals is that the question, "What is the poem about?" is not only an intelligible question but one to which a partial answer can be given. We can supply a paraphrase of the poem. The paraphrase is not the object and cannot exhaustively point to it; it is merely a means by which a reader can be helped to find the object. Further, of two paraphrases we can say that in certain respects one comes closer to revealing what the poem is about than the other. But while the paraphrase points to that

aspect of the object that is revealed *through* the poem, it does not
help us discover that aspect which is revealed *in* the language itself. The language of the poem reveals the object in itself, by
means of its character as language, in the sense that the values and
meanings which constitute the object of the poem are conveyed
to the reader as what they are *in* or *by means of* its prosodic character and the felt morphological structures which make up the
poem. That this is the case is not possible to demonstrate to anyone who does not know how to read poetry and it needs no demonstration for anyone who does. But this need cause us no astonishment, since it would be equally impossible to give a congenitally
blind man an idea of the world of vision. We know, as we progress
in our skill in the reading of poetry, that we have deepened our
grasp of the poem. It is a question of a more lucid yet untranslatable grasp of objective meanings and values. In any case, for
some reason that has so far resisted all effort to elucidate it (at
least within the range of my reading) somehow the linguistic
medium, both through its analytically discriminable elements and
considered as an organic whole, helps to convey or reveal the
values and meanings which are embodied in the poem and which
constitute its object. The most obvious illustration of this fact is
found in onomatopoeia, in which some aspects of the intended
object are revealed in the phonetic properties of the linguistic
medium. But this is only one, and a relatively unimportant way,
in which the object is revealed in the language itself.

Another reason we must distinguish the language of the poem
and its object emerges when we consider what is involved in the
poet's creative effort. The intentional direction of his mind is two-
pronged; it is addressed to a search for the appropriate word or
phrase and for what he wants to say, for the object. The language
sought must fit the object. But the object is not discovered until
the language is found. What is meant by the word "fit" we cannot
here adequately explore without going far afield. Let us be content
with noting that the relation to which the word refers is as readily
evident to the trained reader as it is to the poet. It is not difficult
to find synonyms for the term, but they no more explain the relation than the word "fit" does. We can say there is a "harmony"
or a "congruity" between the language and the object of poetry.

And we can even advance a short step and say that the relation of fitness obtains when the object has been grasped with lucidity and finality—which is to say, when a complete revelation has taken place. But whether a revelation takes place or not is something only a trained reader can tell, and he only by direct inspection. So many variables enter into the discrimination of what the poem is about that consensus as to whether the language reveals its object in a fitting manner or not is something to be prayed for but not to be expected as an ordinary occurrence. But whatever procedure is involved in reading a poem and whatever criteria is agreed on in deciding whether the poem reveals its object fittingly, we must finally come to rest on the ability of the reader to discover what it reveals, and this is an ineluctable datum which aesthetic speculation cannot circumvent.[9]

An allusion to a commonplace of critical theory may throw some light on what is meant by the fitness between the language of poetry and what it is about. We often speak of the poet's honesty. And one of the things we have in mind is that he must successfully resist the lazy tendency to sacrifice the revelation of the object by falling back on ready-made linguistic forms—on stereotypes of imagery or of prosody; he must also successfully resist the tendency to sacrifice the language to a ready-made conception of the object. When he yields to these tendencies "fitness" is lacking. The poet sacrifices language to object—and thus sacrifices his object as well —when, for instance he fails to realize in it the object because the words or the numbers obscure it in some way or other. He sacrifices the object to the language, and thus he also sacrifices the language, when, for instance, he is overwhelmed, as critics say, by passion. In either case what he does is sacrifice the poem. Between two linguistic constructions which to the non-creative ear may seem to be almost identical, the poet chooses one because he feels that it comes closer than the other to what he wants to say. But not until the one that fits satisfactorily is found does he feel that his job is done. In short, his sense of language and his sense of something other than language, control the poet's choice of language. The creative process thus involves a search for language that adequately captures in and through itself the object that, somehow, until it is successfully captured by language, lies tantalizingly just

beyond the reach of consciousness. It is the task of the aesthetician
to do justice to this phenomenon in its full complexity, not to
explain part of it by explaining away or ignoring another part of
it. This is the reason that so-called formalist aesthetics and the
aesthetics of imitation, as the latter is usually interpreted, fails to
satisfy us. The theory of imitation must be rejected by anyone who
grasps firmly the difference between existential objects and the
objects of poetry. Formalism must be rejected by anyone who
grasps the fact that poetry "means something," even if the expression I have put between quotes is not much more than an
unfortunate muddle which is thickened when we try to explain
it by saying that art means itself or that a presentational symbol
merely presents itself, and thus does not represent.

3

Let us, at last, turn to our question and ask, "What status in being
has the object of the poem?" Reflection soon reveals the ambiguity
of the question. I may refer to the object of the poem prior to its
revelation in language, during the time that language imprisons
it and, in view of the effects of the poem on culture, later, after the
poem is no longer an object of aesthetic interest but becomes one
of the forces that shapes culture. Prior to its embodiment in poetry
we discover that the object of the poem has two different positions: in respect to culture, at any time, it may be found prefigured
in it but so embedded and so inchoately realized, and insofar as
it is at all realized, so little grasped at the conscious level by the
members of the culture as to be, for them, practically non-existent.
Insofar as the object is already realized the poet merely imitates—
he is a reporter and not a poet. He is a poet only when his creative
activity discloses values and meanings which the culture is ready
to espouse and adopt, which are knocking, so to speak, at the gate
of history, seeking admission, or have surreptitiously entered history
and become operative in the culture, but have not yet been identified, revealed, given a name and a dramatic mask.

In the latter case—and this is the case in which a man exploits
his poetic ability to the maximum—the object of the poem totally
subsists prior to its embodiment. In the former case, the object is

still in a semi-subsistent state, not fully existent, or to the extent
that it is actually realized in the culture, it is not recognized as
such. To the extent that the object has been fully grasped by the
culture prior to embodiment in a particular poem (and that grasp
is, I would hold, always, in its first instance, an aesthetic grasp),
the object of the poem is an object of mere imitation and therefore of low poetic value. The poet's gift consists in discovering the
not-yet-discovered subsistent values and meanings that make up
his poem's object in the creative act which is the revelation of that
object in and through the language to his own and to his reader's
minds. In any case, when the poet, through his creative gift captures an object in and through the language of the poem, the
object does not, by virtue of such capture, enter into existence.
It has what status it may have, in respect to the poetic revelation
it is the object of, in the poem; and because it is desirable to
identify this status I shall say it *insists in* the language, although
the use of the preposition, dictated, unless I am mistaken, by the
exigencies of the idiomatic genius of the language, is somewhat
pleonastic. The poem itself *exists* as an object of culture, although
ideally, since it is to be found in a book to be read or to be expli-
cated by the critic, or found in a man's mind to be recited, or set
to music. But the object of the poem as distinct from the poem
itself no longer merely subsists, in the sense that it did prior to its
discovery through the creative act. This is my excuse for adopting a
barbaric neologism and saying that it *insists*. Insistent objects are
ideal objects, revealed in and through the language of poetry, and
poetic revelation may be called, if we desire, a kind of representation or imitation—but one which takes place not merely through
but in the language and represents or imitates objects which until
they were captured by the poet were hidden in the limbo of subsistence. It ought to be observed, however, that to call poetic revelation a kind of representation or imitation is a very poor way of
saying what is intended. But it is one to which traditionalists are
loyal, and one which cannot be legitimately objected to so long
as it is merely a verbal expression and does not intend similarities
between what is imitated or represented and what does the imi-
tating, and insofar as it does not obfuscate the fact that what is

imitated or represented does not exist but subsists prior to its expression in language.

Insofar as the objects of poetry subsist prior to their revelation, they have the same status, for ontology, as is enjoyed by the operative invariant relations in nature—the "forces" and "powers" and the actualizing potencies which subsist as the structures of the physical world and which the scientist "discovers" and formulates as his "laws." But we must not forget the all-important difference between the objects expressed through the scientific hypothesis and the objects revealed through and in poetry.

If circumstances conspire, the poem performs effectively its practical role in culture: the values are isolated from the poem and espoused, and the meanings are institutionalized and thus given actuality in men's actions. When this takes place they are no longer dependent on the language in which the poet revealed them, and ostensive language can now refer to them. We can speak of Trojan horse tactics, of a man's quixotism; we speak of a man we know as a Don Juan or a Hamlet; we refer to the vices of a person of our acquaintance as those of a Karamazov, and the infatuation of a lad as that of a Romeo. But as actualized in culture, the values and meanings which constitute the object of poetry are not identical with their insistential revelation in poetry. A historically valorous act inspired by a reading of the Iliad, let us say, or the quixotical character that a man of flesh and bone may happen actually to have, is never in an unqualified sense like the valor or the quixotism revealed in a poem. When the insistent values and meanings presented in and through poetry are by some happy chance actualized in existence, they gain, if "gain" it may be called: they now have temporality and spatiality. But they lose in specificity and in uniqueness at least for ordinary perception, since they become entangled in irrelevant and obtrusive factors which rob them of their distinct boundaries and which in fact impede their actualization to the full. Whether the change from subsistence to existence is a gain or a loss, however, is something on which the doctors disagree. The majority of our contemporaries, loyal inmates of a secularistic culture, are certain that it represents a gain. Plato and many others have considered it a distinct loss.

4

It is desirable to summarize succinctly the import of the preceding remarks before bringing our discussion to a close. I have said that the poem is a linguistic thing which reveals symbolically in and through its medium meanings and values which have subsistent status in being and which are discovered by the poet in the act of creation. Note that the word "discover" is intended literally, for the meanings and values embodied in the poem do not exist prior to their embodiment. They are found by the poet in the creative act, in a realm beyond existence where they subsist. What the poet embodied is not altogether unrelated to his cultural and idiosyncratic experience, and to his poetic training and interests.

Once a poem is assimilated individually or culturally, its readers get the impression that its object imitates meanings and values with which they have been more or less well acquainted all along. But this is an illusion. For the values and meanings of a culture are never known, or never known clearly, or never known in their full density and specificity by those who participate in the culture, until the poem reveals them. When it does so, the symbolic revelation exercises, by virtue of the requiredness possessed by the revealed values, a normative function which leads men to espouse them and to realize them in culture.

Thus, at least at the phenomenal level, the object of the poem is objective, since it is revealed in and through the poem which, being an object of culture, contributes to the culture its meanings and values as potentially operative factors in it. This complex activity through which the poet extricates meanings and values by means of the creative process and gives them to his people who, now, through his formulation of them, are able to use them as ideal patterns of experience, is precisely the activity through which the gradually discovered ideals of the society are first defined and finally actualized, to some extent, at least, in institutions. Only then do they achieve their maximum of effective power in determining the quality of life of men and the direction of their historical development. Because poetry exercises an influence on the values actualized in a culture it has a normative function to perform. Thus to the extent that the poet succeeds in revealing

meanings and values which are actually involved in an emergent
sense in the social process, he becomes the creator of culture and
the meanings and values thus revealed become constitutive of
culture.

The object of the poem, then, has more than a merely phenomenal objectivity. It has status in being, or as I would put it,
"ontic status," since the meanings and values revealed in and
through the poem subsist by themselves and are actually to some
extent at least operative in the culture prior to their discovery by
the poet. There is thus a double connection between poetry and
existence. It is this double connection that defines the function
that poetry performs.

Because an elucidation of the arguments through which we
could justify the contention that the structure and the values of a
culture have ontic status would take us far from the field of aesthetics and because I have attempted it elsewhere, I have here
assumed it, although I know perhaps as well as any man of my
generation that the doctrine of axiological realism is profoundly
revolting to the dominant philosophical fashion of our age, at least
in the Anglo-Saxon world.[10] Without attempting to do again what
I have done elsewhere, let us note, in passing, that the ostensive
reasons for this deep-seated repugnance never quite do justice to
the depth of the feelings involved. The best reason that is offered
seems to be that on methodological grounds philosophers of science have shown that there is no need of any other type of entities
than existent ones and that existence, outside the reach of human
desire and need, is free of values and of purposive structures. But
philosophers of science could not have shown any such thing.
What they could have shown, at most, is that for their purposes
there is no need for positing anything else than existents. To argue
more than this is to assume that the exigencies of a philosophy
of science control all inquiry. And this is in turn to forget or disregard the fact that man in culture is considerably more than a
scientific knower: he knows more than the scientist as such knows,
and he engages in other activities besides those of knowing—he is
morally, religiously and aesthetically active. Each one of the activities he engages in has its own kind of autonomy and is related in
its own peculiar way to the others. Nor can any one of them, with-

out a threat to the total organization of culture, assume the autocracy of a dominant interest. From the standpoint of these other activities, human life involves, as a matter of simple fact, complex and determinative structural relations of a purposive nature which are constitutive of human society, and it is drenched through and through with values which we no more create—although to some extent we can control—than we create—although in our puny way we control practically—the mountains and rivers of the world in which we live.

Our modern mind is instinct with hatred of value.[11] This is part of the suicidal compulsion of our culture. But since it is impossible to do away with value altogether, our modern mind does the next best thing, it tries to reduce value to desire or interest, and beyond this, to biological needs, and beyond these, to the processes of a physical nature which are a partial, if essential, component of human life. To suppose that a structure of meanings and values has status in being independently of the mind that apprehends them, the modern mind takes to be sheer superstition. But we must admit that the poem embodies an object. How then can we account for the seeming objectivity of aesthetic meaning and value? Rather than admit that it is grounded objectively in being itself, the contemporary philosopher invents *ad hoc* a process of "projection," or a totally mysterious process of "emergence," according to which the continuous chain of causation somehow ceases and does not cease at the same time to operate in nature, to lead to levels of existence that are and are not prefigured in the level out of which they emerge. By such means he makes his peace with the fact that in some sense culture is at its heart value phenomena, although he recognizes that, on his ontology, the universe must be maintained to be value-free.

There is, however, this difficulty to be explained: that the values a reader discovers in the poem are often utterly unrelated to the desires and emotions the poem arouses in him. The question, then, "How does the poem appear to embody values?" remains one of the puzzles of contemporary aesthetics. The solution of this puzzle and of a number of others is ready at hand; it is to grant that the poem reveals insistent meanings and values in and through its linguistic medium, which are not merely nominal projections of our desires but are revelations through symbolic representations of subsistent values and meanings, that therefore have status in being. When the meanings and values are embodied by the poet they become potentially constitutive of culture. And it is this relation of poetry to culture that gives it its exalted and unsubstitutable function. Insofar as poetry discloses by creating the operative values and meanings of culture, poetry is constitutive of culture. With morality, knowledge and religion, art is one of the four main activities which the animal employs to transpose himself from the animal level and into the human. Through art, man makes himself into a human being.

1953

naturalism and creativity

A Note on a Naturalistic Theory of Mind

Contemporary naturalists urge the acceptance of their philosophy on the ground that it is not open to the criticism that led to the discrediting of the materialistic philosophy of the Nineteenth Century from which it descends. Claiming to be more sympathetic to the demands of the contemporary world than traditional philosophers, as they frequently remind us (as if sympathy for such a world were something for which one could take credit) these thinkers believe that they are able to avoid the facile techniques of reductionistic analysis of the older naturalism; and thus, they argue, they are able to do full justice to the higher values of religion, morality, and art. As J. H. Randall, Jr. puts it, naturalism "is not only not unsympathetic to the genuine values on which anti-naturalists have insisted. It is convinced that it feels them as strongly and understands them better than their protagonists." [1]

In the following pages one naturalistic theory of mind will be examined—that presented by Y. H. Krikorian in the book in which Mr. Randall makes this assertion. The examination shows that Mr. Randall's claim cannot be accepted, because Mr. Krikorian's theory neglects important data which it is necessary to reckon with in order to do justice to the workings of the human mind. If the criticism is valid, it invalidates, in an important sense, the kind of naturalism defended in the volume to which Mr. Krikorian makes his contribution. Kindly observe, however, that the results of the criticism do not allow for the unrestricted conclusion that all naturalism is therefore invalid. If another naturalistic theory of mind can account for these data, in that respect and to that extent a naturalistic philosophy is possible. Naturalism, however, does not succeed, when its proponents exhort us to employ the scientific method and promise us that if we do we shall solve all our problems. A philosophy cannot base its claims to validity on promissory notes.

Krikorian's view of mind is behavioristic, he tells us, because "behavior is the only aspect of mind which is open to experimental examination." [2] Unfortunately the reader runs immediately into difficulty, because Krikorian forgets to tell him what the naturalist does about those aspects of mind which are not open to the behavioristic approach. That there are such aspects is clearly implied by his statement, but we need not be informed of them by the author to know that they exist. There are, for instance, the purely private aspects of experience—the immediately felt quality of our affective life. This aspect of mind is incommunicable, yet of its importance there is no doubt, since it includes not only the felt quality of mere sense experience but a wide range of affective aspects which determine decisively our valuational attitudes. There are also those submerged processes of the psyche which we dimly envisage by tortuously round-about and fleeting means of a purely introspective, nonbehavioral nature: the field, I mean, which psychoanalysis has preempted. And there are finally the "creative" activities which take place beyond the range of experimental examination and through which men somehow transform their experience—in the fields of science, art, morality, religion, and industry—and, as it seems, add something to it which was not there before.

The decision to use only data that can be brought under experimental examination gives rise to the question whether the philosopher can both neglect the non-behavioral aspects of mind and at the same time offer a complete and adequate theory of mind. If this question is answered with a reply to the effect that the naturalist is better off if he stays within the area of the positively known, we reply that he cannot both claim that he understands better than his opponent those genuine values on which the latter has insisted and at the same time admit limitations of method that block such understanding. A scientist can narrow his inquiry down to such subject matter as his method can properly handle, for he passes no judgment on what falls outside his purview; but a philosopher does not have the same privilege, for he not only sets himself out, as Krikorian puts it, "to understand mind," but he must attempt to give us a comprehensive account of human values and a plausible theory of human destiny. This, his main task, is a pressing one that does not await that remote and glorious day when science shall have found out everything there is to find about the mind. One often hears naturalists, particularly positivists, repudiate the role that I have assigned to philosophy on the ground that the problem of human destiny is a meaningless problem. The answer is that you cannot avoid it by denying it or ignoring it; for all you do in that case is to refuse to face it critically, and instead of an explicit conception open to rational correction you accept uncritically the philistine notion of destiny which is implicit in the organization of values (such as it is) of the day and world in which you live.

While Krikorian claims that on behavioral terms he is able to "understand mind," I doubt if there are many scientists who have looked into the problem of the creative imagination who are as daring as our scientistic philosopher in their boasts. The late Clark Hull, a leading behaviorist who earned his reputation in the laboratory, was under no illusion that he knew enough to be able to give a scientific account of "the highest rational and moral behavior." [3] R. W. Gerard, a physiologist, approaching the problem of the imagination from the standpoint of his own interests, but, unlike Krikorian and Hull, willing to learn from psycho-analysts as well as from rigorous behaviorists, tells us that:

> It remains sadly true that most of our present understanding of mind would remain as valid and useful if, for all we knew, the cranium were stuffed with cotton wadding. In time, the detailed correlation of psychic phenomena and neural processes will surely come; but today we are hardly beyond the stage of unequivocal evidence that the correlation does exist.[4]

In spite of the way in which he prudently qualifies his statement, Gerard seems to be as full as Hull of generous unscientific faith that psychology and biology will some day overcome their limitations. And I, for my part, do not in the least doubt that if we are seeking nothing further than psycho-physical correlations, we shall get them in increasing numbers in the future. That is not what Krikorian and Hull have as final aims; what they want to do is of course to get rid of the category of mind altogether. Whether the correlations that Gerard seeks will tell us all that, as humanists, we need to know about the creative process, is another matter. In the meantime it is only fair to wait for them before passing on their value, remarking in anticipation that until scientists are able to predict by observation of the nervous system or any other part of the body, and of the environment, whether a man is capable of writing an Inferno or an Oedipus Rex, and what the value, moral and aesthetic, of such work will be, the faith of our scientists about the importance of the light which their science can throw on the creative process is only of biographical interest and quite immaterial to our argument.

Since Krikorian may reply that this criticism is external and based on authority and that it makes too much of an unimportant sentence in his essay (that, namely, in which by implication he allowed that there were aspects of mind that the behavioral method could not handle), we must turn to the theory itself, although it will demand that we go into matters of a somewhat technical nature, and ask what explanation Krikorian offers of the creative activity.

Careful search does not reveal that this problem has been investigated by our author. But he no doubt considers that he has adequately handled it in the passages in which he gives us a theory of "reasoning or problem solving." We must therefore turn to this part of his essay to see if it satisfies our demands. Reasoning, which is to say, purposive thought, we are told, is

> an anticipatory schema, a frame to be filled in. . . . The specific ideas that fill the schema are also anticipatory. Ideas are anticipated operations and their consequences in relation to some situation. In behavioral terms, to have an idea is to be ready to respond in a specific way to a stimulus; to reason is to rehearse various anticipatory responses in relation to a problem. The difference, therefore, between reasoning and actual manipulation is that in the former case the operations are preseen and are only possible ones. When one says that one has an idea as to how a certain machine will work, one anticipates the series of operations which one would actually perform were one running the machine.[5]

Krikorian goes on to tell us that as ideas develop, "they become more and more general in their application and abstract in their nature," freeing themselves gradually from specific operations and being performed by symbols. But he insists that "in this whole development of ideas anticipatory operations are basic." The process, however, through which ideas become abstract, and the manner in which symbols come to substitute for operations which in their basic reference remain nevertheless operational, are matters which are not gone into, although the reader suspects that this is one of the points on which strong evidence of a behavioral nature should be brought to bear and which requires the most rigorous analysis; for it is one of the points at which the anti-naturalists have insisted that a break occurs in the natural process. Again, I doubt whether in order to have an idea of how a certain machine works one must rehearse anticipatorily operations performed when actually running the machine; for on this basis it would be difficult to explain how a teacher is able to teach, say, a musical instrument, although he himself cannot play it. Be that as it may, the problem to which we must confine ourselves is whether Krikorian can throw any light on what Coleridge called "the active imagination."

Krikorian holds that the anticipatory responses that constitute cognition or purposive thought, "were previously experienced as

actual consequences of the same kind of stimulus." But this constitutes a virtual denial of the possibility of creative increment.
That this is not a mere slip of the pen on Krikorian's part is shown
by the fact that elsewhere in the essay he tells us that "a physicist
in his experimental work is guided by future results involved in
his experiments; and a physician in making a prescription is controlled by the expected consequences of his medicine." This is
unquestionably true of the physician in writing the ordinary prescription; but it is not true of the research men in medicine, nor
is it true of the physicist. The two cases of physician and physicist
are mentioned by Krikorian at a point where he is interested in
emphasizing the futuristic aspect of thought; but they do not illustrate the same type of "prospective cognition," and the failure anywhere throughout his discussion to mark the difference between
them gives our author away. For it is to be hoped that the physician already has identified the nature of the disease for which he
is prescribing and that he knows with reasonable certainty the effects of the medicine before he prescribes it. If he does not, he is
irresponsible and of no interest to us in this discussion. The physicist may be merely checking an experiment that has already been
performed, as a cook does in the kitchen who is not too certain
of her art and is therefore trying to follow literally the directions
of her Fannie Farmer. But as a creative mind, in first conceiving
the experiment and in formulating the hypothesis which it is
designed to test, the physicist has taken a leap beyond the already
known and the already experienced. The same kind of leap of
course is taken by the medical man when he gets a creative hunch.
Krikorian tells us that we need not "make a mystery of the potentiality in the future reference of mind. The future possible consequences were previously experienced as actual consequences of the
same kind of stimulus and were recorded in the neuromuscular
system as 'neurograms'." It is interesting to note in passing that
Krikorian, who insists on observable behavioral data subject to
experimental control, has no scruples in falling back, when he
thinks he needs them, on nonobservable entities called "neurograms" for the existence of which he does not offer the slightest
evidence. Let us waive this point, however, and note the fact that
the sentence which follows the quotation clearly indicates that he

does not have in mind genuinely creative activity but that he is thinking of "problem-solving" at a very rudimentary level; for he says, "Thus, having been conditioned to the stimulus, they are ready to be set off by it when it is met again."

Krikorian is right in emphasizing the anticipatory aspect of thought. Mind is indeed, as he points out, prospective or futuristic; but unfortunately for his theory it is not so in the manner in which he tells us that it is. For thought is controlled, not only by "future consequences of stimuli which function as present stimuli," but teleologically, in a way that Krikorian does not seem to realize. To put it concretely, the thought of the physicist is controlled by a vague and inchoate whole, although at the moment of creative thinking he does not exactly know what that whole is like. The new conception of the creative mind seems to come to birth under the guidance of an inchoate structure of ideas for which, since they have not yet been created, there can be as yet no "neurograms." If they were already recorded as neurograms, proof should be furnished of their presence, as well as of the fact that they are indeed consequences of stimuli previously experienced, for precisely what is at issue is this point, which on Mr. Krikorian's theory is settled by assertion.

Because I am less ignorant of aesthetics than I am of physics I am going to discuss the problem in terms of art rather than science; but the change should make no difference in the result, since it seems safe to assume that, viewed psychologically, the creative acts of both the physicist and of the artist are very similar. Now in art, what the behaviorist has to explain is the control that the new whole, which from the standpoint of consciousness has not yet been fully born, exercises over the artist's mind as he proceeds to bring it to birth. Mysteries are not elucidated by encouraging us not to recognize them as mysteries, and the creative act remains a mystery for the behaviorist in spite of his scientific courage and precisely because, by introducing his neurograms and his anticipatory expectations, he reduces the creative activity to a complex process of shuffling the already experienced. But for all its appearance of contemporaneity, this does not advance the theory of mind beyond the point where Hobbes left it. In order to make a significant advance the behaviorist would have to be able to account in his terms for the intentional mental direction, the purposive thrust of the mind, the mind's ability to follow the lead of something which is not pushing it from behind, so to speak, since it is not yet there. It is this fact, the control by the not-yet-there total situation over the present, that leads the idealist to insist that a factor is here at work of an essentially teleological nature; and until this factor is explained in its own terms and not by reduction (by implication) to simple problem-solving, according to which creative thinking consists in shuffling "neurograms" which were already formed, mind will continue to escape the efforts to bring it into line with behavioristic psychology.

A related difficulty which the behaviorist must face arises from the fact that the creative activity is not observable by behavioral techniques, nor even by close introspection. Consider for instance the celebrated case of Poincaré's successful research into Fuchsian functions.[6] The fact of which this case is an instance is itself very commonplace; if we discount Poincaré's stature and the importance of his discovery, we can say that there is hardly any one who has not had the somewhat similar experience of solving a problem or elucidating a puzzle overnight. But how can we apply a theory of behaviorally observable anticipatory responses to the long unconscious work and the sudden illumination of which Poincaré gives us an account? Since for the behaviorist there is no consciousness, nothing can take place below its level. And yet somehow deep beyond the reach of observable behavior the creative mind transforms and transmutes the matter of experience, so that what it produces is in an important sense utterly unlike what was taken in by experience. If this fact is denied, the burden of proof is on him who refuses to admit it as valid, and the proof would consist in showing that what we take to be new is not truly but only apparently new. In respect both to form and content the mind out of its own intrinsic spontaneity makes additions to its experience in the fields of science, art, statesmanship, morality, and religion. Nor is it possible to dissolve the difficulty by denying the validity of the distinction between form and content, for even if the denial were to be admitted, the problem would remain as to the source of the newness of the created object as a whole in respect to which no discrimination of structure as distinct from matter was admissible. The medium through which the addition is made—the language of the scientist or the material of the artist—resists, for it has obdurate ways over which the creative mind must win. But as the creative idea suddenly illumines consciousness, or slowly comes to birth, the matter yields and grows and is informed with something utterly new.

We know, of course, something about the observable aspects of the creative act—but what we know is superficial and trivial compared with what we do not know. It is not an exaggeration to say that in respect to its hidden factors we know nothing about the creative process, except that it does occur, and chiefly of course because the active imagination performs the synthesis of the old and brings about the creation of its new product unobserved, in the depths of the unconscious, if you will, after conscious effort gives it its first push. That in some minds the idea seems to pop fully formed and quite unexpectedly into consciousness, while in other no less gifted minds it has to be dragged out painfully piece by piece, and has to be fitted no less laboriously into completed wholes—these are all easily observable commonplaces. In the latter case, which is probably more common, it is easier to sense the effect of the not-yet-born whole controlling the process of creation, but that does not mean that in the former it was absent. If the whole is there, in the depths of the unconscious, behaviorism will have to rescind its claims and the psychologist will have to give us an account of the manner in which the synthesis came about. The problem does not consist of the tracing of the old elements and distinguishing them as such, but of discovering the origin of the new, or of the disposal of the claim that anything new came into being. It is in respect to this puzzle that we seem to be utterly in the dark as to how the creative imagination goes about its work. Yet our ignorance is not so abysmal that it will allow us to confuse "the active imagination" with the capacity to solve problems evinced by the merely ingenious, the merely inventive mind. The difference may be only one of degree, though that is on the face of it doubtful; but a few degrees more or less mark an important difference in kind between the quick and the dead in body and may mark the difference between the mind of the genius and the merely ingenious mind.

It is true that we speak of the solution of problems on the part
of both the creative scientist and the artist. Of the former it may
be proper to speak in this manner, although there are reasons to
doubt it. But of the artist, in spite of the fact that the expression
is used idiomatically, it is not proper, and the acceptance of the
phrase uncritically is likely to mislead us as to the actual process
to which it refers; for only in a very qualified sense does the artist
have before him a "problem" whose solution can be verified in
terms of conditions objectively set *before* the "solution" is proposed. In the process of artistic creation the formulation of the
conception and the solution of the problem are, I suspect, identical,
and the creative process consists at once in creating and discovering
what one wants to say. If the object thus "discovered" or "created" is a genuine product of art it is as strange and fascinatingly
new and unexpected to the artist when he finally brings it forth
as it is to a competent audience. The activity of the artist has these
two aspects—contradictory though they may seem—because the
product presents itself to the artist, as he gradually "hits it off," as
having an objective existence which controls the artist's activity
and which resists his control, and yet as being, at the same time,
the product of subjective propulsions and tensions that the artist
can recognize as his own.

Perhaps the reason that we so readily talk about solving an
artistic problem is the fact, already noted, that the for-conscious-
ness-not-yet-there whole somehow tyrannizes over the artist, dic-
tating what is admissible and what is not. However, although in
ordinary discourse the phrase is not objectionable, when we are
seeking the best light we can get on mental activity the expression
can be a source of confusion. There are indeed difficulties that the
artist can overcome and which, with little danger of confusion,
may be spoken of as "problems," in the sense that the artist knows
what he wants before he has found the way to achieve it. Such
"problems" present themselves in regard to the manipulation of
the medium when the artist feels that he has not yet come close
enough to effects he clearly wants to achieve because he has clearly
imagined them, but has not succeeded in quite hitting them off,
or when he has to judge of the adequacy of a given form to a
subject matter not yet informed that has begun to take shape in

his mind. This is the case, for instance, when a poet thinks he can say what he wants in a sonnet and it turns out that a different "form" is required, or when he attempts a drama and after much labor discovers that his "matter" can only be handled in a novel form. But even these so-called "problems" are not problems in the same sense that a technological problem, controlled by conditions of an objective nature publicly definable prior to the solution, is said to be a problem.

What has been said agrees only in part with Croce's doctrine that conception and expression are identical, because it recognizes that the activity of imagining takes place through and in a material medium which resists the artist's efforts, and without intimate familiarity with which no purely mental imagining would be possible to him. To suppose, however that the creative process is a hit-and-miss matter of following the suggestions which the medium somehow originates, is either to give evidence of complete ignorance of the creative activity or of honorable but purely deductive loyalty to a theory irrespective of easily available facts.

The reason for this discussion is the need to point out the complexity of the creative process by showing how notions of simple problem solving, particularly of the behaviorally observable type, fail to account for the way in which matter taken in by the senses is literally added to while it is also to some extent merely reshuffled. It indicates a purely external and inadequate knowledge of what is involved to assume that creative activity consists merely of the reshuffling of discrete elements or of atomic contents and experienced forms into other combinations. The product of the creative mind is not a mere combination, but a creation in a sense that no behaviorist or mechanist can admit and remain true to his theories. Creative activity takes place very rarely; but when it takes place it adds something new to the content of experience.

There is, it would seem, very little excuse for contemporary naturalists to neglect the creative imagination in their view of mind, since Dewey has given it a prominent place in *Art as Experience*.[7] Dewey acknowledges that the artist produces something *new*—and as I read him, he means something literally new, since the product of the creative imagination goes beyond the forms and matter received from without and thus involves an addition to the fund of informed meanings that are brought to the act of composition. As against the tradition headed by Hobbes, which virtually denies the active imagination, Dewey takes his position with the idealists who, with Leibnitz, assert that there is nothing in the mind that does not come through the senses—*except the mind itself*. The content of experience is not merely shuffled by the poet but is transformed and transubstantiated. He advances on what he takes in; he does not merely recombine his funded meanings ingeniously into patterns that have themselves been suggested by shuffling experience. The issue of such a process of mere shuffling is mechanical and imitative: but art does not imitate nature; instead it breaks up its meanings and forms, so to speak, under the impact of experience, and then fuses the whole into something utterly new.

This is not the place to ask how Dewey reconciles his recognition of the spontaneity of the mind with his naturalism; it is enough for us to point out that his account of the creative activity makes nonsense of the universal applicability of the scientific method. Nor is it the place to ask how he reconciles what he says about the creative mind's activity with his antipathy toward introspection. Dewey's book on aesthetics (which in many respects seems to me to be the least instrumentalistic of his books and to contain therefore the soundest part of his philosophy) is referred to in order to make concretely an important point: namely, that the genuine and first-hand interest in one of the important activities of the human spirit forced him to take seriously the spontaneity of the mind, thus leading him to transcend, at one point at least, the limitations inherent in his scientistic methodolatry.

It may be retorted that the assumption of spontaneity blocks inquiry—we should try to get at the possible determinations that control the creative act, the search for which it is wise to encourage. To this criticism two replies, at least, should be made. The first is that this is a counsel of perfection prompted by a narrow scientistic interest which would interdict all aesthetic speculation until the glorious *mañana* when behaviorists will give us an adequate theory of the creative artist. The second reply is that it was Dewey himself, whose philosophy was proclaimed by one of the contributors to Krikorian's volume as "the vanguard of twentieth century naturalism," [8] who recognized the spontaneity of the mind, and that his recognition was based on close empirical, although not "scientific," analysis of the aesthetic activity. "Spontaneity" is indeed Dewey's own word, and not one merely attributed by the writer to him. And while the writer is in hearty agreement with Dewey in his emphasis on the creative contribution of the mind in the poetic process, it is for the latter, who is a naturalist, and not for the writer, that the recognition constitutes a problem. One of the reasons the writer had to abandon the naturalistic doctrines which he once defended is that he was forced to recognize the mind's spontaneity, an insight to which he was led in part by the study of Dewey's aesthetics. Once you grasp the importance of the mind's spontaneity you can easily see how naïve and simplistic are the efforts of scientists when they try to reduce it to processes of reshuffling with which scientific method can deal. If the scientist must ignore what he cannot observe and measure, let him do so—but why, except as prompted by doctrinaire intransigence, must he deny that which eludes him?

A theory of mind that does not take into consideration the phenomenon of the creative imagination, or that reduces it to complex mechanical reshuffling and anticipatory manipulation, is not a theory of what is distinctive and of chief interest about the human mind to one interested in the genuine values of the human spirit. And if some of us will grant that the only real value of the best explanations of the creative activity now available consists in their revealing the complexity of the problem and thus in a sense of mystifying further what is already mysterious enough, the moral of our admission is not that a naturalistic theory of mind has succeeded where other theories have failed, for the opposite is the case; but that so long as such a phenomenon remains unexplained, naturalists have no ground for the militant and intransigent faith they express in their philosophy. If what they are interested in is the advancement of the truth and not the propagation of a doctrinaire philosophy, the least that can be expected of them is that they admit the limitations and inadequacies of their theories and their method. No service is done science or philosophy by attempting to claim for a doctrine or a method a virtue that it does not have. The sanguine assumption that in the future the creative activity will be understood scientifically is no ground for affirming that at present the methods of scientific psychology are applicable to it. Until they are successfully applied, the naturalistic philosopher's confidence puts one in mind of the little boy who, having borrowed the salt-shaker from his harrassed mother, proudly proclaimed that he had captured the bird.

1948

3

THEORY OF CRITICISM

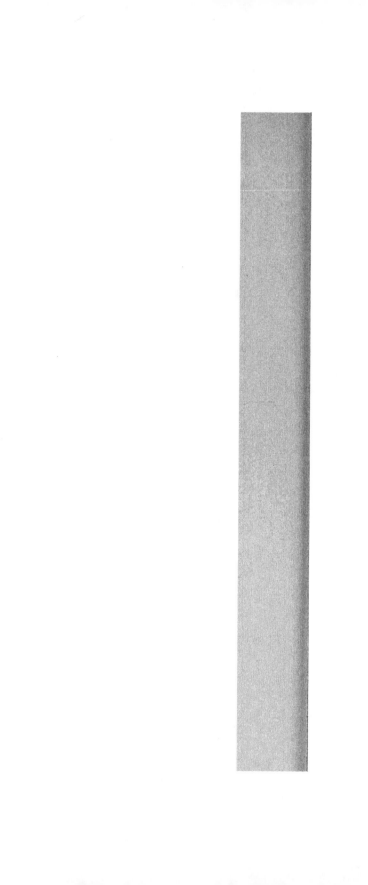

criticism, intrinsic and extrinsic [1]

In spite of the fact that the *aficionados* of the little mags have
attended the numerous wakes and funerals of the late, much
lamented worthy, The Problem of Intrinsic As Against Extrinsic
Criticism, the stubborn old thing will not stay decently buried.
We have seen it put in the coffin and have heard the latter nailed;
we have followed the hearse to the cemetery and have heard the
hollow sound as the first shovelsfull of earth were thrown into the
hole; we have tearfully gone through the appropriate exequies;
and we have returned home relieved that at last the thing was
under to stay and we could go on about our business, only to find
it the next day or next week ringing our bell and saying hello as
truculently as ever. The last critic, to my knowledge, to remind us
that The Problem was not buried but very much around is Mr.
Leslie Fiedler, and it turns out that Mr. Fiedler is very happy,

since it enables him to cut his apron strings and proclaim a revolt of young turks against his old teachers.[2] If I may put it literally, I do not believe Mr. Fiedler has succeeded in solving the problem —at least neither to Mr. Cleanth Brooks' nor to the writer's satisfaction. And the reason, I would suggest, that the problem is still giving us so much trouble, is that the contending claims have not been examined in terms of their underlying assumptions. Critics do not apply the aesthetics they know—when they know any; and aestheticians are so busy with their own autogenic problems that they have little time for the difficulties that plague the critics. Were the problem to be attacked with the theoretical tools at our disposal, it would be discovered that no inherent incompatibility exists between those who claim need for knowledge of context, of whatever kind, in order to read a poem with profit, and those who argue that the reader ought to stay within the poem or it ceases to be poetry and becomes something else. For this conclusion, which commends itself to commonsense, no claim to novelty can be entered. What we know about aesthetics ought to have given us the answer long ago, had we but used it. However, we cannot tell whether this commonsense answer is valid until we have examined it in terms of a coherent, although not necessarily explicit, theory of aesthetics.

It has been assumed by some of our critics that the superiority of intrinsic criticism over extrinsic was established when it was demonstrated that it was fallacious to appeal to the intention of the poet. But the analysis which led to the formulation of the intentional fallacy is hardly sufficient to establish the exclusive validity of intrinsic criticism. The question rests on more complex considerations and can only be answered when we have settled two other questions: whether and in what sense art is autonomous, and whether there is a unique mode of responding to art which can be labeled "the aesthetic response." The question as to the autonomy of art has been debated by aestheticians and critics from every conceivable point of view during the last fifty years, but it has not been resolved. As regards the second problem you will remember that I. A. Richards denied in *Principles of Literary Criticism* that there was a kind of experience which was different from other kinds of experience and could be labelled "aesthetic."

The problem, so far as my reading takes me, has never been considered seriously by any of our prominent contemporary critics and historical scholars. And the upshot of the neglect, I believe I could demonstrate with convincing force, is that critics discuss the merits of the intrinsic versus the extrinsic reference of poetry without regard to the fact that one cannot read a poem as one reads a newspaper account of a flood or a historical account of the fall of a royal head. Let us then take these three problems in the order we have stated them.

We first must review well-known arguments and ask what bearing has the intentional fallacy on criticism? There are at least three reasons the intention of the artist cannot decide without qualification what is the intention of the poem, or, what is the same thing, that we cannot decide from his utterances what the poem intends. The discussion assumes, however, that we can distinguish, although we may not be able to separate, the aesthetic from the non-aesthetic factors that contribute to the writing of a poem. It also assumes that we can discover in the poem itself, inductively, an aesthetic intention which can be put into a formula expressing why the poem is as it is, or why it fails to be what it aims at being. One of the reasons that the intention of the artist does not give us reliable information about the intention of the poem is that the poet is creative, and what he intends is never clear until he has written the poem. But when he has finished the poem he occupies a relatively, not an exclusively advantageous position, in respect to the poem. It is advantageous only in so far as the poet is more intimately in possession of the poem than any other reader. But what we know about the creative activity warns us that all poets do not possess the same degree of self-consciousness and explicitness about their aims. In contrast to men like Poe at one extreme— if we take him at his word—we have at the other the man whose creative processes are almost entirely unconscious and who is not able to speak as a critic about his work.

The second reason the intention of the artist is irrelevant is that even when the poet is able to discuss his work in theoretical terms, he is not always able to make the distinctions about his intentions which the adequate answer to the question presupposes. He tends to confuse (for obvious and good reasons, from his point of view) the aesthetic with the other intentions that cooperated with it in the writing of the poem. The third reason is that only on a rationalistic psychology which ignores the depths and duplicities of the mind can we take what the artist tells us about his aesthetic intention at its face value.

Observe that these considerations do not deny an aesthetic intention to the artist. They assume it but distinguish the actual operative intention which, as telic cause, accounts for the finished product, from the explicit intention, which may or may not be a sufficiently accurate formulation of the actual operative one. Nor do they deny that the critic can find in the artist's biography or in what we know about the tradition to which he belongs, useful and often perhaps indispensable, hints as to the nature of the actual operative intention and what it succeeded in expressing. They merely warn about the risks involved in accepting the poet's report uncritically. Nor do they suggest that the poet carried on his creative act exclusively motivated by a purely aesthetic intention. Little as we know about the creative activity and the virtues and factors which account for it, we know that the artist as man is a complex animal propelled to create by a multiplicity of heterogeneous forces more or less in harmony with one another. Indeed there are cases in which the critic, if he aims at a complete account of the failure of construction exhibited by a poem, must first discover the nature of the failure in the poem and must finally trace it to its genetic factors in the poet's biography. In such cases the distinction between intrinsic and extrinsic criticism can be maintained only through a pedantic insistence on theory for the sake of theory.

Thus, *The Possessed*, in so far as the non-Russian reader is able to judge, seems to fail because the social-theological matter is not embodied successfully in the actions and characters of the novel. But if we seek for the original cause of this failure, sooner or later we have to trace it to biographical data. Nothing less than the dominance of the didactic impulse in the author seems to account for the failure. A similar hypothesis with which you are all acquainted has been advanced by Eliot (unless I misunderstand his point) to account for the failure of *Hamlet*. Examples could be multiplied almost at will. Thus, a complete account of D. H.

Lawrence's failure as artist could not be achieved by any one who refused to look into those biographical factors that deluded him into believing that a poet has a messianic role to perform in the social scene.

But often it is not excess of matter which the poet for didactic or other reasons refuses to jettison that accounts for the failure of a poem, but the opposite, absence of matter. A good illustration of this is to be found—if we grant the validity of the criticism for the sake of illustrating our point—in Leavis' criticism of Henry James' last phase. The defect of the works of this period—"the hypertrophy of technique," as Leavis calls it—is accounted for in terms of what is known about James' biography. James, we are told, "paid the penalty of living too much as a novelist and not richly enough as a man." Note, however, that in both cases—that of too much and that of not enough matter—the fact that initiates the inquiry is established in its own aesthetic terms. The failure, if it is one, is to be demonstrated objectively in terms of an analysis of the way in which the novels succeed or fail as novels. The aesthetic intention is gathered from the work and used to criticize it. But the dialectic of the inquiry does not allow us to remain satisfied with this limited, purely aesthetic, account of the defect, but seeks its cause in the artist, and that means going beyond the poem to the life that feeds it. In neither of the two cases can we claim that we have committed the intentional fallacy. And as such explanations go, they seem (in principle at least) plausible enough.

There may be cases on record in which the artist is a fairly accurate guide to his aesthetic intention. But in order to decide how accurate a guide he is we have first to define what is the intention, and we cannot answer this question by asking the artist or consulting available biographical material, since that is an obvious instance of a circular argument.

If the preceding reasoning is cogent, we cannot choose sides on the intrinsic-extrinsic controversy by reference to the intentional fallacy exclusively. For a complete inquiry as to the causes for the success or failure of a poem takes us out of the purview of aesthetics into biographical and historical areas. Note, however, that I have not questioned that the aesthetic intention of the poet is discovered *in* the poem. This is, however, not the whole story. We must ask in what sense can we affirm the autonomy of art.

A few years ago Kenneth Burke wrote that "the complete autonomy of art could but mean its dissociation from other aspects of the social collectivity." Let us inquire into the merits of this assertion.

Has the claim ever been made by a responsible aesthetician that the artist can dissociate himself from all other aspects of his society than the artistic? I cannot think offhand of a writer who has asserted such an absurd belief and to whom, on other grounds, I would go for enlightenment on problems of this nature. But my ignorance is no basis on which to make a denial. The claim, however, is open to criticism because it is ambiguous. In one sense of the term it is impossible for the poet to dissociate himself from society, since he maintains his physical and his spiritual existence only through the ties that he has with his society. But in another sense it is not only possible for him to dissociate his art from all other aspects of his society, but necessary, since it is only by means of such dissociation that he can function as artist. Just as we can distinguish the lawyer in his professional capacity from the rest of the man—the husband, the father, the neighbor, the man who goes to church and who votes—and just as we can recognize that the proper professional training required by a lawyer need not be harmonious with the training required as a human being—although it may be desirable that it be—so we can distinguish, although we cannot dissociate in the sense of "separate," the poet as engaged in a task that requires special aptitudes and skills from the rest of his relations to his society. Should anyone argue that the best training possible for a poet is to become a small town doctor or a banker, and not a teacher of literature, and that the worst is to exile himself to England or Paris, he would be doing so elliptically, since irrespective of where the poet gathers the substance for his poetry, he requires a specialized training as poet which is distinct from the training required by the doctor or the banker. But the distinction between the poet's training and his medical or banker's training (which I imagine everybody will grant) cannot be made unless we distinguish the purely aesthetic from the non-aesthetic factors in the life of the poet. These non-aesthetic factors, however, enter into the composition of the poem. In one sense, therefore, we must entirely dissociate art from society, although it may be essential also to make certain that the proper training of the poet prevents the dissociation from becoming the kind of actual separation that fosters whatever incipient tendencies some poets may have to feed exclusively from art and to eschew those tougher cuts that come from the rest of life.

Mr. Fiedler has attacked the thesis of the autonomy of art on the ground that if we ask the reader to stay inside the poem we reduce the poem to nothing but words, whereas the poem is an expression through the poet of racial universals of which the poet is the heir. Let us see what is the merit of this claim.

Poetry is, of course, words, in the sense that there is no poetry without language, just as there is no music without sounds. But the doctrine that the poem is nothing but words, if it means what it says, is a patent absurdity, for words are meaningful and what they mean is in some sense distinguishable from the words, the vehicles, that convey the meaning. There is, however, a radical difference between the manner in which a poem means the values and meanings which constitute its object—what it is about—and the manner in which a non-poetic statement means its referend. And if we lose sight of this difference we turn the poem into an ordinary non-poetic statement. What the difference is cannot be explained *en passant*; it is one of the most difficult problems which the aesthetician has to confront. This much can be said here: that since the poem is always more than empty words, whatever may be intended by those who advise the reader to stay inside the poem, only the lunatic fringe of the party could possibly intend the reduction that our young critic has charged the whole party with. Indeed, what he has done is dispose of the weakest case that could be made for the side he opposes. Nor is it at all clear how the dubious doctrine of racial memory bears on the question. Any one hypothesis as to what the poem means—whether it be that based on Jung's psychology or on any other theory—must wait for a hearing until it has been decided what can a poem mean, and in what manner it can be said to mean it. In some legitimate sense a poem can be said to be self-sufficient, and the

proper approach to it can be said to be intrinsic, without falling
into the absurd claim that it is nothing but words.

In view of these considerations it should not be difficult to see
that the autonomy, or, as I prefer to call it, "the self-sufficiency"
of art, is not a question to be settled in a few sentences. Intrinsically difficult, the problem becomes all the more difficult when we
broach it in the fog of contemporary polemics. Stated as succinctly
as I can, a poem is self-sufficient in two distinct but intimately related senses: The poem is self-contained and its meanings and
values are somehow revealed directly by it. If we are going to
make headway with our problem we have to keep in mind these
two senses of the doctrine of poetic autonomy or self-sufficiency.

The poem is self-contained in the sense that it constitutes a
unified whole which supplies and controls the meanings and values which it embodies and gives them their contextual specificity.
This is a well-recognized feature of all art, and while I would argue
that fully satisfactory explanations of this phenomenon are not
available, the fact itself cannot be questioned. It can be accounted
for in part at least by reference to the organic nature of art. I
shall not try to establish the fact, but taking it for granted I shall
make some comments on what it imports. The phrase "the poem
is self-contained" refers to the fact that the poem supplies all the
meanings and values which constitute its object. But if the statement that the poem is nothing but words is interpreted rigorously, the poem ends up by supplying nothing whatever except
the bare physical signs through which it is presented by means of
the senses to the reader. The *Coplas* of George Manrique do not
supply the reader with the knowledge of the Spanish language
which is required to read them. When you ask, "Exactly what
then does the poem supply?" I answer that we cannot state without
reference to a given reader what it supplies. The educated reader
who brings to Manrique's *Coplas* native knowledge of the Spanish
language, brings with it more than mere lean knowledge of the
language. He usually brings with it the social experience which is
funded in the language of those who learned it at their mother's
knees. But if I learned my Spanish at a Berlitz school and you
learned yours as a member of the educated class in Madrid or in
Caracas or Bogota, you bring to your reading of Manrique a thick

and dense language dripping with meanings which, when applied
to the poem, brings out for you, like the reagent in which the spy
dips his letter, the hidden writing between the manifest meanings
of the poem which alone are visible to my lean Berlitz grasp.
Now if we arbitrarily stretch the meaning of the phrase "social
experience funded in the language," as I beg you to allow me to
do in the interest of notational economy, and take it to refer to
the total equipment a reader brings to the reading of a poem—his
knowledge of history and of mythology, of Freud and Jung, of the
Bible and of the Scandinavian Sagas, of billiards and of love and
hatred and of anthropology—in short, all his available resources
moral and religious, aesthetic and cognitive—you can see that one
reader approaches the poem like an American millionaire on safari,
while another, alas, approaches it like an impoverished Bavarian
student on a Sunday outing, carrying all he brings to it in a small
knapsack.

But granted the social experience funded in the language, the
poem supplies all that we need to come into possession of it. You
may retort that I am asking you for a very generous grant. And
I am. For you must grant some knowledge of the language, however lean and Berlitz-school-like it may be. If you do not grant
knowledge of the language your reader cannot get at the poem—
indeed there is no reader. But if you grant knowledge of the language, by the application of what logical principle or material law
are you going to draw the line between what one reader may bring
to the reading of the poem and what the next one brings? Between the reader who comes to the poem like a millionaire on
safari and the reader who comes to it like a Bavarian student
there is no difference in kind; there is only a difference in degree.
Nor need a reader's knowledge be very specific or exact in order
to be able to read with some profit Manrique's *Coplas*. He does
not need to know exactly who the King Don Juan was and when
he lived, or who were the Infantes of Aragon, about whom Manrique asks, what has become of them. All the reader needs to
know, to get Manrique's point, is that the King and the Infantes
were great nobles and that death came to them as it comes to the
humble. If you grant then the experience funded in the language,

the poem is self-contained. Let me illustrate the meaning of the term with other examples.

In Antigone's opening speech, in Sophocles' play, the poet puts into the mouth of Antigone information required by the spectator to grasp the action that follows. The very first speech of Antigone places Ismene as Antigone's sister and refers to the curse of Oedipus. Before the end of the Prologue, Creon's decree is referred to and the battle between the brothers and their death is announced. This quick shorthand reference is all Sophocles needed, because he took for granted that his audience had knowledge of the Oedipus myth. Let us now contrast Sophocles with Dostoevski. In *The Brothers Karamazov* Dostoevski had to supply, even for the Russian reader of his own day, an account of the institution of the Elder. Had he not supplied it, the critic would have had to do it for him, for in the absence of this knowledge one is not able to read this novel with any kind of understanding of the aesthetically revealed oppositions involved in the character of Zossima and that of the Karamazovs. Similarly in teaching *Hamlet* —to take a trite example—we must supply our students with information which the poet took for granted, that the relationship between Hamlet's mother and her second husband was incestuous. To many of our students we have to supply even more elementary information since they do not know that incest was for the Elizabethan audience a sin and not merely a breach of convention of a culture pattern.

How the reader must stock his mind does not matter in the least for our purposes. But two questions are of importance: How much equipment is required and how is that equipment to be used once the reader begins to read the poem. The first of these questions cannot be answered in general terms. It can only be answered casuistically. Obviously, if the historical scholar claims that in order to read a work of the imagination with adequacy the reader has to be conversant with everything the writer may be assumed to have read, he is giving us a counsel of perfection. Had the reader world enough and time, the counsel would be acceptable. But on less than such ideal terms—and that is all we harrassed humans have—were the counsel to be enforced, it would preclude the reading of poetry by anyone but the most erudite specialist. But poetry is for men in general, not for scholars only. How much then the reader is required to know prior to his reading of the poem is best left to his prudence.

The poem is self-contained, then, in the sense that it contains within itself for a given reader, who is in possession of the language of the poem, whatever meanings and specifications are required to grasp it. Nor does the mind employed in reading it need fall back on data the poem does not contain. But the poem is also self sufficient, it also reveals its object—the meanings and values that it is about—directly, in the sense that they are to be found, not outside of the poem, nor beyond it, but in and through it, and there found only by a reader who knows how to respond to the poem in a distinctly aesthetic mode. This takes place when the poem captures the reader's attention and forces him to focus it on the meanings and values which the poem embodies and which it makes immediately available to the equipped mind. I call this responding to the poem *intransitively*. The word "immediately" suggests that the meanings and values are grasped in and through the symbols which present them: in the case of a poem, its linguistic medium. Aestheticians have tried to convey this fact by means of various locutions: Dewey speaks of reflexive meanings. Charles Morris, borrowing the term from Peirce, speaks of icons. Mrs. Langer refers to the same phenomenon by means of the term "presentational symbol." And years ago I used to refer to it with the aid of a borrowed expression: "immanent meanings." What all these terms do is indicate that whatever the poem has to say must not be sought for beyond or outside of the poem itself but in and through it. And exactly what this means and how it is possible is what requires elucidation and constitutes the most difficult problem which the aesthetician has to face. So much for the word "immediate." The term "intransitive" conveys the fact that during the moment of aesthetic apprehension the mind is captive, is completely under the control of the object because the object is so constructed that it does not allow the mind to wander beyond its own self-contained confines. Our attention is intransitive because the object is self-sufficient and because its meanings do not function as signs pointing beyond themselves. But as we have already seen the autonomy of the poem—the fact that the poem is self-sufficient and its meanings are self-contained—does not prejudice the question as to whether the meanings and the values immediately revealed can be apprehended by an empty mind, or require rather a fully stocked mind for apprehension. What it points to is the fact that the poem cannot be read in the aesthetic mode, when the reader uses it as a means to the discovery of meanings and values which are not revealed in and through the poem but are ostensibly pointed out as outside of it. It is therefore the intransitivity of the reader's attention which enables the reader to discover the self-sufficiency of the poem: the self-containedness and intrinsicality of its meanings. The two terms, "poem" and "reader," refer to realities to which ontology assigns distinctive status in the sense that the poem does not create the reader nor does the reader create the poem as objective relativists maintain; but the discovery of the poem's meanings is always—and this is of course a tautology—a discovery by a mind; and the mind that apprehends the poem as poem is a mind capable of responding to the object in a distinctively aesthetic mode.

It ought to be clear from what has been said that there is a valid sense in which we may speak of "a pure aesthetic object." Usually this phrase is taken to mean a merely formal structure devoid of embodied meanings and values. There are no such aesthetic objects anywhere to be found, but if there are, they may be found in the realm of pure design or pure music, certainly not in the realm of poetry. We may, however, use the phrase to signify that the poem is self-contained and its meanings and values are intrinsic to it. But, of course, while these meanings and values function in the poem as pure aesthetic meanings they do not have their origin in a realm of art which is entirely dissociated from the rest of life. The intrinsic meanings of the poem derive from non-aesthetic sources. What these sources specifically are, we cannot say in an a priori way—generally the source is in life as lived by the man who wrote the poem, and if we are capable of inheriting racial memories, as Mr. Fiedler would like us to believe, then these memories also supply meanings and values to the poem. However, from this fact it does not follow, if my considerations hold, that we can shuttle freely from the poem back to the poet and from him to his sources. The assumption that we can, fails to reckon with

what the poet does to the content of his experience before he embodies it in the poem.

If what I have said is valid, it is wise to advise the reader, if he
is to read the poem with profit, first, that he equip himself as best
he can, and second, that he stay within the poem and do not go
outside of it. There is a proper time at which to bring to bear on
the reader's mind the extrinsic resources necessary for reading of
the poem. That time is when the reader is preparing himself to
read a poem by enlarging his funded experience. And this he does
with whatever aids lie at hand that seem to him pertinent to the
end in view. His job is to assimilate what he acquires and to learn
to use it so thoroughly that he does it with the ease with which
he performs any natural function. During his reading of the poem
he should stay inside of it, if he is interested in poetry and not in
something else. Not to encourage him to stay inside the poem is
to cheat him of what the poem can do for him as poetry—and
that is something for which no substitute can be found in human
culture.

1952

the objective correlative of T. S. Eliot

In his study of T. S. Eliot in *The New Criticism*, John Crowe
Ransom has pointed out that though Eliot is endowed with "an
immediate critical sense which is expert and infallible,' his judgments are not guided by a body of well elaborated principles, and
the result is that many of his generalizations are at best half-truths.[1]
Ransom supports this observation in an unanswerable way by
means of a detailed analysis of Eliot's critical essays. Yet I hope
that in spite of the fact that the conclusion at which I shall arrive
in this paper agrees with one of his, there is still room for the following remarks on the notion of the objective correlative, on which
Ransom's study touched from a different point of view.

On the surface the notion of the objective correlative seems clear
enough. Devised to explain how the poem expresses the poet's emotion, it also asserts that the poet organizes his sensibility through

the act of expression. The poet expresses his emotion by "finding
. . . a set of objects, a situation, a chain of events which shall be
the formula of that *particular* emotion" which he wishes to express, "such that when the external facts . . . are given, the emotion is immediately evoked." [2] The fact that Eliot holds this doctrine shows that, in spite of his avowed classicism, he accepts with
the vast majority of his contemporaries the modern dogma that
the artist is primarily concerned with emotion. There are other
places in which Eliot indicates his belief that the poet's concern
with objects is only instrumental, only a means of objectifying the
emotion which he seeks to express. But the act of expression is not
an end in itself for Eliot, but is in turn instrumental to the organization of sensibility which expression somehow accomplishes in
the poem, and which is said to correspond (or lead) to a similar
organization in the artist's own psyche. We are not told why or how
expression organizes sensibility, but we are clearly told that it does,
and that unless emotion is objectified it "remains to poison life
and obstruct action." These words refer to Hamlet, but "the supposed identity of Hamlet with his author" is asserted to be "genuine at this point," and Eliot tells us that "Hamlet's bafflement at
the absence of an objective equivalent to his feelings is a prolonga-
tion of the bafflement of his creator in the face of his artistic problem." Thus Eliot grafts a somewhat revamped doctrine of catharsis
on to the popular theory of expression, and uses the product to
justify poetry therapeutically. Poetry is on this theory a psychic
anti-toxin and makes action possible. This is a convenient way of
chasing with the hounds of modernism while running with the
hares of classicism. For in accepting the modern doctrine of expression Eliot is also able to hold that art is not useless, not an
end in itself, as the modern theory of expression is so often taken
to imply, but instead serves a medical purpose.

It is therefore a great pity that Eliot's theory cannot stand up
under close scrutiny, as the analysis which follows will, I believe,
demonstrate. For the sake of specificity, I have chosen for comment a single passage of Eliot's, in which the notion of the objective correlative receives as full a treatment as in any that I know
of among his critical essays. I refer to the third paragraph of Part II
of his famous "Tradition and the Individual Talent." [3] But while

my comments are addressed to this passage specifically, the ambiguities and confusions which are charged against it appear where-
ever Eliot, implicitly or explicitly, has used his notion of the
objective correlative.

In the two paragraphs preceding the one I am about to quote
Eliot tells us that the mind of the poet is like a catalytic agent
by means of which the "passions which are its material" are
"digested." And in the third paragraph he continues:

> The experience, you will notice, the elements which enter the
> presence of the transforming catalyst, are of two kinds: emotion and
> feelings. The effect of a work of art upon the person who enjoys it is
> an experience different in kind from any experience not of art. It
> may be formed out of one emotion, or may be a combination of sev-
> eral; and various feelings, inhering for the writer in particular words
> or phrases or images, may be added to compose the final result. Or
> great poetry may be made without the direct use of any emotion
> whatever: composed out of feelings solely. Canto XV of the *Inferno*
> (Brunetto Latini) is a working up of the emotion evident in the situ-
> ation; but the effect, though single as that of any work of art, is
> obtained by considerable complexity of detail. The last quatrain
> gives an image, a feeling attaching to the image, which "came,"
> which did not develop simply out of what precedes, but which was
> probably in suspension in the poet's mind until the proper combina-
> tion arrived for it to add itself to. The poet's mind is in fact a
> receptacle for seizing and storing up numberless feelings, phrases,
> images, which remain there until all the particles which can unite
> to form a new compound are present together.

We must first notice that Eliot distinguishes between emotions
and feelings, and that the distinction seems to be an important
one; but how he intends it to be taken cannot be gathered from
the content. Though psychologists often use the terms 'emotion'
and 'feeling' in different senses, they are not at all agreed as to
their import. I have decided therefore not to introduce the distinction into the following discussion, first because I do not know how
to take it, and second because it does not appear in other places
where the notion of the objective correlative is used, and our interest centers solely on those aspects of the above paragraph that
are representative and not on those that are idiosyncratic. We must

notice next that according to Eliot's opening sentence, the stuff
which makes up the poem consists of emotions and feelings. This
statement can hardly be taken as a mere slip on Eliot's part, and
yet it is hard to believe that he actually means what he says, for
he, of all people, must know that ideational materials of all sorts
regarding objective situations are also part of the poet's material.
I rather suspect that historical inquiry will show that the dichotomy
on which Eliot is here operating lines him up with the traditions
in poetry which his criticism has taught us to disparage. But let
us pass by this and let us rather notice that in the first few lines
of the quotation, up to the reference to Canto XV, Eliot speaks
both of the poet and of the feelings and emotions inhering for him
in words and images on the one hand, and on the other of the
reader. Seemingly he is not aware of the difficulties which the
shift brings with it. And this is the source of a serious confusion.
For it would seem as if the feelings which inhere for the poet in
the phrase or image which he chooses also inhere in it for the
reader. Yet we are not told whether for the latter the inherence
consists in the fact that the image arouses the same feeling in him
as it aroused in the poet; or whether the feeling is perceived as an
objective quality of the image, which may be grasped as inhering
in the phrase or image, though it need not be subjectively aroused
in the reader for him to grasp it objectively.[4] Now it is perfectly
possible that a phrase or image may arouse emotion or feeling
and very likely it often happens, even in the case of readers who
are more interested in poetry than they are in emotional experiences. But it also happens that a poem or any other object of art
seems to possess among its objective characters emotion or feeling
values, which "inhere" in it irrespective of our reactions to it.
Whether Eliot means one or the other alternative or both is not
clear, yet the difference is radical. On the latter alternative, exactly
what may be meant by a feeling "inhering" in a phrase or image
is anything but self-evident, and is precisely what requires explanation. But this is not the only difficulty that we encounter in
this passage, for in the sentences following his reference to Canto
XV he seems to distinguish between the emotion worked up in the
Canto and the effect on the reader obtained by the complexity

of the detail that Dante put into the Canto. But the statement that an emotion can be worked up in a Canto is, as it stands, unintelligible, since it cannot be taken literally. You just do not work up emotion into poetry the way a cabinet maker works up boards into a table.

The statements following the reference to the last quatrain pack a bewildering puzzle. Feelings stored up in the poet's mind, which is in fact a storage receptacle; words for which feelings wait in order to attach themselves at the time of composition; the pre-established harmony that must be assumed to exist between the waiting feeling and its verbal garment; the very assumption that a feeling can exist by itself in the mind and wait without symbolic expression of any kind whatever—all this is very dubious psychology. But let it be for the moment. Let us rather note that Eliot says that the quatrain gives an image and a feeling attaching to an image. We have to ask once more whether he means that the quatrain *expresses* or that it *arouses* a feeling. And exactly how can feelings, something subjective, attach to images, something quite objective? This is precisely what requires explanation. Eliot is not the first writer to defend the expression theory. Numerous aestheticians before him have also tried to defend it. But whenever the effort has been seriously made to explain just how emotions or feelings happen to "attach" themselves to phrases, or "inhere" in them, the doctrine of expression has usually run into difficulty, and *has ended up by offering us as an explanation the fact to be explained.*[5] This is just what the doctrine of the objective correlative does.

It should now be clear that Eliot hesitates between the following two propositions—or perhaps it were better to say that he has not considered the important differences that exist between them: I) Poetry arouses emotion in the reader; II) The poem expresses emotion in and through the poem itself. The first proposition needs qualification, but does not require an explanation; the second, however, does. We must therefore take up these propositions and see in what sense each can be held.

I) There is no question that poetry can and often indeed does make us sad, or compassionate, or angry, or fires us with patriotic fervor. It may even evoke or arouse specific but very complex emotions that language is too crude to denote adequately. But in the light of the facts uncovered by psychological investigations in the last fifty years about the diversity of aesthetic responses I doubt whether we can maintain that art always arouses emotion in every spectator. It depends on the art and on the spectator, and on the quality of his attention. Not all spectators are dionysian or want to be. But even if poetry always did arouse emotion, we would still have to ask whether poetry ought to arouse emotion—for we cannot confuse the merely descriptive with the normative question. And it would also be a question whether, if we did hold that poetry ought to arouse emotion, we would not make it entirely impossible to draw the distinction between art and something else—between the aesthetic transaction and some other mode of experience. For the aesthetic experience would now be defined functionally by the presence of emotion, but the emotion aroused could only be ordinary emotion, since psychology does not recognize *sui generis* aesthetic emotions. Should we hold that poetry ought to arouse emotion, we also run up against a statement of Eliot's in an essay entitled "The Perfect Critic" [6] in which he tells us that "the end of the enjoyment of poetry is a pure contemplation from which all the accidents of personal emotion are removed." And yet that the arousal of the emotion in the reader seems to be the way in which at least at times Eliot conceives the expression of emotion is to be gathered from the first statement of Eliot's quoted above, and which Matthiessen considers a *locus classicus* of contemporary criticism; [7] for in this passage we are told that when the objective correlative is presented "the emotion is immediately evoked." Eliot may answer that there is no contradiction between these two statements. For what he is opposed to is the indulgence of *personal* emotion, which is precisely what a correlative that is truly objective controls. But if there is one fact for which we have ample evidence in aesthetics today it is the fact that no artist, however skillful, can possibly control the subjective responses of his readers, and this is all the truer to the extent to which the culture to which either poet or reader belongs (or both of course) is complex and in a state of flux, and where therefore to accidental personal idiosyncrasies must be added the differences caused by heterogeneity of social determinants.

II) Poetry may legitimately be said to "express" emotion in two senses, but the first of these is trivial.

a) In a dramatic scene, you know that the actor is feeling a certain emotion. And you are able to say, "What an intense scene!" Whether or not the actor really does feel the emotion he is expressing through representation is a question we need not ask here. It would seem that some actors need to feel what they are acting, while others act poorly when they are the victims of the emotion they must represent. In any case, all that an actor needs to do to be faithful to the exigencies of the drama is to simulate the emotion. Consider, let us say, Giotto's *Lamentation*. The figures represented clearly express by their gesture the intense emotions that they are supposed to be feeling. This sense neither furthers nor interferes with critical analysis of art.

b) Poetry may also express emotion in another way. The poem may be about a situation or an object which is socially connected or invariably associated—whether naturally or conventionally—with an emotion. This is perhaps the only legitimate and unambiguous meaning that we can give the term "objective correlative." But in this case all the term means is that poetry refers denotatively to emotions, not by means of direct verbal reference, but through the whole poem itself—and how this takes place is precisely what calls for explanation and what the term "objective correlative" perhaps labels but otherwise leaves us in the dark about. Somehow, because of a complex connection which is not yet understood, or which at least has not yet been publicly explained the poem presents itself as a composite symbol, but not as a neutral, merely semantic, one; rather, as one which refers reflexibly to a fully qualitied, self-consistent whole, more heavily loaded with value than things of ordinary life usually are. These values not without some reason, *may be called* emotions, though they are objective characters of the value-freighted reality present for the experiencer, since they seem to be the factors in the object that account for the rapturous quality of the experience. But to suppose that they alone function in this manner seems to me utterly erroneous, since the poem and its parts function as a whole whose

form and content cannot be separated from each other. It is
however in this sense that the poem denotes a specific and unique
complex of emotions. But semantically (not psychologically) the
relationship of denotation between poem and emotion is the same
as that which exists between the word "cat" or "unicorn" and
the animal to which it refers, whether one has had an actual experience of it or not. But just as words may be meaningful for us
though we may not now experience or may never have experienced
their semantic referends, so poetic symbols may denote emotions
clearly and distinctly, though we may never have experienced them
ourselves, and though we do not experience them as we read the
poem. Indeed one of the moral values of imaginative letters consists chiefly in their ability to widen imaginatively the horizon of
our parochial experience. This is not to deny that in so far as
we have ourselves experienced emotions similar to those denoted
by a poem, our experience with that poem will have psychological
connotations that it would otherwise lack. But it is to assert that
adequate communication is possible though the areas of subjective
experience may differ considerably as between poet and reader.
And unless we insist that the function of poetry is to arouse emotion, we must grant that it does not fail simply because it may
refer to an emotion which it does not happen to arouse in the
reader. In any case poetry may legitimately be said to express emotion for any member of a group for whom a connection exists—
conventionally or naturally—between the situation or object used
by the poet and an emotion; and it expresses it whether it arouses
it or not.

In order to make this clear, let us take a poem in which the
emotion is strong and the connection between situation and emotion obvious. Garcia Lorca's "Llanto por Ignacio Sanchez Mejias"
has been translated into English and, I take it, has been widely
read and discussed in this country in the last few years.[8] It is an
Elegy on the death of a bullfighter called Ignacio Sanchez Mejias.
I translate literally the opening lines:

> Five o'clock in the afternoon,
> It was five sharp in the afternoon.
> A boy brought a white shroud
> At five in the afternoon.

One need not read the poem too closely to realize that the man
who wrote it is lamenting the death of a bullfighter and that he
feels very strongly about that death. One cannot name the emotion he feels by any precise term; and for a good reason, since its
full complex specific expression is achieved only through the total
poem; but one may loosely refer to it as a desolate, a deep and
anguishing sense of loss at the death of a great bullfighter whom
Lorca admired greatly. (*Que gran torero en la plaza!* What a great
bullfighter in the ring!) This is the last stanza—again I translate
literally:

> It will take a long time to be born, if one is born,
> As famous an Andalusian, one as rich in adventure.
> I sing his elegance with weeping words,
> And remember a sad breeze through the olive-grove.

Only occasionally does the poet speak directly of his own feelings,
as he does for instance when, referring to the blood on the sand,
he exclaims:

> But I don't want to see it.
> Tell the moon to come,
> For I don't want to see the blood
> Of Ignacio on the sand.

More often than not, the poem refers to objects and situations
directly involved in the death or connected somehow in the poet's
mind with it. The expression of the emotion or emotions—for
there is of course a whole complex of them referred to throughout the poem—is achieved through the presentation of these objects and situations; these are the objective correlatives. And the
reader, whether he reads with interest or with indifference, knows
by means of these objective correlatives how Garcia Lorca feels
about the death of Ignacio. Note however that the emotions that
each reader grasps through the objective correlative are for reasons
similar to those mentioned above in connection with the discussion
of the arousal of emotion, only partially within the control of the
poet. Thus to a reader with strong moral objections against bull
fighting, Lorca's poem will undoubtedly communicate or express

different emotions from those it does to Hemingway or to the
writer of these notes. But in so far as all of the readers share to
some extent certain attitudes towards courage, skill and death, to
that degree do they glean a somewhat similar objective emotional
meaning.

All this should be more or less obvious, though it does not seem
to be for Eliot. What may not be so readily accepted is that the
emotion expressed through the objective correlative cannot be the
same emotion which was originally felt by Lorca when he heard
the news of Ignacio's death or saw the accident at the ring which
he worked into the "Llanto." To establish this contention adequately would take us far afield, and therefore I must state the
reasons that support it briefly and dogmatically. The emotion
originally felt by Garcia Lorca, remembering that he was writing
of a historical bull fighter, was transmuted into something quite
different as he began to produce the poem and began to concern
himself with the problem of poetic composition. What Garcia
Lorca felt before the poem began to shape itself in his mind is
something he couldn't tell us except in the most inexact and inadequate fashion. Of course, being a poet, his ordinary conversation must have shown flashes of his poetical skill. But before he
wrote the poem he could not have told us much more about his
grief than you or I could have told had we been in his place—all
he could have said was that he felt very bad, felt perhaps broken
up over the death of Ignacio. What he really felt could only be
expressed precisely in and through the poem, which is to say that
he had to discover it through the act of composition. But the poem
expresses more than a complex of emotions of which the original
grief is only a part. And this more is at least as important as the
emotions it expresses. For it exhibits for attention a story or in-
cident or object, and does so, if it is an English poem, by means of
meter, imagery, often rhyme, a subtle and complex musical quality,
and a distinct tone. Taken together—and aesthetic apprehension
is not analytic but holistic and naturally takes all these integrated
factors together—they make up the internally consistent unit which
is the poem, and which, if successful, has the power of compelling
intense and intransitive attention on itself. In the case of the
"Llanto" the original grief experienced by Lorca may have been

the occasion of the composition of the poem; if there was such a grief it surely entered into the poem, in the sense that what the poet chose to include in his poem had to be psychologically congruous with his grief. But as the poem got itself written this original grief itself suffered a change, spending itself in the process of composition and sharing the poet's attention with his technical interests, whose stubborn exigencies had to be satisfied. The result, in our example, was an objective whole, the "Llanto," in which the problems of versification which Lorca encountered somehow were solved satisfactorily to his interest as poet and congruously not only with the feelings, but also with the opinions and ideas, which he had of his friend and which demanded expression when he heard the news of his death.[9]

Between interest in form and interest in content there is always a tension which for the artist, I take it, defines itself as a problem of sincerity or of integrity. We all have felt sometimes that the administration of justice is mocked by the forms and conventions of the law, and that there is a vast difference between justice and legality—if we could only wipe off all convention and precedent, all technique and all artificial court procedure, how much closer we would get to the justice we all crave! And so the artist in regard to his original emotion: how outrageously do the demands of form violate it, how deeply do they transmute it! For no form really suits it, no public means through which it can be uttered brings it successfully out of the shadow of its own ineffability. But isn't this the tragic fact which philosophy since Descartes has made its central problem, without succeeding in resolving it—the mind's need to reach beyond itself and its failure adequately to satisfy that need? In any case, neither can justice be administered, nor can emotion be expressed, without some means, and the means exact their price and violate the pristine integrity of that which they administer or express.

Why a poet feels that one object rather than another can serve him as an "objective correlative" is an important question, but one in regard to which we seem to be very much in the dark. Association was suggested above as the reason, but that was done merely to avoid raising at that point the difficulty which we must now face. Mrs. Langer may be right and there may be a correspondence between the "dynamic patterns of human experience," the "forms" of emotion, and the objective characters chosen by the artist to express it.[10] But this explanation does no more than assert the fact and explains absolutely nothing until it is able to make adequately clear what is meant by the key phrase "dynamic pattern of experience" or "form of an emotion." In any case, association will not explain the process of choice, since the poet is not really choosing one image as against another because the former happens to correspond to a pre-existing feeling; what he is doing is creating imagery and conceiving novel situations. Association cannot explain the pat congruity that exists from the very first moment of conception between our symbol and the feelings or emotions which, outside of their symbolic embodiment, the artist neither understood nor could define. Be this as it may, as the creative activity proceeds, the original inchoate emotion which our poet felt for his gored friend gradually changed; it spent, perhaps, its original force; the dumb anguish subsided or became transmuted into interests of the most heterogeneous sorts, which were, nevertheless, fused together and seemed to possess an enveloping homogeneous tone.

The discussion has proceeded on two assumptions that it is now necessary to investigate more closely. We have assumed first that Lorca's emotion, before the poem was written, was itself something clear and definite. This is indeed what Eliot assumed in the passage already quoted, when he spoke of the feelings waiting in the poet's mind, which he said was a receptacle for storing them. Now in one sense, what I. A. Richards has called "the availability of the poet's experience" is an indubitable fact, however we explain it or even if we cannot explain it at all.[11] But Eliot's explanation is utterly inadequate. For feelings certainly do not wait in the mind like tobacco in a pouch, till they can be used. We are more likely to be closer to the facts if we assume that before writing his poem Garcia Lorca experienced a heavy oppressive feeling or emotion, dumb and confused, inwardly disrupting, perhaps extremely painful, but hardly to be compared with the emotion he expressed through his poem, since it approached a confused physiological chaos, which the creative activity, in bringing to clarity through expression, relieved. The emotion the poem expresses, however, is not merely a clarified development from this inchoate affective mass. It is a more complex affair, since it has been informed by the poet in his poem through devices—meter, rhyme, imagery, etc.— that are in themselves expressive, thus transforming the original inchoate affection into what it now is, an objectively significant, because communicable, object of art.

But is it necessary to assume that Lorca felt genuine sorrow at the death of a real bullfighter whom he admired and that the poem was occasioned by the tragic death of Ignacio one afternoon in the ring? The whole episode, name and all, may have been imagined. Ignacio was an historical figure whom Lorca knew and whose taurine art and courage he admired. But he need not have been. Had Lorca lived in a different period he might have written the poem as a commission from a prince. Consider Bach writing concertos for an insomniac patron, or any court poet celebrating to order the birth of a royal heir. It is not necessary to assume that the actual emotion that is worked up by the poet into the poem is the actual occasion of the creative act.

What then does a poem express? I incline to the belief that the aesthetic of expression is a useless and confusing muddle that mystifies far more than it explains. What has been said above about how raw experience is transformed, or better, *transubstantiated* by the creative process, indicates the direction along which I would seek for a full explanation as to what it is that the artist exhibits for contemplation. But many other fundamental points, for instance, the problem of the freedom of the mind in the creative process, would have to be elucidated before we could arrive at the answer. Here let it suffice to say that the object of aesthetic apprehension is a self-consistent structure, involving an ordered complex of values of a sensuous, formal, and of an immanently meaningful nature, which satisfy the alert mind turned towards them for two reasons. First, because they are, in the isolation of the aesthetic experience, final values, inherently interesting for their own sake and not as means. And second, because beyond them we perceive an authentic vision of the structure of reality. This structure we sometimes catch a glimpse of in our daily world, when we peer beyond the chaos of our moral relations and beyond the onrush of natural events. But in art, as in philosophy, and I imagine in prayer, the desire is gratified and the mind, rapt in its full and luminous possession, finds in it consummatory satisfaction. This ordered structure is ideal, in that its apprehension is rare, and that when we succeed in grasping it, it brings with it rewards of a noble kind: peace, serenity, release from the sting of passion and freedom from the indignity of living. That is why Schopenhauer valued it so highly. It is also ideal in that it can be grasped only by a mind fully alert. Yet it has status in being since the poet is no sorcerer, and has no means of going, for his vision of the order he presents to us for our contemplation, to a meta-empirical realm where we unpoetical folk cannot follow him, but finds it subsistent in the same world in which we find our potatoes or our beans. Yet it is not merely in a pickwickian sense that we call poetry ideal, for poetry has about it a flush and a luster which do seem to lift us into a higher or a more intensely "real" world than the tarnished stuff of our daily experience. "Seem," for whether it does in truth or not is, as my people say, flour from a different bag. Be that as it may, a poem expresses all that which the poet presents objectively in it for apprehension; true, among the elements making up the object there are some that we find easier to denote when we wish to refer to them verbally, through the terms which we use to denote emotions. But I see no reason to assume that all else in the poem is put there merely to arouse an emotion in us or to bring about its objective denotation. Surface, formal and ideational elements, are all in their own right of intrinsic interest. And while the emotion expressed is also of interest, it is not, and it should not be, of chief or exclusive interest to the reader.

It is too much to expect that a theory so popular as the expression theory shall be abandoned on account of its ultimate unintelligibility. But since, in spite of this criticism, it will continue to be used, just as the term "imitation" and the notion for which it stands, continues to be used in certain retardatarian quarters, it is of the uttermost importance for criticism to realize that the emotion expressed through the objective correlative is not that which the poet felt before the poem was written. The emotion as well as the correlative, are *found* through the process of *creation*. But if the term "creation" is taken seriously, the consequences for

Eliot's critical approach are devastating. For it means that once finished no one can go behind the poem, not even the artist himself. Otherwise put, the emotion itself, naked and unexpressed, cannot be had for comparison with its expression through its objective correlative. And the assumption therefore that we can criticize "Hamlet" by comparing the emotion expressed in the play with Shakespeare's emotions, or that through the play we can discover the emotions that went into it, is a confusing illusion. The vocabulary of the emotions is thus confusing, if not indeed irrelevant, to literary criticism; and if it were dropped, and the critic confined himself only to the objects and situations and values communicated by the poem, there would ensue an enormous clarification in the practice of criticism.

1944

the objective basis of criticism

Criticism seeks, legitimately, to perform several functions: it tries to guide and improve public taste, to disclose the relations of art, considered purely as art, to non-aesthetic activities and values, to determine the comparative worth of the aesthetic qualities embodied in objects which may compete for our attention, and to enlighten the artist on the true nature and meaning of his created object, since the artist may do better or worse or quite differently than he intends. For its many ends contemporary American criticism is well equipped. Critics approach their tasks with no small measure of sensibility, discriminative power, historical knowledge, and by and large, a proper feeling for the importance of art. Yet contemporary American criticism suffers from a serious defect: it ignores, sometimes truculently, the need for a systematic philosophy of art. The fault, it must be said in fairness, is not entirely the critic's, since contemporary aesthetics tends to be an autonomous discipline concerned chiefly with problems of philosophic method and with epistemological issues, and to ignore the problems of criticism and the contemporary situation in art. But it is my impression that aestheticians today are more apt to learn from critics than the critics from the aestheticians. Be that as it may, often it appears as if critics were enemies of theoretical consistency.

What aesthetics should be able to offer the critic is not an academic discussion of purely philosophical problems of method and of epistemology, although these cannot be altogether avoided, but an examination, carried on in technical terms, of the underlying assumptions that the critic must and does make about such problems as the nature of art, its relation to other modes of activity, the categories with which it can be approached, its function. Such an examination must remain in the nature of the case a dry, abstract, purely theoretical analysis. Critics, impatient with the difficulties of technical inquiries whose relevance to their work is not immediate or obvious, tend to scorn them and to fall back on a shabby hand to mouth pragmatism which does not avoid but merely ignores them and which therefore inevitably generates confusion. Contemporary critics, with a few notable exceptions, do not have a clear idea of the theoretical foundations of their discipline, in spite of the serious sense they have of the importance of art for human life.

Nowhere in the field of criticism is the need more urgent for an adequate theoretical clarification than as regards questions about the validity of the judgment of comparative merit. What validity or justification does the critic have for his judgments? Does his judgment express merely his own taste, his sensibility, his own private knowledge and wisdom, or does it claim somehow to discriminate, by means of such equipment, values that are objective and about which one can fruitfully dispute? And if he does make the claim to objectivity where do these discriminated values reside: are they located in the object or is the latter merely a means to bring them into existence through the satisfaction the object gives to the spectator? The complex problem which these questions formulate is, of course, a very old problem. But for all its antiquity its solution is no less urgent today than it ever was, for without some sort of clear opinion on it, the critic's practice is apt to be characterized by the inconsistencies and ambiguities which are the usual consequence of unexamined assumptions.

No matter what he takes his function to be, the validity of the critic's analysis depends on the validity of the *aesthetic* judgment that he must make. For even if he should not be interested in pure aesthetic values, but should seek to discover the relation of the art object under analysis to other interests, he cannot discriminate with clarity the relationship between art and anything else— whether it be politics or morality or religion or science—unless he has a clear knowledge of the value as art of the object whose relationship he is seeking to disclose. To assume, as moralistic or sociological critics seem sometimes to do, that the moral or political value of art can be decided independently of its aesthetic value, is simply absurd. For if an object acts on us morally in total independence of its aesthetic value, it is not as art that it thus acts, but as a moral object; and the specialized aesthetic discriminations of the art critic are totally irrelevant and may even be in the way of his apprehending its moralizing message. But if it acts on us morally by means of its aesthetic quality then a clear examination of the latter would seem to be a prerequisite to an adequate examination of its moral efficiency. The critic of art then, however he may conceive his task, depends for the success of his activity on the validity of the aesthetic discriminations he is capable of making. But the converse is not true. For an object may function solely as aesthetic and in the discrimination of its aesthetic value no other considerations need then enter than merely aesthetic ones. It may be, of course, that since we are human beings and not exclusively aesthetic animals, interest in purely aesthetic objects may be an incomplete diet for us, incapable of sustaining our complex and heterogeneous needs. Indeed a wise critic would recognize this as elementarily true. But the fact is no justification for confusing aesthetic values with moral, religious, social and any other kind of values.

But what does the validity of the aesthetic judgment itself depend on if not its objectivity? For an avowedly subjective judgment is one with which no one in his right mind would undertake to quarrel theoretically, since all it asserts is a private and arbitrary preference. You may point out to the subjectivist the consequences of a given preference and, on this basis, you may seek to dissuade him from opinions you take to be dangerous to him. But you cannot find a rational argument against a preference that claims no rational ground and demands no jurisdiction beyond itself. But how can we, in view of the stock arguments of the subjectivist, defend the objectivity of the aesthetic judgment?

The aesthetic judgment is objective in the sense that it asserts the presence in an object of an aesthetic value-trait which is open to public inspection. This view is rejected on various grounds. Mr. Pepper, for instance, rejects it on the ground that the value of the object depends on the observer's taste, and C. I. Lewis on the ground that the value of the object consists of its potentiality for giving immediate satisfaction in experience. In this discussion such issues cannot be gone into and it must be assumed that the presence of aesthetic values in objects is a matter of *prima-facie* experience. When I say "Jane is beautiful" it is of Jane I am speaking, of the beauty that somehow resides in the shape of her face, her eyes, mouth, in her fresh skin and in her neck, and not of myself; her beauty is certainly not *in me,* nor in my reactions to her, although, of course, I cannot discover it unless I somehow react to the features in which it resides. If beauty reveals itself only to an individual and does so in an incommunicable way, so that no one else can discover it, nothing more can be said about it, except that, unless the person who claims to descry it is a liar, it is there for him. Correction of such taste is impossible. But the objects of art with which criticism busies itself are not of this kind. And the critic, in engaging in his activity as critic, asserts thereby tacitly that they are not, but that they are values that are discoverable by others besides himself. Otherwise why does he publish his opinions? It may well be that the critic will discover in the objects of his preference, after analysis has done its best, an ineffable quality which helps give the object the specific value that it has for him, but which somehow eludes his power of analysis. But if the critic starts with ineffables instead of ending with them when he can do nothing to exorcise them, he condemns himself to emotive grunts of no interest to anyone but himself.[1]

Now an objective judgment of an object not only refers to a

value trait, but does so because the object possesses some sort of
discriminable structure on which the value depends. This is so
by definition, for art involves material that possesses an inherent
capacity for organization, shaped intentionally by the artist in
order to capture a determinate congerie of aesthetic values. If the
presence of the value is not controlled by the object's structure,
there is no question of art and the object is of no interest for
criticism, although such an unanchored value may be within the
grasp of enraptured and immediate apprehension for some men.
But, you may object, why could we not talk of values that reside
in objects but that do not depend on structure for their presence
in them? If and when one finds them, he can no doubt talk of
them, but he could not share his experience with his neighbour
unless the latter had already, by the same happy accident, apprehended the same values. No artist could have controlled their
presence in the object; nor could critics make objective reference
to them. For it is only through reference to the structure to which
they are anchored that reference to aesthetic value is possible;
otherwise the presence of a value in an object is altogether for-
tuitous and miraculous, to be apprehended only by those who do
so accidentally and forever closed to those who do not.

That values reside in objects and that they depend for their
presence in them on the latter's structure seems to me a matter
of common experience although often denied by philosophers. But
it is also a matter of experience that values reside in objects independently of their structure. Consider for instance a picture of a
"Virgin and Child" almost utterly devoid of aesthetic value, such
as one sees in religious store windows, and which no doubt appears
to some believers as beautiful as well as holy. It seems to be a
difficult question as to how values which are not, so to speak,
"anchored" to the structures of objects, get to reside in them. It
is usually said that they are "projected," and with this utterly inadequate problem-begging metaphor many aestheticians and psychologists seem to be satisfied. But this is fortunately not a problem
which we need to discuss here, for whatever answer we give to it,
it remains a fact that "unanchored values," so to call them, are
on examination found to be different in kind from those which
depend on the object's structure for their presence in it. It is true

that some aestheticians have held that all aesthetic values are projected; but even if they are, they cannot be indifferently and arbitrarily projected upon any object, and on this theory the critic still has the problem of discovering those structures which are hospitable to aesthetic values. The point is, obviously, that there is a relationship of some sort between aesthetic value and structure, even if no one has yet successfully formulated it. A faded snapshot of a dead child may wring the same feeling from his mother as a portrait of his done by an artist of distinction. The value of either object, for the mother, need not depend on its intrinsic structure but may entirely depend on the extrinsic and purely accidental power it may have of reminding her of her lost child. In an aesthetic object, however, the structure subtends the value and communicates it, irrespective of purely accidental relationships between the subject who will grasp it and the object in which it resides. Indeed an aesthetic structure is one which successfully excludes the irrelevant values and controls rigorously the values and meanings it communicates.

The assertion of the possibility of objectivity of aesthetic judgments does not mean that such judgments are absolutely correct but merely that they are corrigible. The correction of judgments involves greater difficulties in art than it does in science, where techniques of abstraction, isolation, quantification, and controlled experiment enable the inquirer to confine his attention to the precise phenomena to which the judgment refers and to exclude idiosyncratic irrelevancies. In art, in the absence of such instrumentalities, corrigibility takes place through the give and take of criticism of the object. In such give and take the criteria of criticism are themselves open to criticism. And only by means of a criticism of such criticism is the presence of a value in an object isolated and related to its structure. Through such a process the specific nature of the structure is itself defined by critical analysis, the value it subtends is isolated, and the criteria which governs its presence in the object exhibited. Thus the utterance of the judgment "This object is beautiful" is in a sense the least important part of a critical effort, since challenge of the judgment involves an examination of its basis, and this examination may disclose that the judgment rests on insufficient grounds. If the "verification" (a most inappropriate term to use for these activities) consisted, as some simple-minded positivists hold in respect to moral judgments, merely in the statement of formulae expressing intrinsic values and the logical deduction of specific valuations from these, discussion would be futile and criticism would consist in the clever conditioning of another's taste by one's own. This is in fact what criticism often undertakes to do: arbitrarily to recondition another person's taste. But discussion of beauty is also addressed—although of course it rarely is—to the discovery and exhibition of values subtended by aesthetic structures which for some reason we have either overlooked or misconstrued. The assumption on which such discussion is carried on is that the exhibition of the structure will allow the value to come forward and that its presence will then draw forth our interest. For value exists prior to interest and more often than not creates it. This is always the case as regards non-inherited interests, all those, that is, above the biological level. But even congenital or inherited interests do not create value, they merely discover it. The correction of criteria is possible because the determinate structure which subtends value and which controls our perception of it can be appealed to. The criterion is an inductive statement of an empirically discovered normative transaction between a mind and an object embodying a value, but once stated the criterion enters into the situation and acquires normative force, clarifying and governing taste. In no case however is it more than empirically related to the situation over which it rules. Our formulated criteria are susceptible of correction because a pre-existing structure, conflicting judgments about the value it subtends and the very examination through which both structure and values were discovered can be appealed to in order to correct each of the factors involved in terms of the others when conflicting judgments reveal the need for such correction.

Value judgment, then, is objective, first, in the sense that it refers to a quality of an object and not to the subjective quality of satisfaction, fulfillment, enjoyment, or pleasure which may be derived from its grasp. One of the most frequent forms of the subjectivistic fallacy consists in confusing the value of an experience with the value of an object in an experience. Both object and experience of it may be endowed with value. But to deny value to a thing because it does not happen to enter into an experience, or to attribute to it the value which may belong to the experience, is to fail to make distinctions essential to the clarification of our subject matter. Aesthetic value is not the quality of an experience but of an object in an experience; the only value experiences can have for the subject undergoing them is moral value, although objectively viewed one man's experience may have aesthetic value for another. It is true that the aesthetic object which is of interest to the critic is always an object in an experience, but so are all other objects which may be the objects of judgment; the predicament holds of scientific objects and not only of aesthetic objects. Of course the adequate possession of a positive value should in the majority of cases involve subjective satisfactions. But when these are present they are by-products of the activity which resulted in the possession of the objective value, and if such satisfactions are also considered by the subject in possession of the objective value as adding to that value, as they indeed do, the critic must insist on the distinction between the value of the object, and the added values in terms of satisfaction that its possession brings with it. The residence of the aesthetic value in an object can be ascertained through the fact that it is available for public inspection. The judgment is valid to the extent that it can justify itself to those adequately endowed judges who are interested in discovering the value to which it refers; but it is not objective in that it can do so but because it can: I mean that it is objective because it refers to objective traits but we ascertain their presence publicly and only by thus ascertaining them can we be sure that the values are there.

But—and there are of course several "buts"—the word 'beauty' is much more ambiguous than words which designate physical properties, since, first, that to which it points is not apprehended by but through sense; and second, and this is the source of the worst trouble, the discrimination of beauty, as resident upon specific structure, depends on our ability to descry in the object's construction, its aesthetic purpose. Our failure to discover in a poem of Hopkins the beauty so readily found in one of Keats is not infrequently caused by the fact that we approach the former with expectations acquired through our acquaintance with the latter. Modigliani will not give you what a Titian will nor does Picasso try to do what Goya did. How then shall we determine the artist's aesthetic intention? Will we discover it from what he says in his letters or from Boswellian records that we may be fortunate to possess? Even if we had such records for all artists we could not use them without checking their statements against the artist's work considered in the context of the aims and directions of his tradition or school. What artists say about their work all too frequently depends on aesthetic theories which may not be relevant to their practice; or if they are, may not have been fully elucidated, or may not be consistent. In any case the artist's statements are only a part of what he had to say and, as artist, not necessarily the most important part. What he has had to say is best found in his art. The criteria of validity of a statement about an object must be whether the statement represents the object truly. The artist's statements about his object must certainly occupy a preferred place in our decision about his intentions. But they cannot be accepted at face value.

Examination of the object with adequate knowledge and sensibility may yet reveal no value in the object for one examiner, although for another it may be there. I can agree with you that the structure was conceived for the purpose you ascribe to it and agree, as far as discrimination can carry it, as to the structural traits you so perspicuously describe. But for all that I do not find in the object the value that you find in it. On the very grounds that you find value I may even find the very opposite, a disvalue. Does that mean that it has value for you but not for me? Does it now follow that we both are right? This conclusion would legitimately follow from complete knowledge about yourself and myself; until we possess such knowledge the source of the failure must remain an open question. The disagreement may mean that factors as yet undiscovered—either in you or in me or in both—are interfering with an objective grasp of what is there to be grasped. You may be "projecting" values on the object which are not truly there; or I may be made blind to them by my lack of sensibility or ignorance or by deeply grounded prejudices; or we both may be at fault and may be perceiving more and less than the object's structure subtends. And the reason for this is of course that judgments of value, as ut-

tered, are never beyond challenge. The law says that a man acquit-
ted at court can never be tried a second time for the same crime.
But his value judgments do not have the same privilege he has and
they can always be called a second, a third, and a fourth time, to
justify themselves. Error does not thereby impair the objectivity of
the judgment. What objectivity requires, besides the objectivity of
the value, is not that we have consensus, but that we have on hand
means of checking the validity of our judgments. Infallibility is not
possible but it is not necessary either. And the means to check the
validity of conflicting judgments are difficult of application, inefficient, and take more time and patience than we usually have at
our disposal. But they are there to be used if we want to use them.
This is a most important point and it would be well to dwell on
it longer, at least to the extent of suggesting that a theory of
objectivity cannot be made responsible for the sins of omission
and commission of specific judgments. A certain subjectivistic aesthetician not long ago made a historical study on the basis on
which a very famous Italian painting has been praised by various
critics since Vassari; and because of the heterogeneity of the demands clearly made by the various critics which he studied he
concluded that there is no way of choosing between the various
conflicting modes of criticism. But the conclusion is a total *non-
sequitur*, since it has assumed that there is no way of criticizing
across the boundaries, so to speak, of incompatible conceptions of
the intention of the artist. The analysis assumes, as all subjectivism
seems to, that each individual's reaction is absolutely valid, and we
must take it at its face value.

The claim of objectivity depends, then, secondly, on whether it
is possible to disclose the means by which conflicting judgments
can be corrected when discrimination has done its best and has,
through a perspicuous analysis of structure, called forth contradictory value judgments. We have already noted that in cases
where seemingly inerradicable disagreements are encountered
neither of the conflicting judgments can claim initial superiority
or validity over the other. By what means then shall we correct
these judgments? Notice first that the rational correction of judgments involves, as a guiding condition, the desire to arrive at the
truth. In practice this is an ideal more honoured in the breach

than in the observance. But unless the condition is assumed no further discussion of the problem is possible. And in practice to the extent to which we fail to realize this ideal there can be no possibility of correcting conflicting value judgments, not because the techniques for so doing have failed, but because other objectives have been substituted for those of rational inquiry.

But, the reader will press, what techniques do you have in mind? The answer, I am afraid, will disappoint lovers of novelty as well as those addicted to scientifistic methodolatry, for the techniques in question are those which were used by Socrates in his own moral inquiry: the mutual interrogation of claims and counter-claims in order to elicit from them the evidence on which they rest and the clarity on which they count; in short what Plato called a "dialectical" inquiry. In the give and take in which a dialectical inquiry consists, the judgments in conflict are corrected by confronting them with the facts to which they pretend to refer, and the principles on which the judgments are based are themselves subject to criticism by reference to the objective values, as critically apprehended, to which the inquiry is addressed, and which remain the ultimate basis of appeal. It is important to notice, however, that what is purely idiosyncratic—whether in the artist or in the judge of his work—is irrelevant to an objective judgment, and gradually emerges when the conflicting judgments are put, in Plato's phrase, through the gauntlet of the argument. Criticism seeks to reveal the aesthetic value of an object, to relate it to the structure that sustains it, and to relate the object to the traditions to which it belongs and define the intention of the artist. Thus the critic tries to put himself in a position from which he can evaluate objectively an artist's achievement in relation to the achievement of other artists who may be members of his tradition and even of other traditions. The total process, carried on against all comers, results in the gradual crystalization of opinion from which the errors of subjectivity have to some degree been expurgated. This doctrine may be maintained while admitting freely that the process is not one from which error can be thoroughly removed.

The foregoing account will no doubt seem to be infected with circularity to those readers who, not adequately acquainted with the actual complexities of criticism, will think of the problem

solely in abstract terms and will demand logical rigor and elegance
above fidelity to the complex facts. But the account is not circular
since it holds that the criticism of the judgment and of the criterion
which rules it is always controlled by objectively given facts to
which final appeal is made. First hand acquaintance with the actual
procedure of criticism will reveal it to be characterized by ineffi-
ciency and confusion, but not by radical circularity. In the give
and take of criticism, through which gradually the true values embodied in objects emerge, the intention of the artist is more or less
clarified, and his contribution to taste is slowly digested.

One criticism that has been made of this account must be met.
The doctrine has been called conservative because, it has been
argued, it calls for a criticism which is guided by the criteria of
well established taste. But this is not a fair interpretation of what
the view intends, since established taste is not on this theory a
fixed affair to which art must conform. If however it should be
insisted that the theory is more likely to give comfort to a conservative artist than to a revolutionary one, since it seems to put
so much emphasis on established taste as a source of criteria of
value, it were well to remember, in justice to it, that taste itself is
not treated in this doctrine as if it constituted the final criterion,
since taste is held to be responsive to values presented, to beauties
actually embodied. If it is open to criticism, it is not because it is
conservative, but because it sounds like Deweyism. But the similarity is specious, since the final criterion is held to be the objective
value, the beauty embodied, or the abortive failure before us which
somehow suggests the intention of the artist. These are held to
exist prior to their discovery and to be regulative of taste. We can
depend on taste only when it is impeccable; but any serious challenge to it immediately puts it on the defensive. It often happens
that taste for some reason ossifies; in such cases the error carries
with it its own punishment, since the tradition it sustains soon dies
instead of developing. If on the other hand, taste becomes too
fluid, too ready to welcome all innovation, as is the case in our
day, the error also carries with it its own punishment, for it becomes distracted, queer, eccentric, unintelligible. In such periods
those to whom art should minister become even more distracted
than they already are by contemplating objects that are hermetic

puzzles and keep the secret of the artist's intention within themselves against any serious and honest effort to wrest it from them; and men who need art wander starved amidst the plenty. Art, one of whose most important functions is to bring order, harmony and lucidity into a man's vision of his world, adds to the chaos and speeds up the social disintegration that produced it. The individualistic intuitionist, the man who repudiates all tradition on the authority of his inner voice, condemns himself and, insofar as he is influential, his fellows, to shallow experimentalism. Such a man acts as if he carried in himself his own self-validation. But the very conception of self-validation is a contradiction. For this reason, while we must agree with the subjectivist who has insisted that private factors do in fact enter into valuation, and must add that they serve to individuate one's taste, we cannot agree with him in so far as he seems to suggest that they ever "justify" it. When a judge falls back on them he has withdrawn his judgment from all criticism and has asserted that he is interested in the expression of his arbitrary will rather than in the objective justification of his taste. Note however that if the argument of this essay has been made clear the phrase "objective justification" should be taken as pleonastic, since the effort to justify a judgment consists precisely in exhibiting the objective and sharable basis on which it rests.

It is also necessary to remember that the notion of tradition, as T. S. Eliot has pointed out in his well-known essay, "Tradition and The Individual Talent," does not call for an inert and frozen past in terms of which we must judge the present irrespective of the differences in interest and orientation which may be found to exist between yesterday and today. Eliot pointed out that the appearance of a new poem involves a reinterpretation of the tradition. He writes as if the past changed—and that involves a conception of time that commits us to a weird metaphysics. But if he allows us to read him as if he had meant, not that the past changes but that our interpretation of it changes, I would willingly subscribe to all that he says in the first part of his essay. Now the literary humanists—I mean, Irving Babbitt and his now almost totally extinct followers—as I read them, bring the present to the rigid norm of the past and instead of judging it, in Eliot's distinction, they amputate it. For them the differences between the practice of the modern artist and that of the ancients was traced to contemporary aberrations and the devils of modern history, Bacon and Rousseau. The complimentary error, that of the individualist, because more virulent at present, is much more dangerous today than that of the humanists. The individualist denies the jurisdiction of the past over the present and assumes the right of the artist to unrestricted originality. It ignores the fact that we owe loyalty to our past because we are absolutely nothing without it. The repudiation of the past is justified on a philosophy of history according to which there can be a radical break between our age and another. The repudiation of the past involves a misreading of history which is both egregious and obvious. Those who have contempt for the past counsel us to bind ourselves to wilful, upstart movements which express the transient needs of men without piety, restrained by nothing but the limitations of their own willfulness. We need expect nothing from *guerrilleros* either in art, in ethics or in politics; we are much better off if we take our chances with the tradition than if we appeal to the latest *apparat*, whether it be positivist, instrumentalist, or Marxist. In contrast with these two extremes, a genuine empiricism allows for the progressive transformation of the past in terms of the present, even to the rejection of aspects of the tradition that can be shown to be genuinely in error. But it also insists that the past must judge the present, for we cannot define our own contemporary norm without its aid.

These remarks cannot be taken as an exhaustive treatment of the problem of aesthetic revolutions; not even of those minor revolutions which are frequently accomplished—as it would seem—by your strong individuals and which result in a marked deflection in the direction of taste. A complete treatment of this phenomenon would take us far afield, and would involve investigations of regions as yet unexplored, to my knowledge, in order to discover the relationship between the social processes and artistic creativity. Nor do these sketchy notes touch on another problem, a much more difficult one, and one which an exhaustive treatment of the problem of aesthetic value would have to face. For moral phenomena cannot be satisfactorily elucidated unless we distinguish between the conditional and the categorical moral imperatives. But in art we do not find, so far as I can see, a similar dualism.

We are now in a position to gather our results: the discussion has been grounded on the belief that it is of the essence of truth to give an account of its grounds, submitting these without strings to criticism. In the exact sciences, discussion is carried on in terms of techniques and procedures that in part are devised in order to locate the idiosyncratic in observation and the ambiguous in formulation. In art these techniques are not available, but through persistent discussion and criticism failures and limitations of commission and omission on the part of the artist and his critics emerge, and their exhibition constitutes the process of corrigibility. If judgments are corrigible, or rather in so far as they are, they are objective. But it would be impossible to speak of corrigibility if the discussion had not sought to make clear what is meant by asserting that value traits are objective and dependent on structures which can be discriminated objectively and which can be intentionally devised to subtend a complex of values. However, the connection that we have discovered to exist between a physical structure and the value it subtends is a purely empirical, *a posteriori*, one. If such a connection does not issue in subjectivism it is because, in spite of cultural conditioning which tends parochially to blind a man to the alien, an earnest inquiry into alien values will frequently reveal to him that those values are objectively present. In aesthetics however, the desirability of arriving at uniformity of judgments remains and is likely to remain in the realm of the possible, whereas in ethics—not in moral judgments—uniformity and universality of agreement is in fact a reality, at least among those men who have not been, as Bishop Berkeley put it, debauched by philosophy. The empirical, contingent connection, then, between physical structure, embodied value, and a spectator's capacity under favorable conditions to discover it, makes criticism an intelligent objective activity, which is capable of guiding taste and correcting the artist's practice. We also saw, in passing, that criticism entails a complete theory of aesthetics, since it operates on a notion—whether explicit or implicit—of the function of art and of the meaning of the purely aesthetic. The failure to define the purely aesthetic and the function of art is what gives the subjectivist a plausible ground for his belief that about values there can be no rational dispute. This paper was based on the assumption that in concrete critical activity the purely aesthetic can be isolated, and that the resident function of art can be distinguished from its non-resident functions. That a discussion of the basis of criticism —to which an essay on the aesthetic judgment really is addressed— depends on a general aesthetic theory is worth while pointing out because in no field does a hand to mouth pragmatism seem to be more entrenched than in the field of criticism. But serious and responsible criticism would acknowledge freely its dependence on the wider philosophic enterprise which is aesthetics. Our criticism is bound to remain erratic and inconsistent insofar as it is informed by embryonic conceptions of the uses of art and of the validity of the critical judgment.

1948

4

AESTHETIC THEORIES

four notes on I. A. Richards' aesthetic theory

> . . . *everybody knows the diminution of energy, the bafflement, the sense of helplessness, which an ill-written, crude, or muddled book . . . will produce, unless the critical task of diagnosis is able to restore equanimity and composure.*

Very few contemporary writers on aesthetics in English occupy Richards' authoritative position. Since the publication of *The Principles of Literary Criticism* [1] his theories have gained increasingly in prestige among theoretical writers as well as among practical critics, and he seems in the process of gathering a school. [2] Those interested in aesthetics or in practical criticism will generally admit, I believe, that his influence has already had some very salutary effects. He has been instrumental in sobering speculation; he has called attention to a number of problems hitherto inadequately dealt with, notably the problem of communication; and

with profound conviction he has insisted on the need we moderns
have of art. No doubt these achievements explain in part the prestige his doctrines enjoy. But the felt need, inchoate and confused,
for a 'scientific' aesthetics, the meagerness of experimental results,
and perhaps also the imperial manner Richards has of dismissing
as mere verbiage theories with which he disagrees and of bravely
hacking at very difficult intellectual knots rather than patiently
unravelling them, must also be accounted factors. A critical examination of his theories will, however, reveal that they often
suffer from defects similar to those he has noticed in others. Under
undoubted excellences one discovers a number of incoherences and
confusions which need probing, and this all the more urgently on
account of the militant intolerance not only of his followers but of
Richards himself.[3]

1

Richards holds that the function of art is to produce an organization of impulses and attitudes through which the individual comes
into a competence and sanity he could not otherwise acquire.[4]
His theory no doubt contains important truth. But as one reads
his account of it one is left with a large number of insistent questions for which no answer is found in his pages. Three of these
difficulties will be here pointed out.

1. We must first note the abstract manner in which he describes
the processes of organization and the absence of specific illustration
which would give the theory reality and precision. Only once is an
illustration offered. In *The Principles* [5] the attempt is made to
show how the contradictory impulses of pity and terror are ordered through tragedy. But this single illustration does not satisfy
the expectations of the reader, for he is led to expect from the
formidable psychological equipment of the preceding chapters
something less stale and less rhetorical. One does not object to
Richards' purple passages on tragedy or even to the profuse use
of capitals with which he punctuates the periods of his emotive
efforts. But one does object to rhetoric offered as illustration of
actual psychological processes by a psychologist who has made the

explicit claim that he writes strictly in the scientific spirit, and who has subjected rival theories to such pitiless strictures because they are not criticism but "inferior poetry. . . . Too much sack and too little bread." [6] What Richards has to show to put his own outside the reach of the charges he makes against other theories is specifically what impulses are engaged, what attitudes come into play, in the case of the various arts. If the only specific result of the theory is merely to rewrite Aristotle, the tremendous effort is hardly worth while.

It must be noted in fairness to Richards that he is aware of his inability to illustrate his theory specifically or even to give a satisfactory account of it. The apologies he offers however cannot take the place of the needed facts. He warns us that although organization is the result of all genuine aesthetic experience, we must resist the temptation to analyse it, because these "opposed impulses from the resolution of which such experiences spring cannot usually be analysed." [7] Elsewhere he has told us that we do not know much in specific terms about impulses and attitudes because "psychology is not yet far advanced." [8] If no account of the process is possible, how does he know about it? May not his theory be open to the charges he makes against previous nonscientific aesthetics?

2. Another observation must be made about the theory of organization. Descriptive aesthetics has come increasingly to feel that there are "varieties of aesthetic experience." Let us consider Nietzsche's classification of the types of art and experience because it is the simplest. It will be remembered he distinguished two types. Now it seems that Richards' organization refers to the type of experience which Nietzsche called Apollonian. When organization is accomplished through art, we are told, " 'the film of familiarity and self solicitude' which commonly hides nine-tenths of life for man seems to be lifted and he feels strangely alive and aware of the actuality of existence." [9] The result is that contrasting impulses are balanced, and that we gain in competence and in serenity. Richards almost uses Nietzsche's very words. The latter writes:

Contrasts are overcome, the highest sign of power thus manifesting itself in the conquest of opposites; and achieved without a feeling of tension; violence being no longer necessary, everything submitting and obeying, and doing so with good grace. [10]

Nietzsche believes, it will be remembered, that there is another type of aesthetic experience, called by him Dionysian. This type he describes in dithyrambs one blushes to quote. It is an "orgiastic" state, characterized by the superabundance of "sensuality, intoxication, cruelty." Dionysian art is the expression of overpowering strength, and a "stimulus" to the yea-saying qualities of existence from which it springs, terrible and destructive though these be. Richards has nothing at all to say about this type of art and the aesthetic experience it brings about; yet the burden is clearly on him either to prove that the Apollonian experience is the only valid one or to give us an account of the Dionysian.

3. Richards bases his conviction of the importance of art for society not so much on the intrinsic value of the aesthetic experience, as on the effects which the organization of impulses of which it consists can have on our daily life. Yet his ideas, on scrutiny, appear to be more the expression of a hope than the assertion of irrefragable fact. "Finer adjustment," he tells us, "clearer and more delicate accommodation or reconciliation of impulses in any one field, tends to promote it in others. A step in mathematical accomplishment, other things being equal, facilitates the acquisition in a new turn in ski-ing." [11] And although he warns us in the following sentence that "other things are rarely equal," the doctrine remains questionable in fact and ambiguous in formulation. "There is," he tells us, "abundant evidence that the removal of confusion in one sphere of activity tends to be favourable to its removal elsewhere." [12] But he fails to tell us where such abundant evidence is to be found. There are sound theoretical reasons to suspect that success in a particular specialized field of activity does not necessarily carry over in such way as the illustration from mathematics seems to imply, for specialized activity involves the development of a definite technique applicable only in fields similar to it. It is this technique and not a formal general aptitude which is developed. What indeed does it mean to speak of a formal or general aptitude? In any case, the matter is one of fact about which psychologists are still undecided, and which would take more than the mere mention of available evidence to establish. Richards circumvents the difficulty of adducing positive evidence either of an ex-

perimental or of a theoretical kind, by putting the burden of proof
on the negative. "But what would have to be shown before the
principle is invalidated is that, granted equal specialization, the
successful specialist is not better fitted for life in general than his
unsuccessful *confrère*." [13] One wonders what "better fitted for life"
means. Again, how can equal or relative degrees of specialization be
determined? In any case, the number of highly trained specialists
who are duffers out of their fields, who outside of their offices or
laboratories bungle and err, is too large and too notorious to bear
repetition. The inability of scientists to think vexing political or
religious issues clearly through, even when the facts are not lacking, is a type of case in point; and certainly artists have not gained
in "the mastery of life" because of the supreme achievements in
the field of art. Though there have been great artists who by commonly accepted standards lived successfully, there have been too
many on the opposite side, great artists, too, who under no reasonable standards could be said to have achieved "mastery of life." For
every Shakespeare there has been a Villon. This shows that as far
as our evidence goes no correlation between the aesthetic activity
and what is loosely called "life" can be established. All we can say,
if we are speaking of things as they are and not of things as we like
them to be, is that we have no adequate grounds for positive
opinion on either side.

2

In one of the first chapters in *The Principles* Richards makes an
important distinction between *the critical* and *the technical* parts
of the aesthetic judgment. The critical refers to the value of the
aesthetic experience, the technical to the means through which
that experience comes about.[14] Now one of the most irreducible
confusions in Richards' doctrine results from the fact that through
his extreme intolerance of any other approach to aesthetics than
the psychological there is no legitimate place in his system for technical analysis of an objective kind. But without objective technical
analysis it is difficult to imagine what answer can be given to the
question why good art should be preferred to bad. The different
degrees of organization produced by good and mediocre poetry

respectively presume objective distinctions between the two poems in question. Otherwise we should have to maintain that *any* objective means may produce a satisfactory subjective condition of organization. And this in turn would be tantamount to maintaining that the distinction commonly made between good and bad art is, technically speaking, of no critical importance whatsoever. In some places this seems to be the only possible construction which the reader can put on Richards' speculations. But this construction cannot of course be consistent with other aspects of his theory. For he maintains that there is a difference in technical quality between different art-objects, and has much to say about the deleterious effects of mediocre or bad art on society.[15]

Yet Richards' psychological method precludes any reference whatsoever to the object. For the object we are asked to substitute psychophysiological processes, thoroughly reducing it thereby to subjective phenomena. We are thus confronted with a radical contradiction. On the one hand the distinction between the technical and the critical parts of aesthetic theory necessarily implies an object, capable of giving rise to the subjective phenomenon of organization, with which the critic is concerned, and on the other the object is destroyed by the psychological method insisted on and one is left with no objective *point d'appui* for a critical judgment.

The radical nature of the defect reveals itself in its full complexity when one notices the ruthless ease with which Richards discards objective categories currently employed in "technical" description as altogether useless and meaningless—categories which he is forced later to reintroduce surreptitiously into the system. Richards maintains that we have no use for

> such terms as 'construction', 'form', 'balance', 'composition', 'design', 'unity', 'expression', for all the arts; as 'depth', 'movement', 'texture', 'solidity', in the criticism of painting; as 'rhythm', 'stress', 'plot', 'character', in literary criticism; as 'harmony', 'atmosphere', 'development', in music.[16]

This "verbal apparatus" with the aid of which we have always endeavored to describe the art-object will be found on examination to come "between us and the things with which we are really dealing."[17] These terms are invalid because they are based upon an assumption of objectivity which is utterly fallacious. We currently use them as if they stood for qualities existing outside the mind, whereas all there is outside is "an assemblage of pigments" in the case of painting: and, in the case of poetry, it is difficult to discover "what thing other than print and paper is there for these alleged qualities to belong to." [18] Thus we get accustomed to saying that a thing is beautiful when all we should say is that it is causing in us an experience which is valuable in certain ways. This is the fallacy of " 'projecting' the effect and making it a quality of its cause." [19]

One wonders what makes Richards stop with paper and print and pigments, what forbids him from carrying his excursus one step farther and maintaining that the paper and print and pigments also are really within the mind. This half-way logic leads one to believe that the real reason for discarding these objective categories of description has a deeper source than the "fallacy of 'projecting' the effect." Indeed the objectification with which Richards takes issue assumes the character of a fallacy only when considered from the view-point of the psychological method which he advocates. Under it "beauty" becomes a meaningless term. For the aesthetic judgment of beautiful we must substitute a correct psychological analysis of the aesthetic experience. If we wish to speak of an art-object, we must not forget that we are not confronted with form, color, deep space in a two-dimensional canvas; all we really have are stimuli and muscle-movements which give us the illusion of a house, meadows, sky in the picture we are looking at. In Richards' own words:

> It remains conceivable, that a work of art should have some one quality in virtue of which we recognize it as such though there are very strong general reasons against the assumption. It is plain that a description of what happens when we feel an aesthetic emotion (if ever we do) would fall into two halves. There must be a long psychological story about the organization of our impulses and instincts and of the special momentary setting of them due to our environment and of our immediate past history on the one hand. On the other a physico-physiological account of the work of art as a stimulus, describing also its immediate sensory effects, and the impulses which these bring into play.[20]

Nothing at all remains or can remain of the object when the method has been applied with any thoroughness. All the objective features of the work of art become physico-physiological stimuli. Rhythm becomes "expectancy," which in turn becomes "a thing which must be thought of as a very complex tide of neural settings, lowering the threshold for some kinds of stimuli and raising it for others." [21] Metre likewise becomes "increased expectancy"—relatively to nonmetrical language—of a narrow, definite and unconscious kind.[22] In painting, again, depth, volume, and solidity must be thought of as produced by "relicts of eye movements, kinesthetic images of the convergence of the eyes and accommodation of the lenses according to the distance of the object contemplated." [23] Similar instances of the reduction of objective phenomena to subjective terms could be cited in the case of sculpture and music.[24] But all these phenomena, interesting no doubt in themselves, can throw no light on *the character* of the experience and the fact that in some cases kinesthetic movements of the eyes lead us to say—as we often do say, and, as I shall presently show, Richards *demands* that the critic be in a position to say—that, *as art*, we know one particular specimen is more competently executed than the other, that Matisse draws better than Grant Wood. Though the aesthetic experience then may be sufficiently accounted for in terms of impulses, instincts, and sensory effects, somehow or other the work of art has vanished, has become mythical. Of what use then technical analysis? Of what use the work of art? Yet the objective categories which are merely fallacious "projections" of the mind cannot be so easily dispensed with. They—or synonymous terms—are the only ones we have for referring to those objects outside of the mind which are one of the sources, at least, of the stimuli which give rise to the experience. In other words Richards is forced to take notice of the technical "ways and means by which our experiences arise and are brought about," [25] unless he is to maintain that the mind manufactures them out of its own impenetrable depths. And for this reason he is forced to bring back, disguised under new names, or, in a large number of instances, lumped together under the heading of "formal elements," the categories which earlier he so unceremoniously disqualified. He has to reintroduce such terms as rhythm, metre, pitch, timbre, and movement in verse; and in painting texture, volume, structure, picture-space, weight, tensions, color-harmony, plastic rhythm; and a host of similar categories are reintroduced in sculpture and in music.[26] But though they are pressed into service by him, they have no business whatsoever within the scope of his theory.

The issue however involves more than the matter of a hopeless logical contradiction; it involves the legitimacy of turning aesthetics into psychophysiology. When we are concerned with the technical aspect of art we are concerned with the validity or adequacy, the goodness or badness in Richards' terms, of a work of art. We do not wish to know whether it produces in us a certain kind of organization but whether the means used by the artist are adequate, better than those someone else used, or not as adequate as those he could have used. We are interested in the work of art objectively, and no subjectivistic epistemology or psychological analysis can tell us that our interest is not a legitimate one. It seems as if a psychological approach to criticism leads not only to neglect of the technical side of aesthetics, but also to the denial of its claim to our interest. Nor may any one plead that his interest is in criticism, for that misses the point of this observation, namely that the valid distinction between the technical and the critical does not free the critic from the burden of grounding his speculations in a thorough consideration of the complete aesthetic phenomenon. To maintain that the critic is concerned with value alone would be like maintaining that the practical engineer need not know theory. Richards, it must be noted, in spite of the hopeless confusion into which his method throws him, does not defend so sophomoric a position. Chapters Sixteen to Twenty of the *Principles* show this. Here we see that he is conscious of the fact that aesthetic criticism presumes a technical evaluation of the art-object. And yet psychology does not provide either the categories, or the criterion, or the method, involved in that evaluation.[27]

3

Another one of the difficulties into which Richards is led by his psychological method appears when we turn our attention to the problem of the standard. The critic must be able to judge the relative value of the different organizations which various aesthetic experiences are capable of producing.[28] But in order to do so he must be in possession of an objective standard or criterion of the worth of an experience.[29] We must inquire whether Richards' system can offer such a criterion.

The value of the organization is determined by the object in spite of the fact that his method, as we saw above, does not permit of commerce with it. Now there are two reasons why one may say that art is bad: Art fails either technically, as an instrument of communication or, from the critical standpoint, because the experience communicated is worthless.[30] Can we tell objectively whether the means of communication are at fault? We must note, first, that success in communication is partly determined by a number of subjective factors. For instance various levels of aesthetic response must be recognized. This means that various judgments of a work of art are always possible. Again, in artistic creation subjective factors enter, such as the artist's 'normality' and, in the experience of art, the normality of the spectator. We must also consider the divergence of possible readings—a possibility of divergence which exists not only in poetry but in all the arts.[31] All these are of course factors which increase considerably the difficulty of discovering the objective standard.

Richards attempts to resolve the difficulty through the appeal to a "competent reader" or spectator, who decides when the means of communication employed by the artist are capable of producing a valuable organization on the normal beholder.[32]

The objections to an appeal to a competent reader are of course obvious. The objectivity thus gained is specious and the problem has merely been pushed one step back, not at all resolved. For how is a competent reader defined? The discrepancies in the judgments of competent readers are too notorious to need mention. And how do we determine their normality, their objectivity and the impartiality guiding their judgment? Shall we succeed more readily if we attempt to determine the worth of the experience communicated? Richards suggests a method for this determination only in the case of poetry, nor is it clear how we could apply it to the other arts.[33] But even in poetry it applies only to those cases in which the vehicle is not "sufficiently adequate and the critic sufficiently representative and careful for the response to be a good index of the value of the poem";[84] in other words it ignores the issue at the very start. But this is not the only difficulty. Let us proceed. We must first define the poem carefully to make sure we are speaking of the same object. What then do we mean when we speak of a poem? We may mean four things, he finds:

> We may be talking about the artist's experience, such of it as is relevant, or about the experience of a qualified reader who made no mistakes, or about an ideal and perfect reader's possible experience, or about our own actual experience.[85]

But, since we cannot take any single experience to be the poem, we must take a class of experiences, occasioned by the particular poem under judgment, "which do not differ within certain limits"[86] from the artist's experience. The latter is considered as standard. The rest follows quite easily. In his own words:

> Anyone whose experience approximates in this degree to the standard experience will be able to judge the poem, and his remarks about it will be about some experience which is included in the class. Thus we have what we want, a sense, namely, in which the critic can be said to have not read the poem, or to have misread it.[87]

The objections to this solution are both of a logical and of a practical nature. The standard experience by which he is judging the readers' experiences—that is, the artist's experience—cannot be recovered, even by himself (speaking generally), except through the poem; and Richards has already admitted that this experience cannot be recovered by anyone else, "since nobody but the artist has that experience."[88] In other words, he is simply begging the question of an objective criterion, by bringing in one which cannot be defined or had for inspection. Without the standard we cannot know how the class of experiences which define the poem differ among themselves. Our judgment remains therefore entirely subjective. Also, there always remains the purely practical yet insurmountable difficulty of obtaining a class of experiences by which to define the poem. How, otherwise than by counting heads, can such a collection of documents be obtained? But counting heads obviously will not do.

We are left in a quandary. We have a theory of the function of art in society, which demands that we be able to determine values objectively. This demand is fundamental. And yet the theory fails to offer us any criterion through which alone we could claim objectivity for our judgments.

Aware of this failure, Richards seems to have repudiated in *Practical Criticism*, virtually if not explicitly, his previous position and doctrines. He does this by redefining the function of criticism. The critic has become a teacher now, and his most important task is to improve communication. How he is sure his judgment is correct we are not definitely told. But we are told that only after such improvement is he to concern himself with judging the value of the experience. The problem of finding an objective criterion of value is given up. "Value," he tells us, "cannot be demonstrated except through the communication of what is valuable." [39]

4

Underlying the whole structure of Richards' critical theory lies his misconception about the nature of value and our ability to derive it from a psychological description, which vitiates all his conclusions. "Critical remarks," he says, "are a branch of psychological remarks" and "no special ethical or metaphysical ideas need be introduced to explain value." [40] Were it possible successfully to demonstrate this proposition the result would of course be of the greatest significance, for it would enable science to annex ethics, and ideals of conduct could be determined to the third decimal place in the laboratory.

Value, we are told, consists in the satisfaction by the individual of the broadest and most important system of positive appetencies. And we are further told that the conduct of life is throughout an attempt to organize impulses so that success is obtained for the greater number or mass of them, for the most important and the weightiest set.[41] "That organization which is the least wasteful of human possibilities . . . is the best." [42]

Whether the conclusion be acceptable or not is irrelevant for our purpose. The following remarks will examine the logic underlying the means by which the results are arrived at. We may disregard of course the use of question-begging terms like wasteful, important, and weightiest, and attend directly to a more serious matter. Has Richards *extracted* value from a psychological description, or has he injected it from without? In what sense is his value-theory psychological? Is there anything upon the face of the described situation which tells him that a wider organization or even a wider satisfaction is more valuable than a narrower one? Psychology has shown him that there are systems of impulses in conflict; it may have shown him also that some of these go under in the Darwinian struggle of daily life and are never satisfied. But it has not at all shown him that one type of satisfaction is "better" than another unless an *a priori* valuation has been injected which deems a wider organization better than a narrower. Richards, along with many men today happens to have a naturalistic and humanistic attitude towards life. But he does not *derive it* from science, as he thinks,[43] although in an entirely different sense it might have been science indeed that led him indirectly to accept such an attitude by making it impossible for him to retain a supernatural conception of the world and the other worldly values which were attached to that conception.

The upshot of this rather elementary consideration is twofold. Firstly, the necessary connection between a valuation and its psychological ground has not been shown. And secondly, the *ethical* aspect of that valuation has not been obliterated, as Richards claims it has. A prudential judgment remains—for all the apparatus of psychology brought out to save it from the stigma—just as *ethical* in character as it ever was. The connection is a preference, for which psychology gives no warrant, for psychology describes, if indeed it does, the impulses and how they behave.[44] Being a modern, and not inclined to asceticism, Richards happens to prefer vitalism to otherworldliness. But the reason for the choice of either —erroneous and foolish as it may seem to the other—depends not on the description of impulses but on standards of preference and excellence which description of impulses cannot account for, and which are logically, and very often temporally, prior to the choice made.

1935

a note on the emotion in Dewey's theory of art

1

Stated in general terms one need not quarrel with Dewey on account of the role emotion plays in his conception of the aesthetic experience.[1] But if one examines his statements on this subject carefully, difficulties will come to the surface which appear quite formidable; for he seems to oscillate between three, or at least two, quite distinct views, which cannot easily be made consistent with one another. Nor is it merely a verbal question. The verbal difficulty, arising from the use of shifting and unprecise terminology for the presentation of content which demands nicely fixed terms, is there indeed. But the writer expects to show that besides this, one encounters essential defects in conception which give rise to insuperable difficulties.

Emotion, we are told, "is not *what* is expressed" by the artist; and a few lines above this statement he informs us that "just be-

cause emotion is essential to that act of expression which produces a work of art, it is easy for inaccurate analysis to misconceive
its mode of operation and conclude that the work of art has emotion for its significant content." [2] With this point of view a large
number of students of aesthetics would find themselves today in
unqualified agreement.

And yet, in innumerable passages—too many to give here exhaustively—Dewey perplexes his attentive reader by statements
like the following: In cases of inspiration, the emotion called out
by the original material which engages the artist's interest "is modified as it comes to be attached to the new material"—that is, as
it comes to be "attached" to the artistic product which is the result
of the artist's creative activity.[3] A page following this statement
Dewey tells us that what the artist possesses over the ordinary man
"is the capacity to work a vague idea and emotion over into the
terms of some definite medium." And in the next page, he tells us
that emotion is aesthetic "when it adheres to an object formed by
an expressive act." In still another passage towards the end of the
book Dewey tells us that sounds "have the power of direct emotional expression." Elsewhere we find that music "denotes" the
accompanying phases of emotional movement. Somewhere else we
are told that emotion is "informed" in the material. Obviously the
use of words like "attached to," "adhere," "attend," "denote,"
"work into," "inform," would indicate that, in conflict with the
statement above quoted to the effect that emotion is not "*what
is expressed*," art does have at least in part, emotion for its content.

Side by side with these two views we find a third, which seems
distinct from the other two, but which, although it may be compatible with the others, increases nevertheless, on account of the
manner in which it is presented, the reader's perplexity. According
to this view emotion does not "adhere to," nor is it "formed into"
the object, but is said to be "aroused" or "evoked" by the object
in the spectator.[4]

It is not only difficult to harmonize these views with one another,
but, taken separately, they do not hold without important qualifications which Dewey forgets to make. The view that art arouses
emotion in the spectator is a popular one, and is not only generally
held by laymen but has been sanctioned until not so very long ago

by a large number of writers. And yet it is not true that all art, always, arouses emotion in every one who enters into effective commerce with it. The term 'effective' must be emphasized, for what is here asserted is that it is possible to have an *adequate* experience with art without having it arouse emotion in one. The popular view is no doubt true of almost all popular art for the people who enjoy it, and of some good art for almost everybody. But not every object of beauty arouses emotion; nor does the same object arouse it in everybody, or in the same manner always in the same person. We find in recent "experimental aesthetics" the basis for our opinion. Witness on this the experiments of Bullough and those of Myers, to mention only two. The best evidence, however, is furnished us by a type which Vernon Lee calls in her last book the "thorough-paced listener." Of about one hundred and fifty persons examined, Vernon Lee found that about one half stated "that wherever they found music completely satisfying . . . anything like . . . emotional suggestions, was excluded or reduced to utter unimportance." [5] It is not true then that art always produces or arouses emotions in everybody. What we may properly say regarding the arousal of emotions by art is that some times, some objects of art arouse emotion in some people. The three terms are variables, and whether we find the law of their behavior or not, the fact remains amply demonstrated.

The view that emotion "inheres" in the material, or is "attached," to the object, is a view to which Dewey has long been committed on the basis of his objective relativist epistemology. It is true that phenomenologically "emotions" seem to inhere somehow in the object during the aesthetic experience. But in aesthetics the term 'emotion' must be guarded most carefully from confusion, and we must therefore distinguish. What the objective relativist or any one else has the right to find *in* the object, during a distinctly aesthetic experience, are the object's objective characters—if the pleonasm be permitted—and not "emotions." We find characters like "morbid," "jovial," "dainty," "graceful," "mystic," "sombre," "tragic," "heroic," "hateful." Some of these characters bear names which we use sometimes to denote emotions. And these objective characters sometimes do arouse emotions in some spectators. But to call the objective characters emotions is to court a confusion which is utterly unnecessary.

The critical reader will find of interest to note that not only does Dewey sometimes deny that the content of art is emotion but in a number of places he tells us, quite unequivocally, that art's significant content is an "objective something." In one passage we are informed that the meanings of a work of art "present themselves as possessions of objects which are experiences." [6] The important thing about this statement is that meanings are considered possessions of objects. Again, when speaking of art objects in specific terms, Dewey discusses them as if he were indeed a thorough-paced listener. Thus in Chapter VI, where the relation of substance to form is studied, the discussion is carried on as if the content of a work of art were utterly objective. In the analysis of a passage of Wordsworth's "Prelude" the writer does not find any reference to the emotions.[7] And in the analysis of an unnamed picture, a few pages below, there is reference to masses, movement, rhythm, pattern, weight, colored areas, depth, and so forth, but no mention of emotion.[8] There are other instances further on. In his discussion of music, however, Dewey does not seem to be a thorough-paced listener; for he tells us that "sound agitates directly as a commotion of the organism itself." [9] Although these statements cannot be accepted as generally valid, we may take them as true of his own experience of music.

2

Defenders of Dewey will object. "Your criticism," they will say, "leans on the distinction between subject and object of which the whole of *Art as Experience* is so thorough and eloquent a refutation. And it is your implicit acceptance of this dichotomy which accounts for your misunderstanding of Dewey. For as he has written, 'the uniquely distinguishing feature of aesthetic experience is exactly the fact that no such distinction of self and object exists in it, since it is aesthetic in the degree in which organism and environment coöperate to institute an experience in which the two are so fully integrated that each disappears.' " [10]

To this the critic of Dewey replies that with the belief that in the aesthetic experience the difference between object and subject disappears no one will quarrel. But it is precisely *the disappearance of self in the experience* (which is a more exact phrasing of the phenomenon in question), that militates against the opinion that the object expresses emotion either in the sense of arousing it in the self or of emotion inhering in the object. An adequate understanding of this point will reveal that the difficulties we are discussing cut much deeper than may appear at first sight. For if the self disappears, emotion, if the word is used in a technical and not in the popular sense, should disappear with it; and if emotion is used as synonymous with objective characters, as sometimes it seems to be, it could not be "aroused" in a spectator whose self has disappeared. The difficulty increases when we remember that for Dewey "emotion is the conscious sign of a break, actual or impending," and that it is "the discord . . . that induces reflection." [11] But surely when the self has disappeared, when all there is is an object, no "reflection," in any appropriate meaning of the word, is possible, and the disappearance of self indicates harmony rather than break.

At this point it is necessary emphatically to assert that the disappearance of emotion does not leave us with a cold and uninteresting experience. The objective characters of things will hold our interest, and the object will appear to be bathed in a glow or feeling which is an inevitable tonality of all intense and successful experiences. But this feeling should not be, in an adequate aesthetic experience, a central object of attention. The central object of attention ought to be the object; while the delight itself is a pervasive medium, thoroughly ambient.

With this account Dewey would, no doubt, find himself in substantial agreement in many important respects. That the object defines the emotion is a very Deweyan view with which current experimental psychology concurs. Disagreement might perhaps arise on account of the distinction which this writer makes between feeling and emotion, and which Dewey seems to deny in *Art as Experience*.[12] And Dewey would not agree with the proposition that with the disappearance of the self, emotion also disappears. Yet this seems to have been Dewey's belief in 1895, and it is attested by the experiments mentioned above.[13] Of course, moments when the self disappears are not frequent even for thorough-paced listeners. What usually happens is that attention upon the object is never so intense, so rapt, that a more or less quick oscillation to the self does not take place. Complete disappearance of self is then impossible; some awareness of inward events does remain, though in the fringe; and this awareness enables the emotion to define itself through the object which aroused it. But we have good evidence that complete disappearance of the self occasionally does occur, and theory cannot leave this fact out of account.

The difficulties to which attention has been called rest on two serious oversights on Dewey's part. The first consists in his failure to distinguish between *emotion* and *feeling* and *objective characters*. The second consists in his overlooking the importance for the definition of the aesthetic experience, of the empirical researches of recent decades into the various "types of aesthetic response." This oversight leads him to read into the aesthetic experience aspects which are not universally found in it. It hardly need be pointed out that these two defects are closely interrelated. Serious, however, as they may be, it should not be forgotten that in *Art as Experience* Dewey gave us probably his best book, one which is profoundly stimulating, and from which writers have already begun to quarry unstintingly.

1938

Jordan's defense of poetry

1

With the publication of Jordan's *Essays In Criticism*,[1] a contribution of importance has been added to American aesthetics. It will
take some time and considerable labor before its quality is assayed.
But those acquainted with Jordan's previous work and with the
powerful mind back of it, are justified in expecting that this
second book in aesthetics—written, it would seem, some ten to
fifteen years after *The Aesthetic Object*—will be of the same quality as the rest of his work.

It cannot be denied, however, that the difficulties that confront
the student of Jordan are almost insuperable. Some of these inhere
in the system itself, and a few among them will be examined below. It would seem that Jordan's system lacks the degree of
perfect coherence and the diaphanous quality that the thought of
each philosopher possesses to perfection but which each finds lack-

ing in his fellows, particularly in those with whom he disagrees. Some are defects of composition; and among these, at the most superficial level, we find editorial flaws. These defects may seem trivial, until we consider the difficulty of grasping the structure of the argument.

While these difficulties can be endured with charity, this virtue is hard to summon when we have to face another type of difficulty which Jordan himself seems to throw in the reader's path with perverse gusto. There are passages in this book which will make many readers remember nostalgically the irenic anaemia of a Hume. It is a pity that Jordan on occasion did not show some charity for the smaller animals among his richly stocked zoo of *bêtes noires*. When he picks off certain contemporary critics because, as he puts it, they are philosophers in their own conceit, one admires the absolute accuracy of the marksmanship but wonders why Jordan had to use his elephant gun—he never goes hunting with anything lighter—on sparrows and chipmunks. Many of his readers will find embarrassing the peevish and uncontrolled utterance of prejudices expressed as if they constituted the articles of a new dispensation just brought down from Mount Sinai. And many will deplore Jordan's egregious intolerance towards contemporary poetry (using the term, as I shall throughout, in its widest acceptation). But it is not alone intolerance of, but perhaps even lack of acquaintance with, contemporary poetry, that one suspects Jordan of. For while one sees him liquidate such poets as Joyce, Yeats, "James (preferably Henry)," Mann, Pound, Eliot, Hemingway, Gertrude Stein, and T. E. Lawrence, one remembers all the other writers that on his grounds should have been liquidated but that Jordan lets go scott free.

I bring up this indictment because it must be faced. But I move that it be quashed. For a man who thinks of Dante, Shakespeare, Donne, Goethe, Wordsworth, Shelley and Hardy when he is theorizing about poetry, (even if he also takes *The Raven* seriously) is a man who has more than the necessary amount of empirical data from which to generalize. Let us remember in this connection that an apparent lack of acquaintance with the best art of his day did not prevent Kant from defining (was it not

Victor Basch who made the claim?) the problem of aesthetics for his successors.

2

On the common usage of the word "aesthetics" Jordan's work may not be considered a contribution to the discipline. If the aesthetician's primary responsibility is to the practical critic and through him to the artist, and if he should not allow himself to be pushed into centrifugal inquiries, Jordan is no aesthetician. For he is not interested in what Blackmur calls "executive techniques," nor in developing a comprehensive theory of the arts or even of poetry. He works away from such problems towards their philosophical foundations, inquiring into the role that poetry plays in culture and into the factors that enable it to fulfill its function. It would be proper to say that Jordan is centrally concerned with the metaphysics of value and the philosophy of culture.

Wherever we pigeonhole the inquiry no one can deny its importance. Since Matthew Arnold's day we have been looking with a feverish urgency incited by the threat of a new barbarism, for an elucidation of the value that we so deeply feel art has for man. What we need is an "apologetics" of art in the theologian's sense of the word. For reasons that cannot be gone into here the older defenses of poetry are inadequate when not actually worse than no defense at all. It would be better to leave its end unaccounted for than to degrade it, as the Chicagoans do, by defining it as pleasure, or with the early Richards, as therapy, or with the Deweyeans, who are ill concealed hedonists, as pure experience. My own high estimate of Jordan's aesthetic theory is based on the conviction that he has offered us a defense of poetry that reveals the unsubstitutable end that poetry performs in the rearing of culture, and which is therefore more serious and liberal in scope than those popular with us today, in spite of the fact that in Jordan's own exposition of his doctrine it often appears to be nothing more than a Nessus shirt.

Jordan holds that art is constitutive of culture. As I read him, this is his central thesis. This doctrine, it is well known, has its roots in idealistic philosophy; and an elaboration of the initial insight, in terms of different theoretical presuppositions, constitute one of Cassirer's contributions to contemporary philosophy. From another point of view, and considerably farther away from the salt-cellar, the present writer has sketched out a somewhat similar account of the thesis. But however phrased, and on whatever theoretical basis it is reared, I know of no attempt to answer the question as to the role art plays in culture as deep-rooted, and as broad-branched, as Jordan's. Its value is based on the bold manner in which Jordan has grasped the implications of his thesis. Audacious, perhaps foolhardy as it may seem to some, and absurd and even perverse as it will seem to others, Jordan seeks to demonstrate that poetry "is literally the creator and legislator for the real world" (44).[2]

In order to elucidate his theory Jordan points out that the primary function of language is not to communicate meanings but to constitute objects. The objects so constituted are not *about* reality but are themselves reality, are a real world of objects that is sufficient unto itself and which makes up the world of culture.

> Man sought to give form to his world, and thus to infuse his words with meaning, long before he was curious to understand it, and this urge to form was the largest determinant in the development of language. . . . His first making instrument was his words in any case, and what he made with them first was the world of objects about him. (43).

And some pages later:

> The substance, stuff, of art is not merely one of the realities along with that of religion, science, industry, etc., but reality itself. And it is reality in intelligible form, reality made intelligible by the form that art imposes upon it. Art is not about experience, not about life, not about nature, not about God. It is concerned with a reality that gives to experience, life, nature, and God whatever substance they have, and it has its existence upon a higher plane of being than these. Its substance matter is reality itself; its specific or individualizing relation to experience, life, nature, and God is that it is the synthetic identification of all these in a world, a universe to which it gives constitution and form and so substance (79).

Jordan is not satisfied to speak of the constitutive function of language in general terms. In *The Aesthetic Object* he attempted a deduction of the *a priori* forms of functions of thought through which the elementary color-tone or feeling content of experience is transformed into objects. These forms are the categories of value. The color-tone content is for Jordan the stuff or feeling which poetry structures into its objects. In the present volume no formalistic "deduction" is attempted and we are not given tables of categories, as in the earlier book, but essentially the same problem is faced: How does poetry come into being and out of what is it made up. The imagination does not create out of its own absolute parthenogenetic spontaneity, and the process should be analyzed if the thesis is to deserve serious consideration.

3

Jordan's first job is to make clear how poetry creates reality. It is the imagination that achieves the synthesis through its organon, metaphor; and the imagination derives the materials with which to make reality from the medium in which it lives. About it lies a content of unlimited variety, from which the imagination gathers free of the principle of contradiction, and which it synthesizes into reality. The stuff it gathers has, prior to its synthesis, no apprehensible form; it is feeling or quality, as yet unordered and undesigned. "In the beginning was the Word" (44). But this does not mean that words or language created man who uttered the word which creates the world—a thesis which could be called second order nonsense. Nor does it mean that until any one man spoke there was no world for him. At any time in history there is a constituted world of culture, populous with all sorts of objects and rooted in a physical world that makes it possible. But the world, such as it is for us—the world of culture—has in the order of history no less than in that of logic, as its fundamental and pristine principle, the creative activity of language that began it and now keeps it going.

Through the double role it plays, as the stuff of the world and of experience, "feeling," or "quality," mediates between both and gives the mind immediate grasp of reality. The synthesis thus accomplished by language is the basis for the distinction between aesthetic objects and other kinds of objects—moral, religious, and practical. For the aesthetic mode of apprehension

> mind and its object are one, in accordance with the principle of analogical identity, and in their oneness they cease to be *as* mind and object; and this indicates the basic condition of art. Mind disappears and is consummated in the life of the aesthetic object. . . . The identity of mind and object in the Individual indicates also the bounds of 'the arts.' All the arts thus are activities in which 'mind' comes to completeness and fulfillment and realization and so annulment as mere mind in an appropriate object, or activities in which that which is quantitatively objective and unformed mere matter is informed by the suffusion of it by the mind operating as the principle of creative agency. This is the primordial act of assertion. The result in every case is the identification of mind and object and the disappearance of both as such and as particular, so that this identity, as the form of the Individual, becomes the principle of discrimination and criticism for all practice. The ultimate standard for both thought and action is thus the aesthetic, since the aesthetic principle is the law of the creative act (51).

It is this objectivity, which is the result of the annulment of mind, that defines the aesthetic experience in which the poem is present to us immediately, or, as I phrase it, self-sufficiently and intransitively. A poem, Jordan tells us, "does not have meaning." But Jordan adds, "it is meaning" (57). A sunset, an aesthetic object, *asserts*.

> The sunset does not address itself *to me*, nor does it 'express' itself to or for any being whose claim to its recognition lies only in the consciousness of it as a sunset. The sunset has no purposes, no ends; its design, both as determinative of its form and as delimitative of its intention, is its own constitution and the continuity of that constitution with the design of the universe. It asserts its being to itself and to the world that it, together with other such, constitutes, and in that assertion it is. It creates itself an object, and this object is what it means and all it means. This does not mean that it creates an object for itself, an object other than itself which it proposes to 'mean' . . . (20-21).

This is so important that it bears reiteration. The meaning of the word "assertion" ought to be clear from this quotation; others employ for the same purpose the word "revelation." Through the term, Jordan intends to convey, it would seem, that the aesthetic object, the poem, refers to nothing outside itself, does not "communicate," is reflexive in meaning, or, as I put it, that the poem, when beheld intransitively as poem, and not as something else, means what it is and is all that it means. That this is a distinct mode of experience and one we sometimes enjoy, at least in degree, it is too late to question. That it ought to be called "the aesthetic" is a purely verbal matter. Whatever we choose to call it, it is still structurally different from the moral, the religious and the cognitive. What is doubtful is whether anyone has as yet done more than isolate it; whether anyone has analyzed it successfully. Jordan's explanation, as we have seen, adds up to the claim that the poem is reality, but I shall try to show below that this claim, for all the irrefragable truth that it expresses, cannot be accepted because of all the puzzles which it brings in its train and that Jordan does not resolve satisfactorily. In any case, the assertion that the poem does not refer beyond itself, that if beheld intransitively it is its own meaning and means what it is, marks a basic distinction between things that are and things that are not aesthetic. If we do not draw it we commit ourselves, in our relations to art, to sheer sentimentality; art becomes referential or associative and in either case ceases to control our attention. In practice this means that we substitute our own irresponsibly constructed objects for the carefully structured and organically related self-sufficiency of the object the artist presents us with.[3]

But those who assert the self-sufficiency or intransitivity of art often overlook its complexities. The aesthetician cannot deny that the mind cannot grasp the object if it is a Lockean empty tablet, a simple reflecting mirror. Whatever Jordan is, he is not simplistic; he asserts that words have "cosmic implications." He tells us that

the relevance of words that have meaning is to a system of objects and relations and qualities, and it is only through these objects and relations and qualities, considered as objective and independent of mind, that the meaning of a word is to be determined (16).

But he also tells us that words "are elementary constituents of the system of the nature of things" (16); that words are not about objects but are the objects we contemplate.

It is in the light of this complex notion of the self-sufficiency and intransitivity of poetry that we must interpret many passages that otherwise seem unintelligible if not altogether silly in *Essays*, of which the following is a representative sample:

> "The poem constructs itself, or *is* through all eternity, and dictates to the poet the form for which it demands assertion, and it chooses the words and phrases and 'conceits' from out of the qualities of its own design" (24).[4]

4

To the unqualified realist, whether scientist or philosopher, indeed to those who have utterly forgotten certain fundamental insights of the idealists, the notion that the poet "creates" culture must seem utter nonsense. The realist accepts Mario Pei's conviction that the fundamental function of language is to transfer meaning; and this in turn involves the belief that meanings are already there waiting to be transferred—as leaves might be found in the backyard in Autumn, waiting to be raked into the compost heap. This conception of language is in turn grounded on a naïvely realistic epistemology, according to which the organization of the world in which we live—the world of culture, through whose forms we seek to penetrate beyond it to the world which is prior to culture and makes culture possible—is determined wholly by the world itself: we accept the world as it is in itself nor do we contribute anything to its definition in apprehension.

Today, however, we need not depend entirely on idealistic philosophers for grounds on which to question these realistic assumptions. Psychologists and ethnolinguists have given us *prima facie* evidence for the plausibility of the idealistic thesis. Empirical science cannot "prove" the thesis; that could only be done by means of a transcendental deduction. But scientists can present us with data that pose the problem, thus indicating that the claims of the idealists do not arise entirely out of idle speculations.[5]

Jordan, however, working at the foundations, faces problems the ethnolinguists do not even suspect. Thus he tells us that words employed in their primary functions are not *about* objects, but that they are *about* objects when they refer to scientific or moral objects; for the scientific objects are abstractions while moral objects have to be realized through action, and are thus never as fully real as the objects of poetry. If this interpretation is correct, Jordan is a realist in epistemology, not a phenomenalist, and his problem is to harmonize the idealist principle of the constitutive role of the knowledge process with objectivity, or to qualify his realism by the idealist principle. This, along perhaps with a manner of exposition that shifts the burden of grasping his thought chiefly on the reader, is the reason that, while he tells us that poetry is literally the creator of the world of culture, he also tells us the reality created by the poet obtains from beyond itself the stuff—the feeling or color-tone or texture or quality, as it is in various contexts variously characterized—to which the poem gives form and thus reality. The world of art

> is not a figment or fiction of the imagination, although it is created by it; but is a discovery by the reason of what is there in reality. But is it the world of sense? If so, sense must itself relate to art only as a presupposition. . . . Such it is: sense is the presupposition of experience, the presupposition of substant matter, that by which, as basic medium and background or *Urgrund*, the world of time and space is transformed into the concrete materials of art (108).

There are many passages that can be cited to show that Jordan is seriously asserting the seeming paradox that mind both creates and discovers reality. References to passages in which he tells us that the poem creates reality have already been given. Let us look at a few of the statements in which he asserts that the poem discovers reality. He tells us that a metaphor "is . . . an identic (sic) replica in language forms of a real object . . ." (133; see also 110 and 137). In this passage Jordan not only distinguishes the poem from what the poem is about—the realities of which the poem is a replica or which it contemplates—but by calling them *realities*, he is saying that they are not constituted by the poem.

I agree with Jordan that an aesthetic which is not looking for facile verbal consistency, one that stubbornly sticks by the facts no matter how self-contradictory they may appear, will assert the two propositions Jordan asserts: the poet creates reality, or as he would probably prefer, reality is created in the poem, and the poet or poem discovers reality. But faced with a paradox so poignant we have a right to ask our writer either that he give us reasons that will convince us that the paradox is not generated by his interpretation of the data, or that he do more than exhibit it helplessly, that he attempt to resolve it. I do not believe Jordan would take the first way out. I believe he wants to solve the difficulty and in the book we find tantalizing hints as to how he would go about it. What they add up to, so far as I can discover, is that the stuff or texture or quality which is external to the poem comes into the poem by the principle of analogical identity, and thus, it seems, mediates between an existent world and the reality of poetry. But this solution presents, in turn, a number of serious difficulties for the reader, one of which I shall state succinctly: I refer to the fact that this principle of analogical identity is conceived and employed by Jordan in a prodigiously protean fashion, and from its manifold uses and the several attempts at definition of it which we find in the text—as well as in *The Aesthetic Object* where it appears under several aliases—it is not possible to get a clear enough notion of what is intended by it.

Part of the difficulty is terminological. What Jordan seems to mean is that other objects of culture are not as real as the poem because not as fully realized but are "mere existents." In several places Jordan seems to have in mind some sort of contrast between "reality" and "existence," and at least in one passage, between reality, existence, and actuality (215, 234). If my reading is correct, the "reality" of poetry includes existence (202). But if this is the case, the solution is not adequate, and for two reasons: a), the term "existence" is not explicitly defined, and one is left to infer its meaning from texts that are anything but luminous; and b), we are left wondering about the ontological status of objects that lack "reality" and are mere existents. The problem is further complicated by the fact that not only does art require matter or stuff that is not created by the poet and as to whose status one is in the dark; but that "form" which structures the matter and en-

dows it with reality, is not given by the words or through the
synthesizing act of the imagination but is found in things (248).
The stuff of reality is feeling, what lifts feeling to the plane of
reality is form. But if form is in things, how can the creative act
of the poet give them reality? How can art be literally the creator?

However we manage to dispose of this puzzle, Jordan is emphatic
in his insistence that the activity of the imagination is "cognitive"
in the sense that its processes are accomplished by reason, and
that the object created is known "as distinct in nature and character by virtue of its relational structure, from the object of mere
sense" (91). The organon of the imagination is "metaphor," but
this word is not employed by Jordan in its ordinary sense, to refer
to a figure of speech wherein a word or phrase denoting one object or idea is applied to another in order to suggest a likeness. He
uses it to designate the organon through which the imagination
creates reality. It is "the formulation in words of the design of an
object as that design is implicit in a complex of mutually appropriate qualities" (112); and a few pages later we are told that a
metaphor is "the assertion of an individuality; the assertion by
which a complex of real quality becomes an individual or asserts
itself as real" (117; also 115, 124, 125, 361, among others). It
would seem therefore that "poem" and "metaphor" refer to different aspects of the same activity. The poem is the language object,
as synthesized, out of circumstantial qualities, by the agent, the
free imagination, and "metaphor" refers to the means or organon
employed by the agent to bring about the synthesis.

5

But at this point, one reader at least is forced to come to grips
with an embarrassing perplexity. For Jordan maintains two propositions whose compatibility is not self-evident: the imagination
operates freely (88), and the imagination has its own logic (101-
102). The perplexity is intensified when we notice that he also
maintains that the activity of the imagination is the activity of
reason in one of its modes, and is therefore "cognitive" in essence.
To explore this puzzle, let us first note that in the narrow sense in
which in these post-positivist days we have become habituated to

using the term "cognitive," the activity of the imagination is not
cognitive. For we cannot "verify" the object that the imagination
produces by comparing it with anything that exists external to it,
since Jordan, as we have seen, emphatically asserts that the object
of the imagination is "the one real . . . object," that the imagination is "literally the creator and legislator for the real world." What
then can "cognitive" mean? It means, it would seem, that the
object is grasped as real, as objective, and that in coming to be it
obeys the logic of the imagination, which latter is in turn a function of reason. But if the imagination obeys its own logic, how
can we say that in creating the poem, it does so freely? What
Jordan seems to mean is that it is free from the laws which govern
scientific and speculative or philosophic knowing. In the terminology of the earlier *The Aesthetic Object* the "contemplative" function of reason is distinct from, and independent of, the "cognitive"
function. In the terminology of *Essays* the "imagination" functions in its own way, not dictated to by the logic of science or
the logic of metaphysics (101-102, 139-140). Doubtless this is
what he means when he says, as he does several times throughout
Essays, that the poem writes itself (20, 24, 29, 36, 347, and many
others). There is more than an echo here of the Socrates of the
Ion. And in the context, it is not an unreasonable way to put it.
In a review of Reginald Pound's *Arnold Bennett*, we have been
recently told that Bennett boasted that he "never let a character
get the whip-hand of [him]." What Jordan is saying is that unless
a writer lets the poem get the whip-hand of him, he is no poet
and the result is not poetry.

   In the broad sense in which Jordan uses "cognitive," the poetic
activity can legitimately be called cognitive. But Jordan would
have been more enlightening and more convincing if he had given
us at least a sketch of the rules and devices of the logic of the
imagination. What are the laws, principles, regulative operations,
formulable processes, which guide the work of the imagination?
One need not be an Aristotle, a Mill, or a Boole, to know that
there is a logic of reasoning or knowing, in the ordinary sense of
these words. But Jordan does not offer us anything to compare
with these rules and techniques. All he gives us are general considerations about the principle of analogical identity—as regards

which Professor Mack gives the impression in his "Introduction"
that it is used by Jordan univocally; but as I have already observed, that is not the case. Therefore it is not easy to define this
important principle from the context, by discovering the uses he
makes of it. Its meaning seems as variable as the proverbial
chameleon's color. The long quotation which follows is the most
extended discussion given by Jordan of the nature of the logic of
the imagination:

> There is, then, a logic of the values of imaginative thought in art
> just as there is a logic of the values of speculative thought in philoso-
> phy and a logic of the values of reflective thought in science. Each
> issues in its specialized form of knowledge: the logic of speculative
> thought issues in pure theoretical formulations of the principles
> upon which or in accordance with which reality is constituted: the
> logic of reflective thought issues in generalizations which state the
> various forms of the 'law' of averages which governs the rules of
> practice and technique in every field; the logic of imaginative
> thought legislates the law by which all value structures are created
> and all value substance is given form. Each logic has its organon, a
> unified system of concepts which mediates the approach to reality
> in that aspect of reality which it contemplates: the logic of specula-
> tive thought has its system of the categories all integrated within the
> principle of the syllogism; the logic of reflective thought has its
> system of rules integrated within the 'law' of causation and the
> methodology of induction; and the logic of imaginative thought has
> its system of concepts integrated within the law of analogical identity
> and expressed in metaphor. Metaphor therefore has the same status
> in the function of imaginative thought that the syllogism has in the
> functions of speculative thought and that the inductive methodology
> has in reflective thought. The logic of speculative thought has its
> principle of contradiction; the logic of reflective thought has its prin-
> ciple of causation (in cultural connections generally stated in sub-
> jective terms as the principle of purpose); the logic of imaginative
> thought has its principle of analogical identity (139-140).

I am not raising the more difficult questions which will occur
to the professional philosopher when he reads this passage. I am
asking only the easiest and most obvious question: If metaphor
has the same status in the function of imaginative thought that the
syllogism has in the functions of speculative thought, why can't

we be given its rules, so that when a poet uses metaphor wrongly we can point out to him his error as we point out his to the man who tries to make his syllogism work on four terms or forgets to distribute its middle at least once?

Grounds are not lacking to assure us that the reason aestheticians cannot give us a sample of "the logic of the imagination" is that the imagination of the creative artist works in a genuinely free fashion, in the sense at least that it obeys no laws which can be inducted from extant works of art. In spite of this—be it noted in passing—the critic still can find ground for his judgments, not in inductive laws formulating the principles governing past accomplishments, but in a grasp (an Aristotelian induction, so to put it) of the intention of the work as gathered by the critic from the work itself. In any case "the logic of the creative imagination," is a term whose meaning Jordan does not succeed in conveying, since it is used as a metaphor whose tenor he cannot exhibit. The most important difference between the so-called logic of the imagination and ordinary logic lies of course in the fact that the former lacks the normative force of the latter. I do not know before I enter the classroom what thesis a student will defend but I know that if he fails to distribute his middle he is wrong. There are no rules in poetry that can be gathered from past accomplishments and can be applied in the same manner to future ones. If I approach the work of D. H. Lawrence with principles of construction gathered from the work of Jane Austen or Henry James it is not Lawrence I condemn but myself. The history of art is the history of a succession of triumphant nose-thumbings by artists at the rules of the critics and the grammarians. The work of each poet has its own logic, and frequently the logic of the work of youth is abandoned in the poet's maturity. The logic of Shakespeare's imagination is not that of Marlowe's or Jonson's; nor is it the logic of the Spanish theatre of the Golden Age. If I approach *Ulysses* with expectations derived from *Dubliners* I deprive myself, not Joyce.

This question is not merely theoretical; it has practical implications of great moment, for it is directly related to the question as to the basis for criticism. And while it is necessary to make the stubborn attempt to discover the objective basis of criticism rather than seek exclusively, as skeptics and nihilists do, for its subjective and idiosyncratic components, the search must be carried on with great circumspection. For back of facile discourse about the logic of the imagination and the principle or principles of metaphor, one can all too frequently sense lurking the presence of a dogmatic will disguised in the robes of Reason, which uses the logic of art as the commissar uses his forty-five, to liquidate those works that it does not happen, for some idiotic reason or another, to approve of.

6

The realist who doubts that language is constitutive of the world points out, adapting to our purposes a recent phrase of Charles Hartshorne, that language was not invented and preserved primarily by artists but by the more agile and "practical" individuals. Nor can it be denied that the constitutive theory seems absurd to common sense. How can we reply to this realistic objection? Let us first observe that, whether we call those who employ language in its constitutive function "poets" or anything else, does not make any substantial difference. This is why it was important to point out that the constitutive hypothesis is not one which has been fathered by idealistic philosophers alone. However, the common sense argument cannot easily be dismissed. Are we then faced with a contradiction? No, if we accept a distinction which Jordan does not employ, or at least does not explicitly elucidate, and without which great confusion can come about. We must distinguish, on the one hand, between the self-conscious and specialized making of poetry that we are acquainted with in our society, the activity, that is, of the poet as fine artist, and on the other the pervasive, continuous, and to some degree unconscious use of language in its primary or constitutive level, although not employed in activities which are, or are recognized to be, the specialized activities through which the self conscious poet creates his poem.

For Jordan's thesis does not commit him to argue that it is the self conscious, specialized poet—the poet in the narrower sense—who creates culture through the constitutive use of language. All it requires of him is that. he distinguish between the primary or fundamental or constitutive use of language and the secondary or practical use, whose function is communication. Nor does it require that he conceive of the constitutive function as earlier in time. Jordan suggests that it is "earlier," but this claim is not essential to his argument. We can say that where there are animals discovering values, and embodying them in institutions, and thus creating culture, these animals are featherless bipeds, and they use language constitutively, and where there are such bipeds, using language in this manner, there a human culture is recognizable. In the narrow sense of "poetry," it need not be one of the activities of the group, although Franz Boas maintains that actually art is an activity of all known primitive groups. But for Jordan's thesis Boas' claim is not essential.

The distinction between the broad and the narrow sense of poetry is implied, I noted above, by Jordan. But he does no more than adumbrate it and his failure to elucidate it adequately leaves us with a constellation of problems on which the reader would like to have much more light than he gets. I am not suggesting, therefore, that the failure to draw the distinction is an insuperable difficulty. It could easily be obviated along lines already intimated in the preceding paragraphs. And one defending Jordan could point out that the search for the conditions which lead to the growth of poetry in the narrow sense, is a task for the historian and for the social scientist. But I do mean to suggest that the failure to draw the distinction explicitly is one factor that adds to the reader's trouble in digesting a book which is difficult enough.

7

But if it is true that poetry is literally the creator of the world of culture, this fact is not easy to harmonize with the conception of poetry put forth in Chapter IV, entitled "Poetry and the Stability of Culture." For in this chapter, it turns out, the poet no longer creates the real world, but (and I am following the text here almost word for word) all he does is to use the philosopher's "product," the philosopher's "ideas" and polish them and refine them and adopt them to the generality of men. The philosopher does not have command of the devices whereby the ideas may be presented to men in the mass. It is the task of the literary artist, whose genius is that of the technician, and his activity the expert handling of formal and methodological devices in the shaping of materials furnished him, to translate ideas into the language of men (161-162).

This seems to be a far cry from the exalted position of the poet as creator of and legislator for the world of culture. And a number of observations are in order. The first is a relatively unimportant one. Speaking of Dante and Milton, Jordan tells us that "it is not the fault of either that the picture of the world he presented was incorrect and distorted and false. They had been given false ideas to work with, but that did not prevent that they both created significant imaginative forms for the mass of men" (161). But if the poet has to work with the ideas given him, and if his genius is that of technician, and his activity is the expert handling of materials furnished him, how can we blame Hemingway, or Joyce, or "James (preferably Henry)" or "poor Yeats"? The Swiftian wrath of Jordan should have been reserved for the philosophers—who are responsible for giving our poets the wrong ideas. It is true that Jordan has castigated his colleagues in this and other of his books. But if Jordan is right he should address to them his whole gravamen. If you hire a man to design and build a house for you with the materials you give him, you cannot blame him for using rotten timbers and mortar that crumbles when it dries, if that is what you provided him with. You can blame him for the design he employed. But it is not on formalistic grounds that Jordan criticizes the poets. For all the drumhead justice with which he disposes of contemporary literature, he acknowledges he is not competent to do the critic's job of examining executive techniques, and his indictments are all based on the fact that "the bulk of recent literature" is an attempt "to build a structure of filthy particulars, filthy, however decently refined in presentation" (155). But isn't all the artist can do, according to Chapter IV, to refine his particulars in presentation?

It would seem, moreover, that it is not merely for "ideas" that Jordan would have the artist go to the philosopher, but for the typical elaboration these may be given. Speaking of the subjectivity of modern literature and of the way in which it is excessively preoccupied with love, Jordan writes:

"Since no state of mind is capable of universality, being always particular, the attempt to universalize love results in a legion of abstractions and falsifications. The proper objectification of love, and the
only manifestation of it that is capable of aesthetic expression, is
the family as a cultural object. The Holy Family is the type; but no
form can be given to the mere psychological feeling of love" (155).

The poet's genius is that of technician—so long as he objectifies
love in the proper manner. Sapho, Catullus, the Provençals, Boc-
caccio, the Arcipreste de Hita, the Shakespeare of the sonnets, his
fellow Elizabethans, Swift, the author of *Lady Chatterly*, the
writer of *Remembrance of Things Past*, and that of *The Counter-
feiters*—bring the brooms and let us sweep the whole mess into
the garbage pail where we have already thrown Yeats, Joyce, James
and "the bulk of the moderns." If a poet is going to sing of love,
let him sing of Mary and Joseph and the Child, or of variants in
modern dress of Mary, Joseph and the Child, on penalty of liquida-
tion in the name of the philosophy of Jordan.

This point, however, is a relatively minor one. For if the poet
cannot let his will get the whip-hand of his poem, neither can he
let the philosopher, and he cannot because, as Jordan so truly remarks, the poem is not written by the poet, (and *a fortiori*, least
of all by a philosopher), "but writes itself by decree of the universe" (347). But minor as is this point, it has its source in what
I take to be a radical inconsistency in Jordan's doctrine on which
it is essential to touch, however hurriedly. That the poet would be
advised to get his ideas from the philosopher is not only inconsistent with Jordan's profound analysis of the manner in which
the imagination works freely to create objects, and creates the
world of culture, but it also suggests that the adviser has failed
to grasp the limitations of philosophy *vis-à-vis* his own view of the
function of poetry. The poet has his own limitations, and one of
them is that, *qua* poet, he has no way of telling "ideas" from
verbiage. If the philosopher wants to give him—as the Spaniards
say—cat for hare, he takes it innocently and adds it to his pot.
But the reason for this is that he takes ideas as he takes experience,
life, nature and God. As regards this tetrad, Jordan clearly shows
that they are not the reality the poetic imagination synthesizes but

are used by the poet "in some way and in some sense and to some degree and are all to be exhibited in form and design by the techniques of art" (288). One could go farther. "Ideas" have a way of often lying heavy in the artist's mind, like the stones in the wolf's belly in the fairy tale, and not feeding him. When they do feed him they do so in a peculiar way. For what he is interested in is not "the truth" of the philosopher but the "reality," in Jordan's term and, I believe, in his sense, of the object of his imaginative synthesis. If "the truth" of the philosopher were the reality or "the truth" of the poet, why did he have to distinguish them and assign its own proper logic to each, as we have seen he did? To reverse the order and to suggest to the poet that he go to the philosopher for ideas is to give up the thesis as to the constitutive role of mind or language in the creation of the world of culture. Nor can these observations be set aside because in one long passage (175 ff.) Jordan collapses the functions of the philosopher and the prophet into those of the poet and constructs a composite man who has all the virtues of the three and none of their limitations. Even if poets, to the extent that they are poets, were also prophets and philosophers—a doctrine that can only be accepted by straining to the maximum the coefficient of elasticity of these terms— it would still be necessary for Jordan and everybody else seriously interested in the questions that he discusses in his book to distinguish in mind if not separate in fact the roles of each.

There are many other comments, criticisms, qualifications, one could make about this forbidding and challenging book. I have said nothing about Jordan's criticism of the place given "experience" in modern thought, his behavioristic discussion of genius, his remarks on taste, and his analysis of the relation of morality to poetry. Other critics would have treated, of course, the place of "objectivity" in Jordan's aesthetics differently than I have done. There is much left to be said, all of which must be left to others or to the writer at some future date. I doubt, however, whether any future criticism by whomever undertaken, if it is serious, could manage to dismiss the tremendous achievement of Jordan's contribution.

1954

aesthetics and theory of signs[1]

1

It happens sometimes that a writer fathers a theory that later he would like to disown. If I may judge by some casual remarks made in the midst of a crowded party, something like this seems to be the case with C. W. Morris in respect to his contribution to aesthetics. It is possible that because of the noise and the milling of guests, I may have misunderstood him; but I gathered the impression that Morris is today highly amused by the seriousness with which his paper on aesthetics has been taken by literary critics and men to whom he refers as "humanists." But it is easier to abandon an illegitimate baby in an alley than to disembarrass ourselves from the children of our brains, once we have acknowledged them in print. Whatever his present attitude towards it, Morris' paper on aesthetics has remained to plague us with its specious resolutions of extremely difficult problems. It has been the object of numerous objections and adverse criticisms. But for all the refutations of which it has been the object, like an un- buried burro that is exposed to every shift of wind, it effectively interferes with our business as aestheticians. This is my excuse for my attempt to give it decent burial.[2]

Morris acknowledges that what he did was translate the language of Dewey's aesthetics into the terminology of Peirce's analysis of signs.[3] But Morris reduced Peirce's classification to the distinction between aesthetic icon and non-icon. He further modified Peirce by injecting into the latter's analysis a behaviorism which, I sus- pect, Peirce would not have found acceptable; and he added a claim about the beneficial results he anticipated if we applied the theory of signs to the problems of art (149-150, also 144, 147). These hopes have not been realized. The failure must be traced to the fact that in spite of Morris' promotional drive in favor of his ideas, no philosopher has undertaken to develop semiotic aesthetics beyond the original sketchy and programmatic stage at which Mor- ris left it. But it must also be traced to the fact that semiotics is not a tool for empirical investigation and the problems of aesthetics are fundamentally empirical problems.

Although the theory and the terminology of semiotics is by now fairly well known I hope it is not deemed impertinent if I review it briefly. For semiotics, the reader or listener of a poem becomes the interpreter of a system of iconic sign vehicles which is the poem. The term "iconic sign vehicle" refers to a system of signs which is like, or has properties in common with, what it denotes or designates (136). Since Morris is—or in the paper under consid- eration was—an objective relativist, the aesthetic object is said to emerge from the transaction between the physical object and the spectator; translating into semiotic terms, the object of art emerges from the transaction between the iconic sign vehicle and the in- terpreter. Morris tells us also that the iconic signs denote or designate values which are conveyed by the vehicle because it is an iconic sign. He does not include meanings, but this is a relatively minor defect. When the iconic sign vehicle refers the interpreter to a class that has no actual members, the latter, the non-existent members, are called "designata." But the notion of designation is used by Morris both in a wide and in a narrow sense. In the wide sense the term refers to the semiotic process in general—the process through which someone takes account of something through something else functioning as sign. In this sense "designatum" refers, therefore, to the members of a class whether that class has members or not.[4] This fact, coupled with the desire to avoid clumsiness of expression, leads me to employ the term "designatum" on many occasions when preciseness of diction would call for writing sometimes "designatum or denotatum," and sometimes "designatum and denotatum." When the reader of the poem, then, apprehends an iconic sign, "he apprehends directly what is designated . . . put in other terms, every iconic sign has its own sign vehicle among its denotata" (136). But, Morris adds, we must draw a distinction, because the definition of iconic sign just given includes not only aesthetic but other objects, like maps and photographs and scientific models. The aesthetic object differs from these in that its designatum is a value (138-9). Morris recognizes that the aesthetic object is made up in part of "secondary signs" which are non-iconic, and refer to other signs in the object, thus building up a complex iconic sign. But the object of aesthetic apprehension is at least in part iconic. Morris says:

> What is taken account of through the complex esthetic sign is thus a complex value property which is partially indicated by the value properties of various component sign vehicles, other signs of nonesthetic and even non-iconic sort serving as secondary symbolism to build up the esthetic sign vehicle . . . (139).

As a result Morris concludes that:

> In esthetic perception value properties are taken account of both mediately and immediately: mediately in that they are presented by signs, immediately in that the sign vehicles used embody in themselves in varying degrees the value properties which they present. In such perception the sign vehicle is not simply used as an instrument to direct the interpreter to some other object with the property in question, nor as an occasion for contemplation in reverie of the indicated value; esthetic perception, as perception, is focused upon objects, and it discerns—even if only partially—in the very object itself that which the object signifies. In this process there is a consummation because the object does embody the value it signifies, but

the consummation is in another sense incomplete, since it is mediated by signs, and often by signs, which are not themselves iconic of, or are only partially iconic of, what they signify—and the work of art, as a whole, still remains a sign (139).

2

Morris informs the reader that semiotic aesthetics is not open to the criticism that has been made against theories of imitation. He tells us that

> . . . if art is itself a sign, then by definition it has a designatum. Such a doctrine seems to run foul of the oppositions which theories of 'imitation' or 'representation' in esthetics have encountered (140).

The central opposition that these theories have encountered is that they cannot do justice to the creative activity of the artist. Morris is aware of this and tells us a page further on:

> It may be added that the recognition that signs may be built up which have no denotata (or none other than their own sign vehicles in case the sign is iconic), frees the artist . . . from the literal representation of the actual world which such a semiotically grounded esthetics might at first suggest; the creativity of the artist is fully protected (141).

Our task is defined for us by these two statements. We must inquire whether semiotic aesthetics succeeds in avoiding the criticisms to which theories of imitation have been subjected and whether the creativity of the artist is fully protected. But the second question will hardly engage our extended interest, since it will have already been answered by implication in the answer to the first. The discussion of the first will be carried on in terms of painting and poetry chiefly, instancing now one and now the other, as convenience dictates. But what is said for either art holds, with appropriate changes, for all of them.

It will make our work easier if we begin by considering the objection that has been brought up against the theory of imitation —or at least the objection that in my opinion needs be pressed against it. But note first that I speak of the theory in the singular.

If the purpose of writing on aesthetics were that it allowed one to exhibit his learning, I would have to distinguish among the various versions of the theory of imitation that we find in the history of criticism and of aesthetics. But since the purpose is to get at the truth, it is proper that I speak of the theory in the singular, since I refer only to that which all properly called theories of imitation have in common; namely, that what the work of art is about (or as I call it, its object) is something that exists independently of the means which exhibits it. The theory of imitation is wrong on at least two counts 1), the work of art gives evidence of novelty, originality, or freshness, which aspect constitutes the addition the artist makes to the forms and the matter he takes from experience. Creativity, therefore, is no mere making, but a special kind of making that deserves its special name, unless we are to obfuscate important distinctions; 2), the object of the work of art can only be exhibited with adequacy *in* and *through* the work itself, and any paraphrase or rendition of it outside the work itself involves loss to the object and in this respect, the destruction of the work itself.

If this is true, it is not the literalness of the representation that the artist achieves that makes his work an imitation, since in the sense that a thing is a work of art it is not a representation and in the sense that it is a representation, whether literal or not, it is not a work of art.[5] There are works of art which, considered as representations or imitations, are more literal than others, but that are nevertheless better works of art than the stereotypes of non-representational works that are exhibited by the hundred in the galleries of our large cities. A Chardin, a Courbet, a Dutch portrait or genre picture, can be and often is a better painting than the imitations of cubism and later art styles which are the stock product of our studios.

If it is not the literalness of representation that a theory must avoid endorsing in order to distinguish itself from the theory of imitation, what is it? The answer has already been given: It must not assume, as the semiotic theory does, that the designatum of a painting can be apprehended both by means of the painting and also independently of the painting.

What Morris seems to mean is that we can do both. This cannot

be shown by means of a single quotation, however extended, but
must be gathered from the context of the total discussion. The
closest it comes to explicit expression is in a footnote that Morris
attaches to a sentence already quoted. We are told that "the
painted man is not fully a man and all that the picture designates
is not there in the picture for inspection" (136). But if it is not in
the picture but elsewhere, it is not on the picture that we must
attend, and the picture is only a representation or a mere mnemonic
device. It is of course true that the painted man is not an actual
man. But in a much more important sense the statement is false,
since the painted man is not *about* an existing man, but is something utterly different from one, in spite of the traits which the
painted man may happen to have in common with a certain actual
man or number of men. The statement is still false for a more important reason: the object of the painting, which is revealed in
and through the medium, is fully there for direct inspection and is
nowhere else but there; and if it is not fully there, the painting is
not an aesthetic object but an associational or mnemonic device or
an indexical sign. Morris is among those who agree with a commonplace of contemporary aesthetics that holds that the picture is
not a springboard to something else (136-137). It is not easy to see
how he can maintain this and hold at the same time the semiotic
theory.

That Morris believes that the designatum of the work of art can
be apprehended independently of the icon vehicle which reveals it
in art can also be shown by examination of a section of his paper
entitled "Esthetic Generality" (140). Morris faces the question
that arises from the fact that if the work of art has a value designatum, it has a semantic dimension, and the value which it designates must exist independently of the poem. Morris is emphatic in
his recognition that the "semantical dimension cannot be denied,"
for if the object of art is an iconic sign it has designata. Yet he
holds that his is not a theory of imitation, because the value designata do not exist outside of the work in the manner in which they
are iconically designated in it. But who ever claimed they did? Not
even the most realistic imitationist would claim that the object
imitated by the work of art is the same as the object of imitation.
However, value designata do exist, and we have to ask, How do

they exist? Morris tells us that the artist builds up "elaborate sign structures the elements of which may be suffused with the values of many things, and yet which as a whole present a value complex which has no realization elsewhere. . . ." (141). Verbal clarifiers will ask, and with justice, What can it mean to say that the elements of things are suffused with values? I leave Morris to their mercy as regards this matter, in order to consider another point: True that Morris tells us that as wholes value complexes have no realization, but does he not assert that their components have it? The unicorn that the artist paints need not actually exist; but the defender of imitation will remind us that its horn and its slender beauty and its equine form and its strength and fleetness exist as parts of other animals. In other words, it is difficult to see the difference between the iconic theory and the theory of imitation since Morris holds that in building up the sign structure which is the painted unicorn what the artist does is to imitate parts of two or more animals and to suffuse his imitation with the values possessed by the animals he imitated, adding to the picture, perhaps, other values—the gentleness, let us say, he once saw in the eyes of his sweetheart.

Morris confirms this interpretation when he tells us that art has generality of semantic reference and abstract art has the highest degree of generality. By "generality of semantic reference" is meant that the components of the iconic sign and the total sign are such that their range of possible denotata is very large (140). In other words, a sign is iconic because it is like not one single thing, or the properties of that thing, or the values with which those properties are suffused, but many things and their properties and values. Nor would it have made any difference had Morris spoken of designata instead of denotata, for he holds that "the values embodied in the component sign vehicle are instances of value found elsewhere (even if the value of the whole has no other embodiment)," and that "in its capacity as sign the work of art presents these values mediately" (147).

We are in a position to gather our discussion into a summary statement: The difference between art that is imitation (and hence is bad art) and art that is not, is not to be found in the degree of literalness of the representation it may involve. The difference lies in the fact that the object of the work of art—what it is about or says—is revealed, when it is not mere imitation, *in* and *through* the work of art. The language of semiotics is not adequate to express this formula, since it assumes that the iconic sign vehicle is like something which can be apprehended independently of the iconic sign that reveals it. Because this is a crucial point I believe it is desirable to state it in still different words: I cannot read poetry or look at paintings in the same way in which I look at a photograph or read history. In the latter cases, through the representation I think of the sitter of the picture or of the actual events the historian is describing. In poetry and in painting this is not the case, and were, for instance, all extant copies of *The Iliad* destroyed suddenly and were the language in which it is written utterly forgotten, but were we to retain the translations into the European languages that we now have, *The Iliad* would be destroyed forever.

In defense of Morris the reader might counter that he stated that the sign vehicle is not an instrument which directs the interpreter to some other object. And in the sentence following this statement he tells us quite clearly that aesthetic perception "discerns—even if only partially—in the very object itself that which the object signifies" (139). But we retort that Morris does not successfully avoid the objections to the theory of imitation, since he holds that the object of the poem has existential status independently of the vehicle through which art reveals it; whatever we may choose to call it, his is a theory of imitation.[6]

3

The same criticism must be made of Morris' discussion of "esthetic truth," which we find in a section entitled "Esthetic Semantics" (143-145). Morris acknowledges that if an iconic sign has "a semantical dimension" it must say "something about something." Hence we can ask for a rule governing its use. "The semantic rule for the use of an iconic sign is that it denotes any object which has the properties (in practice, a selection from the properties) which it itself has" (136). We have all we need in order to ask of a poem whether it is true or not. But can we ask this question and conceal from ourselves the fact that we are making the very assumptions that makes our doctrine "run foul of the oppositions which theories of 'imitation' or 'representation' have encountered"?

To avoid this criticism Morris tells us that an iconic sign in isolation cannot be taken to be a statement and that therefore a work of art conceived as an iconic sign cannot be true in the semantical sense of the term. But this does not meet our difficulty. Notice that Morris is assuming that what makes a thing a work of art is the manner in which *we* look at it. The portrait of Bolivar is not a work of art if we think of the fiery Liberator and the great lover; it is, if we do not choose to think of him or do not know anything about him, and the tag in the frame, "Bolivar" means nothing to us. This is psychologism, and is inadequate because it fails to answer the question, What enables us to look at a painting for its own sake, intransitively? Of course any iconic sign can be regarded in isolation from that to which it refers, and is not then a statement. But the question is not whether we choose to disregard at certain times and for certain purposes the designata of certain types of signs, but whether these signs do in fact have a semantical dimension and what can we say about its status in being. If they have semantical dimension they are statements whether we choose to regard them as such or not, just as the typography of a well printed page of Hebrew, let us say, or a medieval manuscript, is a complex statement although a man ignorant of Hebrew or Latin may look on it as only a pretty design. If a system of iconic signs has a semantical dimension we can inquire whether its designata exist or not, and if they exist, we can inquire whether the relation of adequation holds between the sign and that to which the sign refers—whether the referend be an actual existent, a denotatum, or an ideal or imaginary existent, a designatum. The person of whom we ask this question can always answer that we can, if we apply the rule for the use of an iconic sign, decide the degree of truth involved in the relation between the sign and its referend, whether designatum or denotatum. I do not pretend there is anything in this discussion that we could not have anticipated from the views already examined. It is desirable, however, to go over the point in just this manner because it enables us to call attention to a corollary of it which involves even a worse defect than that already pointed to.

The discussion can conveniently take off from the last sentence of a paragraph already referred to. In it Morris tells us that in the process of aesthetic perception:

> There is a consummation because the object does embody the value it signifies, but the consummation is in another sense incomplete, since it is mediated by signs, and often by signs which are not them-
> ⸴ selves iconic of, or are only partially iconic of, what they signify—the work of art as a whole still remains a sign (139).

From this sentence we can infer that Morris believes there are more perfect consummations than the painting could provide if it were not a system of iconic signs but the real thing. But what could these consummations be? What else, of course, but the con-summation provided by the actual denotatum if we could possess it? There is evidence of the sturdy wisdom of Sancho Panza here. *La Maja Desnuda*, on the semiotic view, affords us only an incom-plete consummation, whereas Doña Maria del Pilar Teresa Caye-tana de Silva y Alvarez de Toledo, Duquesa de Alba, might have afforded us, could we have attracted her as she attracts us, a com-plete consummation. That art affords its own complete kind of *sui generis* consummation that has nothing to do in any obvious way with the actual values we might realize with la Cayetana or any other woman—these are woolly claims Sancho could never even entertain. What sort of consummation could that be? Art is mere half-consummatory wish-fulfillment, since it is an iconic sign which is only at best like its denotatum, never the denotatum itself. And how little like its denotatum it is can be easily realized by any semiotician who has seen *La Maja Desnuda* and with the aid of a little imagination extrapolates to the actual maja, the maja of all majas, La Cayetana herself. The moral is clear: A semiotician who knows values knows he can realize them better with a tart than with a Goya.[7]

4

For the sake of the problem to be discussed in this section I pro-pose that we assume that the poem denotes or designates a com-plex of values in the sense in which semiotic theory intends the assertion. It is desirable to examine this question in some detail because the belief that poetry through its phonological aspects refers to, or evokes, values, and even actual situations, is frequently encountered in criticism and is sometimes seriously entertained by aestheticians. Our question is whether, let us say, "Sailing to Byzantium" has something in common with its denotatum. Is the poem's vehicle, its language in its phonological aspect, a qualitative iconic sign? For certainly the structure of the poem has nothing in common with the structure of its denotatum. I am forced to assume in the absence of a statement by Morris to the point, that the designatum of the poem, "Sailing to Byzantium," is composed of the contrasting values with which the imaginary old man is concerned, who leaves the country of youth and goes to another country, Byzantium, where eternal values of the spirit find recognition. It has already been granted that in the case of onomatopoeia there is some sort of similarity between the icon and the denotatum. Can we find other kinds of similarity?

When we ask ourselves exactly what those who assert that poems are qualitative iconic signs mean, we find they do not make clear whether they mean that qualitative icons represent affective states or that the icons arouse the states. If they mean the latter, we are not concerned with their problem here. The claim we are concerned with is the former, the contention that certain qualities of the poetic vehicle, language in its phonological aspect, are like emotions or affective states and hence iconically represents them. All we need do is ask the question to realize that language possesses no property *qua* mere vehicle—which is to say, in abstraction from its designatum—that is like the designatum; neither its rhythm nor its rhyme nor any other phonological component that we are able to discriminate is like the designatum or any of its parts. Much less can we say of the whole poem as aural or visual whole that it bears some resemblance to its designatum.

Those who propose the theory sometimes go so far as to assert that the character of the verse suggests or evokes events or even physical objects. Thus John Frederick Nims in a review of a recent translation of Saint John of The Cross argued that the opening lines of the *Cántico:*

¿Adonde te escondiste,
Amado, y me dejaste con gemido?

reverberating, as they do, with "dark vowels," are "all thoroughly
functional in suggesting the echoing loneliness of the poet and the
stone dungeon in which the lines were written." [8]

I have no doubt that these lines do in fact suggest loneliness and
stone dungeons to Mr. Nims, but they do not do so inherently and
iconically, in the way in which the word "crackling" suggests the
actual noise which this word has been invented to convey. They
suggest whatever they do because Mr. Nims happens to know that
San Juan de la Cruz wrote his *Cántico* in a dungeon, and this
knowledge is associated intimately by Mr. Nims with the aural
values of the lines of the poem. This is an interesting fact of which
Mr. Nims' future biographer should take notice; but it is of no
interest to the critic of the *Cántico*. Had San Juan de la Cruz
written the lines in the cabin of a caravel on the way to Panama
(if caravels had cabins, that is), and did Mr. Nims know that such
was the case, I have no doubt that he could have made the same
claim in regard to the way in which the verse suggests the roll of
the sea and the straining noises of the cables and the whistling of
the gale. Had the lines been written by a man perched high in a
Tibetan lamasery, an ingenious critic could have made a good case
for the fact that they suggest anything they happened to suggest
to him. These remarks are not intended frivolously; they suggest
that the claim that language is iconic of things and events is not
tenable, outside the limited phenomena of onomatopoeic iconicity
of certain words.

There are many reasons to render the doctrine inadmissible,
three of which it is advisable to set down briefly: The first is that
language is an almost altogether artificial construction of the human mind and the relations it establishes between sounds and
things, with the exception of onomatopoeia, is purely "conventional." The second is that the language vehicle is bound up by an
organic relationship with its syntactic pattern, and with the mental
processes and an implicit semantic context within which a verbal
locution functions, so that only the Divine wisdom could discriminate one aspect from another and assign to it its function in pro-

ducing the total effects which language produces. Consider this
matter from the creative point of view, since from this standpoint
it is more easily surveyed. The poet does not start off with disparate ideas of meters, stanza forms, ideas, language and whatever
else the critic is able to discriminate, each in its self-enclosed identity and individuality, proceeding to put these together in the way
in which a child puts together the various parts of his Erector set.
He starts with a confused intention that seeks clarity through verbal formulation. And in the creative act—which may have the un-
premeditated spontaneity of a bird's song, or may extend through
years of brooding and many unsuccessful drafts—the intention
finds its vehicle and its form. In the act of finding, intention, vehicle, and form, lose their identities and become fused into an organic whole, the poem, which reveals its object in such a way that
only the special analytic license of the critic to use his scalpel, and
to use it with the uttermost discretion, allows him to make the
discrimination between object and language, and allows him to
deny its legitimacy only through the assertion that the object is
conveyed in the language and not merely through it. The third
reason is that the same prosodic patterns and the same aural effects, considering them each as distinct, can be and are used to
convey many disparate and even conflicting objects.

This last reason may be questioned, since psychologists find a
close relation between emotional states and rhythmic patterns.
Insofar as there is any such relation, one can claim there is a representation by rhythm of emotional states. But we must qualify,
since a one to one relationship can be discovered only when we
isolate a rhythmic pattern and when we present to a subject an
extreme and characteristic rhythm. In the organic unity of the
poem, given rhythms are capable of suggesting a large range of
the most disparate and mutually exclusive emotional states and
cannot therefore be said to be iconically representative of any one;
and even in the same poem, a given rhythmic pattern can be employed in different paragraphs or even in adjacent lines in the same
paragraph to reveal very different sentiments or emotional states.
The capacity of vowels to suggest whatever they suggest depends
on the idiosyncratic history of him to whom they suggest what they
suggest, but the power of language to reveal objects depends on

the words employed, the rules of their combination, the total semantic context within which they function and many other factors
among which it is desirable to note the aural and rhythmic characters they possess in context and the total associative matrix which
operates below the surface of consciousness for anyone who uses
language. But if the aural and prosodic aspects of poetry, as between
which and emotional states there seem to obtain causal connections, are not iconic, what grounds have we for claiming iconicity
as regards other discriminable aspects of the vehicle and the values
it denotes or designates?

This is not to say that the language of poetry is merely ostensive.
That is the one thing it never is. The meanings and values that are
the object of the poem are revealed in the language as well as
through it. But while they are revealed in the language itself, it is
not by means of any similarity or likeness between the language
and the object, since, outside onomatopoeia, none can be exhibited.
Language, when it functions aesthetically, is similar to nothing and
those aspects of it which have similarities and relationships with
other things in the universe—as we have just seen, rhythm by itself seems to have to affective states—do not function atomically
and separately from the other aspects of language but are organically related to them.

5

It remains only to ask whether the iconic theory protects the creativity of the artist. In substance this question has been answered
already, but it is desirable to make the answer explicit. Morris tells
us that the artist takes elements suffused with the values of many
things, not only of one thing, and puts them together in an elaborate iconic structure which is the work of art. Creativity seems thus
confined by him to the form of the work of art, for the values which
constitute its substance and the elements on which these values
are suffused, are taken, and we are not told that anything is added
by the artist to what he takes from experience. But even in respect
to the form itself, the work of the artist, on Morris' view, seems to
consist of an elaborate shuffling and mixing of elements suffused
with value. Are the forms achieved mechanically? Does the artist

contribute something to them? This is the critical question, but Morris throws no light on it. What we want to know is what does the artist contribute in terms of both form and substance or of the union of them that he did not obtain from his tradition.

We are not yet through with our difficulties under this head. For what Morris is saying is that the object of the poem is not made up of specific, concrete values, but of abstract, generalized ones. This comes out clearly in the following passage:

> There may be a number of incidents in the life of the same person at different times, or in the lives of different persons, to which a poem is applicable, and which therefore are denotata of the poem. There are various degrees of such generality, and abstract art is simply an extreme case of high generality of semantical reference, the generality of the component iconic signs and the total iconic sign being so high that their range of possible denotata is very large (140).

Taken in its context one cannot find out what is meant by the relation of applicability here referred to, unless it be likeness or similarity between poem and external things or events rooted in the poem's iconicity. In any case, this passage flatly denies an important fact that Dewey, along with a large number of contemporary aestheticians, reckoned with: the fact that the work of art, and all the discrete factors that analysis can discriminate as its components, is unique, individual, concrete, specific, not abstract, nor general, nor universal. There may be general terms in a poem. In the second paragraph of "Sailing to Byzantium" we find such a one:

> An aged man is but a paltry thing,
> A tattered coat upon a stick . . .

This is a generalization, if you like, a law, since it says something about all old men; but it functions in the organic whole of the poem not as a general term but as a component of a unique thing: the poem, "Sailing to Byzantium." This poem does not "denote" or designate the general value of art for old men in general. It is a unique thing, to be apprehended uniquely, grasped in its full intransitive discreteness, and when thus grasped, it reveals in and through its linguistic structure a unique object.

6

The original source of the error that has been analyzed in this paper
is not only to be traced to Morris' failure to grasp clearly certain
basic insights of *Art As Experience* in respect to creativity and imitation, but beyond this failure to an inadequate conception of the
function of language. Morris believes that the fundamental function of language is to transfer meanings, to communicate. A
radically empirical approach to the problem of poetry would not
undertake to carry over the results obtained from investigations arising out of interest in the practical and the scientific use of language
into its use in poetry. It would rather seek to determine first
whether the activities of poetry have their own proper functions
and what these are. Anything else is *a priorism*. To avoid this *a
priorism* we must shun employing the categories of a semiotic ori-
ented towards science, and adopt a set of notions that do not
commit us in advance to a denial of the unique function of poetry.
Another way of saying the same thing is to say that in Morris'
sense of the term "designatum" a poem cannot have designata,
although its language is about something. If it has designata
what the poem does is imitate, and the notion of imitation has
been avoided only by translating it into the notion of iconicity.
The object of the poem does not *exist* either as a set of particulars
or of universals, nor can it for that reason be grasped or apprehended independently of it. The object of the poem is presented
in and through its language, nor can we find it or its components
in things in such a way that we can suffuse our language with it.

It must however be said in fairness to Morris that his theory is
more adequate to the complexity of the facts than some of his
critics have succeeded in realizing. Thus Richard Rudner takes
Morris to task because the latter asserts that the aesthetic experience is both mediate and immediate, a patent contradiction.[9]
Of course Rudner is pointing to a *verbal* contradiction; but so was
Kant's disinterested interest a verbal contradiction. And contradictory also are expressions by means of which we often seek to
point to the complexity of data, which without these desperate
devices we might take for simpler than they are. Morris, who is
aware of the data his critic ignores, tries to point to the type of

experience which is distinctively aesthetic, and to the kind of object which is distinctively an aesthetic object. To maintain that the experience is mediate is to assert that the aesthetic object is about something, and thus to assert that if it is intrinsically valuable its value is in some sense different from itself. To maintain it is immediate is to assert that it presents but does not represent anything, that it presents in itself. There are sound objections to both claims when made without qualification and sound reasons for maintaining both, which Mr. Rudner does not take into consideration, at least in his criticism of Morris. To deny either claim is therefore to turn our back on important data which the aesthetician cannot overlook if he is an empiricist whose primary loyalty is to the data and not to merely verbal logic and systemic elegance. Morris does not resolve the seeming paradox but he does grasp the problem.

1953

Allen Tate as man of letters [1]

"The man of letters," a phrase frequently employed by Allen Tate, gives us, I believe, the key to his criticism. The phrase seems obsolescent, but I take it that it has been commonly used in English in the past. Nor can any one claim for it a special force or expressiveness. Again, one might too easily dispose of Mr. Tate's fondness for it by reference to his evidently lively interest in things French, since it is in current use in France; but this fact, although true, does not account for the frequency with which we encounter it in his prose. In any case, its ordinary use in French or English is as a synonym for "writer" or "literary man" or "scholar." But for Mr. Tate the man of letters has a responsibility and a dignity that we do not ordinarily associate with the activities of the writer. And in spite of our critic's instinctive modesty and courtesy, it is not difficult to perceive that he thinks of himself as a man of letters. For this reason, the phrase serves as an index of the seriousness with which Mr. Tate takes his profession; and when we consider it in conjunction with the judgment he passes on the modern world, it also gives us the measure of the desperate courage that is required of a man who makes of the profession of letters the demands Mr. Tate does. This in turn gives us the measure of his stature and the means to define his place in contemporary literature.

What does the activity of the man of letters consist of? In the first essay of his last book, entitled "The Man of Letters in the Modern World," we are given the answer to our question. Our author suggests that we define the man of letters by what we need him to do. His immediate responsibility, "at our own critical moment," is for the vitality of language. It is his task to distinguish the difference between mere communication and the rediscovery of the human condition in the living arts. This responsibility puts on the man of letters the burden of inventing standards by which this difference may be known and a sufficient minority of persons may be instructed. It ought to be clear from this succinct statement alone that Allen Tate is going far beyond what T. S. Eliot conceives to be the task of the poet. For Eliot would have it that the duty of the poet is to preserve and develop the language. But both preservation and development are for Eliot controlled by the need for expression, through the objective correlative, of feelings and emotions. Even when Mr. Tate conceives the immediate task of the man of letters at our own critical moment, he is thinking of that task in objective and not in subjective terms. Sentiments and emotions are no doubt important constituents of the world in which we live, but they cannot give us the key to the whole.

The restricted "immediate responsibility" of the man of letters is conceived by our critic in the context of a larger and more permanent responsibility which is defined by him as follows: The man of letters "must create for his age an image of man, and he must propagate standards by which other men may test that image, and distinguish the false from the true." What Mr. Tate is saying is something that other peoples at other times have known, but that we denizens of a positivistic world have chosen to forget—that the poet is the "seer." I ought to warn the reader, however, that the word "seer" is mine and not the author's. I am reasonably certain that he would not risk its use for many reasons but chiefly, perhaps, because it carries with it all sorts of absurd associations for the contemporary mind. A man of letters is a "seer" but he is not one possessed, he is not an undisciplined madman who allows the Muse or the Holy Spirit to speak through him. But while disciplined, he is not "a specialist" in language, although he is an expert in its use; he does not compete with Jespersen or Sapir; he may know little of the mutations of English from Bede to Shakespeare, or of the difference between the structural devices of Chinook and those of Papiamento; he may find Bloomfield and Sturtevant unrewarding reading, and Mario Pei and H. L. Mencken only amusing. One thing is fairly certain: he distrusts the relativistic attitude towards grammar which seems to be the foundation of the so-called science of linguistics. And, what will be most astonishing to contemporary prejudice, his primary interest is not in language as a means of "communication"; he uses it primarily for the purposes of "communion"—a word which, no doubt, has an obscene connotation to the congenitally positivistic modern mind, but which Mr. Tate does not hesitate to employ. In the essay already referred to, he tells us that:

> literature has never communicated . . . it cannot *communicate*. . . . Our unexamined theory of literature as communication could not have appeared in an age in which communion was still possible for any appreciable majority of persons. The word communication presupposes the victory of the secularized society of means without ends. The poet, on the one hand, shouts to the public, on the other (some distance away), not the rediscovery of the common experience, but a certain pitch of sound to which the well-conditioned adrenals of humanity obligingly respond.

Because the man of letters seeks primarily to participate in "communion" he must take seriously the discipline of rhetoric. But here again the word is apt to be misleading; for as used by the writer, it is not intended to designate the activity of the rabble rouser or the man who has no argument and must therefore fall back on the naked appeal to passion and thoughtless prejudice, nor does it designate the activity of the mere lover of words. It refers to the activity which Professor Richard Weaver has recently defined in his

important book, *The Ethics of Rhetoric.* In the essay entitled, "Is
Literary Criticism Possible," we are told by Mr. Tate that rhetoric
is:

> the study and the use of the figurative language of experience as
> the discipline by means of which men govern their relations with
> one another in the light of truth. Rhetoric presupposes the study of
> two prior disciplines, grammar and logic, neither of which is much
> pursued today, except by specialists.

He goes on to assert that grammar is an essential instrument to
the man who would employ language in order to participate in
communion, since it makes possible the definition of the funda-
mentals of understanding. It does this because "all reading is translation, even in the native tongue; for translation may be described
as the tact of mediation between universals and particulars in the
complex of metaphor." This is an art no longer taught. For the
scientific linguist language is as language does, and what it does
is what men do with it and to it. In an equalitarian society, in
respect to intelligence and culture all men are equal and no one can
be more equal than another. Therefore the most illiterate and in-
sensitive unskilled laborer, whose linguistic requirements are defined by the most elementary functions of social life, has as much
of a right to do with and to language what he damn pleases as the
next guy even if the next guy happens to be a Henry James, a
T. S. Eliot or a D. H. Lawrence.

As to logic, teachers of philosophy will probably disagree with
Mr. Tate. He tells us that neither grammar nor logic is any longer
a prerequisite to the study of philosophy, and he seems to offer as
evidence that an "Eastern university offers a grandiose course in
Greek philosophical ideas to sophomores who will never know a
syllogism from a handsaw." Professional philosophers will answer,
and not without some specious force, that our critic seems to have
generalized from an atypical instance. They may even call attention
to a fact that I believe it would be difficult to deny: that the area
of contemporary philosophy in which probably most creative
energy is at the moment being spent and with most significant
results, is logic. But Mr. Tate is nevertheless right. "Everybody
knows," he tells us, "that modern philosophers, like their brother

scientists, and not unlike their distant cousins the poets, are pur-
suing specialisms of various kinds." What goes by the name of
logic today is not a discipline that can be used by the rhetor; it is
an autotelic discipline cultivated by a small group of esoteric specialists who can no longer talk to one another in ordinary language,
but who communicate among themselves in a script full of wiggles
and waggles, with little relevance to the world of affairs.

If this is how Mr. Tate conceives the task of the man of letters I
do not believe it would take much argument to demonstrate that
what he is expected to do today, as things are for us, at our critical
moment, is a desperately quixotic and probably anachronistic
service.

But does not its anachronistic nature make it false? Let us hear
the positivist's side. There might have been a time, the positivist
will begin, when there was need for the poet's image of man; but
there no longer is. We no more need poets today than we need
medicine men. Surely Mr. Tate will not deny that whatever truth
there may be in the images of man given us by the poets, their picture is ambiguous, incoherent and unverifiable, whereas the knowledge given us by the sciences is systematic, corrigible and universal?
This is precisely what our author denies. Whatever contribution
the sciences may make towards our knowledge of man, it is to the
poet, Mr. Tate answers, that we must go for *the complete* truth
about man. The scientist may be able to tell us what man does and
what he can do, but he cannot evaluate man's actions and elucidate
the nature of his norms, and a picture of man that leaves out this
aspect of his nature is a sadly incomplete and relatively trivial picture. This issue is not one that can be settled or even adequately
defined in a review of a book on literary criticism. But short of a
complete discussion of it, there is an answer that a man like Tate
can give the positivist. It runs something like this: Although positivists have not systematically developed their philosophy of history
and some of them will even deny the validity of such a discipline,
in men like Dewey and Randall and even Reichenbach we find
some of its basic assumptions fairly clearly delineated. According
to what is its most important tenet for our purposes, the new age,
whether we date it from Copernicus, Galileo, Darwin or Freud-
Ford, is distinguished from the pre-scientific past by the fact that

we have finally removed the practical and theoretical obstacles that prevented the full and consistent application of the method of science to the problems of men. Mr. Tate also believes that there is a difference between the new age and the old. On the basis of this agreement he answers the positivist that the image the man of letters gives us is not an objective image—if by "objective" be meant the value-free statistical picture of man which it has been the ideal of the social sciences to obtain, and which still largely predominates. What the man of letters can and ought to give us is a picture forged in his "conscience," in the French sense of this word: an image forged through the joint action of knowledge and judgment. And he explains:

> This conscience has long known a severe tradition of propriety in discerning the poet's particular kind of actuality. No crisis, however dire, should be allowed to convince us that the relation of the poet to his permanent reality can ever change. And thus the poet is not responsible to society for a version of what it thinks it is or what it wants. For *what* is the poet responsible? He is responsible for the virtue proper to him as poet, for his special *arête:* for the mastery of a disciplined language which will not shun the full report of the reality conveyed to him by his awareness: he must hold, in Yeats' great phrase, "reality and justice in a single thought."

Thus, in the final analysis, the heart of the quarrel between men like Tate and the positivists is as to the kind of world that ought to be created: our critic wants a world which will allow us in some measure at least to realize our human destiny; the positivists want the one which is already half born, the louring world of 1984 and beyond it (for the kind of hell we are in for cannot last forever) the worse hell of 632 A.F. In this brave new world of science and of pleasure humanity is not destroyed by forced labor in the frozen tundras of Siberia; it is destroyed by something worse: the social engineer painlessly performs a lobotomy on it and destroys its soul. Otherwise stated, the image of man that is created by the man of letters is not one that can be used by men who are bent on building a secularized society, the *fourmillante cité*—the secularism of the swarm. Such a society, taking God to be a silly and burdensome superstition, will substitute the image of Man for His image and

under the illusion of humanism will worship naked power. This is
the society that we have already begun to rear on both sides of the
Iron Curtain. And if we have not seen in our day what we may
expect from it, we can find it vividly sketched for us in Dostoevski
and in Huxley.

Several reasons have made me emphasize the philosophical assumptions which control Mr. Tate's criticism. The least important
of these is that he has been identified, of course correctly, with the
so-called "new critics." And they are in turn assumed to be for-
malists, because they insist that the substance of a literary work is
to be found by reference not to something outside itself but to
something to be discovered in it. Yet there is a sense in which, in
Mr. Tate's words, "the great formal works of literature are not
wholly autonomous," and in which, therefore, the criticism which
would make them available must be less autonomous than they.
Adapting to our purposes of the moment a phrase of our author,
he is a critic who is concerned with literary questions but who, in
order to be effectively literary, must be more than literary.

There is a second reason for emphasizing the assumptions of Mr.
Tate's criticism. I fear that unless we grasp them firmly and read
him with them explicitly in mind we are apt to encounter certain
incoherences and opacities in his writing that are extremely puzzling. These disappear when we read them in the light of his
philosophical assumptions. Thus, one is puzzled by what seems to
be a lack of consistency in the writer's conception of the role of
the man of letters. In the first essay he recommends that the man
of letters participate fully in the action of society, and in the second, entitled "To Whom is the Poet Responsible?" we are told
that the poet has no business gadding about "using the rumor of
his verse to appear on platforms and view with alarm." There is no
contradiction if we see that Mr. Tate puts on the man of letters a
heavy social burden—that of giving us an image of man—but that
he also holds that this task cannot be accomplished unless the poet
undertakes it as poet and not as statesman or political agitator. But
there is a third and a most important reason for emphasizing the
assumptions on which Mr. Tate's criticism is grounded: unless we
grasp these assumptions and perceive how they guide the direction
of his criticism and inform his actual discriminations, we cannot

appreciate correctly the uniqueness of Mr. Tate's position in contemporary criticism.

Ours, it has been frequently observed, is an age of criticism. Our critics are, one and all, endowed with considerable talent. And they have added to this talent wondrous skills to achieve brilliant discriminations; they are endowed with subtle tools of analysis, they have at their command the insights of the sciences and the pseudo-sciences of today, and those who are put through the academic processing machinery—and most of them are in an age in which education is universal—possess more than enough historical erudition for their purposes. But it must also be observed that our critics are for the most part philosophically pauperized and are, hence, devoid of a coherent sense of the place of man in society, the place of society in history, and the relation of history to the universe. It is no wonder, therefore, that they should have only the most trivial notions of the use of literature. One school of critics, whose ponderous equipment of antiquated theory rumbles over the literary landscape with the terrible noise of a thousand panzers, tells us, in all seriousness, that literature has as its end pleasure produced through the play on the emotions. Another critic tells us that the end of literature is not to give us truth, which is given to us by science, but to give us "pure experience." How experience without content is distinguished from the works produced by the emotional engineers of the Brave New World this critic forgets to inform us. Another tells us that the end of literature is to organize our attitudes. And thus if our critics do not give us the stale vulgarities of hedonism they give us the no less stale vulgarities of therapy. And so on down the dismal catalogue. None of these critics ask of themselves the simple question: How does it happen that art, that seems to be, and in a sense is, the most expendable of activities in human society, is one of the two most ineradicable, most indispensable modes of experience? Our critics cannot ask this question because, for the most part, they work in a philosophical vacuum. And they do because they lack a guiding body of convictions—of *prejudices,* in Edmund Burke's sense of the word—with reference to which the work of art is seen as an indispensable and unsubstitutable factor in the creation and maintenance of the human element in the animal, man.

It is ironic, but it is sadly true, that the only body of men in our day who have had a consistently serious sense of the importance of literature are the very men who in their hearts least of all care for it —the Marxists. Their materialism makes them as blind as the hedonists and the Freudians to the manner in which art actually functions in society; but at least they do not offer us the vulgarities of the hedonists or of the therapists. In contrast with the Marxists, and of course allowing for exceptions, neither conservative nor liberal critics seem to have a sense of the way in which art affects the lives of men. And the reason is simply that they do not base their criticism, whether new or old, whether historical or non-historical, whether sociological or psychoanalytic, on a tenable notion of the destiny of man. If you press them, all they can give you is a more or less dressed-up version of man as an animal essentially motivated by the pleasure principle. The conservative critic may add a sentence or two of pious and tenuous talk about "spiritual values." But what is intended by this notion at bottom is "the higher pleasure": whereas certain Indians of Eastern Bolivia entertain themselves shrinking heads, it is through music, poetry, the theatre that we entertain ourselves if we are civilized. Thus we can expect no more of the conservative than we can of the liberal critics; both are essentially committed to the same secular image of man, and on such a basis anything else than hedonism is absurd. The differences between them consist only in how much pleasure we should allow ourselves, and at what cost. For such men the role of art in human life cannot be central. Philosophically, ours is a bankrupt generation.

In contrast Mr. Tate is saying that art is important because human life is not capable of achieving what virtue or perfection it may achieve unless it is guided by an effective notion of the destiny of man. The poet makes his essential and indispensable contribution when he gives us "the image of man as he is in his time, which without the man of letters would not otherwise be known." Thus it is not an exaggeration to say that our author's fundamental concern as a man of letters is with the values men live by and the ends they serve. In his essay on Dante, what he explicitly proposes to do is "to look at a single image in the *Paradiso* [the image of light], and to glance at some of its configurations with other images." But

when Mr. Tate is through with his analysis what he has given us
is a contrast between the medieval imagination, which does not try
to transcend the mediation of image and discourse, and "the angelic
imagination" which "tries to disintegrate or to circumvent the
image in the illusory pursuit of essence." What is suggested is a
conception of man and, in sketch at least, a philosophy of history.
Because the writer's own words can not be improved on, it is desirable to quote a long passage:

> The symbolic imagination takes rise from a definite limitation of
> human rationality which was recognized in the West until the 17th
> Century; in this view the intellect cannot have direct knowledge
> of essences. The only created mind that has this knowledge is the
> angelic mind. If we do not believe in angels we shall have to invent
> them in order to explain by parable the remarkable appearance, in
> Europe, at about the end of the 16th Century, of a mentality which
> denied man's commitment to the physical world, and set itself up in
> quasi-divine independence. This mind has intellect and will without
> feeling; and it is through feeling alone that we witness the glory of
> our servitude to the natural world, to St. Thomas' accidents, or, if
> you will, to Locke's secondary qualities; it is our tie with the world
> of sense. The angelic mind suffers none of the limitations of sense;
> it has immediate knowledge of essences; and this knowledge moves
> through the perfect will to divine love, with which it is at one.
> Imagination in an angel is thus inconceivable, for the angelic mind
> transcends the mediation of both image and discourse. I call that
> human imagination angelic which tries to disintegrate or to circum-
> vent the image in the illusory pursuit of essence. When human be-
> ings undertake this ambitious program, divine love becomes so rari-
> fied that it loses its human paradigm, and is dissolved in the worship
> of intellectual power, the surrogate of divinity that worships itself.
> It professes to know nature as essence at the same time that it has
> become alienated from nature in the rejection of its material forms.

This is also the theme of the two essays on Poe. In the first essay
the writer demonstrates that Poe possessed the angelic imagination
and used it without qualms and for this reason Poe is "the transi-
tion figure in modern literature," since he is the man who discovered our great subject, "the disintegration of personality, but kept

it in a language that had developed in a tradition of unity and order." In the second essay, Mr. Tate makes clear why he is fascinated by this man of the nineteenth century. He writes, "in the history of the moral imagination in the nineteenth century Poe occupies a special place. No other writer in England or the United States, or, so far as I know, in France, went so far as Poe in his vision of dehumanized man."

One can disagree with Mr. Tate as regards details, and I shall do so presently. But I do not believe the reflective man can disagree with him as regards the substance of the issue. There are, in this quarrel, three possible positions. One can look forward to a totally secularized future, made glorious by science as it extends its sway; one can, with our author, look back on a past in which men, for all their sins, never seriously proposed a purely secular conception of human destiny; or one can deny these alternatives on the ground that the more things change the more they are the same. I take it that this denial of the alternatives is given the lie by the facts and that the disagreement between Mr. Tate and the positivists is as to the proper evaluation of the facts and what they seem to portend. Science has indeed made a difference: it has encouraged a swarm of false philosophies which claim its authority and whose business is to destroy the once solid metaphysics in the light of which we defined our destiny. It is not claimed, of course, that a single system of philosophy enjoyed uncontested supremacy in the history of the West. There has always been strife of systems, and this is a fortunate condition. But Dewey is right when he finds shared assumptions among warring systems in traditional philosophy, although we need not accept his own formulation of what these assumptions are. It becomes more and more clear that the positivist mind—whether in its logical empiricist variety, or its scientific humanist or its Marxist forms, whether represented by the vacuous rationality of a Carnap or an Ayer, or the vulgar hedonistic secularism of the Deweyans, or the threat-filled dialectic of the commissars—will do its termite work, and there is precious little that any one can do to stop it from destroying our culture. I suspect that the muffled despair the reader discerns below the surface of Mr. Tate's essays springs from the fact that he knows that the things he loves are doomed. But Mr. Tate is no man to take the threat lying down. In-

forming his criticism and giving it remarkable consistency and
force, is his protest against the meaning of the present and of the
probable future.

I have to express disagreement with Mr. Tate, however, on a
question of historical interpretation. Following Maritain, our critic
traces to Descartes man's usurpation of the angelic imagination. It
seems to me that this is to credit a philosopher with far more power
than any one man, even a Descartes, could possibly have wielded.
Descartes was not possible without conditions of an extremely complex nature which existed prior to his advent. In history we do not
have parthenogenetic spontaneity. How far back we are going to
go and to what factors we are going to trace the beginning of the
difficulties which are Mr. Tate's basic theme, we need not decide
here; but if we are to seek for them in the realms of intellectual history exclusively and not in the heterogeneous process of the whole
of history, intellectual and material, it would be more exact to
trace it, I suspect, to the Oxford Franciscans of the 13th Century
than to Descartes. For it was these men who began the arduous
preparation of the ground for the complex intellectual movements
which according to Maritain, Descartes initiated. This movement
was made possible by the work of men like Grosseteste, Thomas of
York, Roger Bacon, and their followers and it leads to Descartes
because it leads to the great age of science. To trace it to these men,
be it noted, is not to allocate "blame." The men who in the 13th
Century laid the ground for the scientific upsurge of the 16th and
17th Centuries were not "radicals" trying to destroy the world in
which they lived. They were men honestly trying to expand the
range of knowledge. Descartes was doing something more complex
and more urgent: he was trying to harmonize two constellations of
values that at the moment seemed to be in conflict and neither of
which could be overlooked or denied. The Cartesian synthesis may
not have been satisfactory to the reigning orthodoxy, but what the
latter proposed was neither valid nor acceptable. It is in this respect
that the great work of Descartes—with all its seeds for good *and*
evil—must be appreciated in order not to confuse it with the work
of positivists, who under the pretense of being pure knowers bore
like termites at the foundations of our culture. If we blame Descartes because he made possible the usurpation of the angelic

imagination, we suggest that the 17th Century could have provided
for the development of science and yet maintained the values of
the spirit in some other way than by the Cartesian synthesis. But
what alternatives were there? A decadent scholasticism that had
already lost all power over the creative minds of the century and
a renascent materialism of which Hobbes was the most distinguished representative. But the Englishman was the positivist of
his age—in the sense that he was a man endowed with a singularly
powerful mind but who lacked almost completely an empirical
and, for all his interest in literature and history, a genuinely hu-
mane grasp of the actual complex moral and religious problems
of his age. If therefore the Cartesian dichotomy led to consequences from which we are suffering, suffer them we must, for
there was nothing else that Descartes' contemporaries could have
done but accept his views.

But my quarrel with Mr. Tate is after all a minor one—a question
for erudites, as we say in Spanish. When Mr. Tate speaks of Descartes, I suspect that he is using names in the same manner I do, as
convenient metaphors ready at hand that are (in language that Mr.
Tate has as little use for as I have) "iconic" of the complex movements that they denote. For the disintegration of the modern personality was not the work of one man or of many, nor was it the
work of philosophers or scientists or stupid statesmen—although all
them and all of us share in the responsibility for it. Helpful, therefore, and on certain occasions unavoidable, they are inexcusable
when we take them as an adequate report of the historical reality.
History is not the work of men but of Man, the creature whom we
write with a capital "M"—the animal that stumbles through time
from one stupidity into another, the angelic beast or the bestial
angel, the inhabitant of the city of Man and not of the City of
God, who in the pursuit of truth falls into error, in the search for
virtue embraces sin, in the lust for happiness is led to misery, and
in the search for God often runs into the Devil's arms. If there is
one thing even more false than the belief in progress it is the belief
in progress in reverse. Mr. Tate is philosophically too shrewd to
make such a mistake. He is not a pure philosopher; he is a man
endowed with a philosophic instinct (if I may so call it) that ought
to be trusted more than the skill of the pure philosopher. The

latter, the man who posits a factitious clarity as the exclusive end
of his activity, is a fool who has not taken the first step on the road
to wisdom and does not know that a man ought not to take his
"ideas" too seriously. I take it therefore that when Tate speaks
of "Descartes" he means "Descartes, the man and the icon," by
which is in turn meant, "Descartes and those complex factors,
whatever they happen to be, which made Descartes possible, and
that are, therefore, back of the phenomena which, as literary critic,
I am interested in." And I am not guessing that this is what the
author means. In one of his most impressive pieces, the essay on
"Ezra Pound and the Bollingen Prize," Mr. Tate reminds us that
in "literature as in life nothing reaches us pure." And he continues,
"the task of the civilized intelligence is one of perpetual salvage."
This was the task that Descartes attempted, and if today Mr. Tate
traces the usurpation of the angelic imagination to the Frenchman,
we must read him in the light of the fact that he knows that in
philosophy as in life nothing reaches us absolutely pure.

It would be interesting to look at each of the other essays that
compose this volume and to show how each discloses its center of
gravity, so to speak, when we appraise it in view of Mr. Tate's conception of man and of his philosophy of history. But to go through
each of them picking out their virtues and summarizing their contents is to deprive the reader of the pleasure and profit he should
have at first hand. Instead of attempting to deprive the reader of
what ought to be his pleasure and profit, let me in closing pose the
question that has intrigued me from the moment I unwrapped the
book and looked at its title. Why *The Forlorn Demon*? The ambiguity is rich and it repays notice, I believe, for it throws some
light on the complexity of Mr. Tate's central problem. Mr. Tate
credits Poe with the phrase. But he does not tell us exactly why
he chose the title. I am venturing a guess and it is altogether possible that my remarks will seem absurd and even impertinent. In
one sense, I suggest, "the forlorn demon" is the modern man of
letters, doomed to inhabit Baudelaire's *fourmillante cité*. He is a
demon because he has aspired to become an angel, and by doing
so plunged himself into hell. But the title suggests another interpretation, according to which the demon is now the Socratic
daimon, who is forlorn because we citizens of the swarming secular-

ized city of today disregarded his prohibition and attempted to do something we have no business attempting. The demon is forlorn because in disregarding his prohibition we have betrayed ourselves and thus betrayed him.

1954

NOTES

Notes

Henry and William

[1] The essay on William's moral theory referred to in the text is to be found in the volume entitled *The Will to Believe*, and excerpts from the review of Spencer's *Data of Ethics* are to be found in *Collected Essays and Reviews*.

Kafka's distorted mask

[1] Edited by Angel Flores (New York, 1946).

[2] In his notes to *The Great Wall of China*, Rahv has also published psychoanalytic and sociological interpretations of Kafka in the *Kenyon* and *Southern Reviews*.

what is a poem?

[1] This is a revised version of a paper read before The Graduate Philosophy Club of Yale University, 18 March 1954.

a definition of the aesthetic experience

[1] Compare with my essay, "A Natural History of the Aesthetic Transaction," in *Naturalism and The Human Spirit*, ed. by Yervant H. Krikorian (New York, 1944) pp. 96-120. This essay was written in 1939 at the request of the editor. Although it is a more extended treatment of the problem, I do not reprint it in this collection, because to bring it into accord with my more mature philosophical views would require a major job of revision. But the phenomenological analysis that both it and this shorter paper undertake seems to me to be valid still.

[2] John Dewey, *Art As Experience* (New York, 1934), pp. 67, 68, 79, 91, 237, 238. The treatment of the emotion by Mr. Dewey is extremely baffling (see below pp. 223-228). D. W. Prall, *Aesthetic Judgment* (New York, 1929), pp. 213 ff. *Aesthetic Analysis* (New York, 1936), Chapter V, especially pp. 141 ff.

[3] The evidence alluded to is to be found in Vernon Lee, *Music and its Lovers* (New York, 1933), Chapters I and II, and corroborating evidence will be found conveniently summarized in Albert R. Chandler, *Beauty and Human Nature* (New York, 1934) Chapter 6, Chapter 12, pp. 230-236. T. S. Eliot, *The Sacred Wood, Essays on Poetry and Criticism* (New York, 1930), "The end of the enjoyment of poetry is a pure contemplation from which all the accidents of personal emotion are removed . . ." (p. 15).

[4] This is the conclusion at which Vernon Lee arrives, *op. cit., passim,* especially pp. 543 ff. Note how subjectivism as regards aesthetic judgments follows naturally from this position.

[5] *Loc. cit.*

[6] Dewey, *op. cit., passim,* but particularly pp. 16 and 249. Louis Arnaud Reid, *A Study in Aesthetics* (New York, 1931), pp. 85 ff.

[7] Carroll C. Pratt, *The Meaning of Music. A Study in Psychological Aesthetics* (New York, 1931). Parts II and III, esp. pp. 157 ff. and his article "Objectivity of Esthetic Value" in *The Journal of Philosophy*, Vol. XXXI (1934), pp. 38-45. Mr. Eliot's explanation of this problem in terms of the objective correlative is examined below, pp. 175-189.

8 The values and meanings which constitute the informed substance of the poem have a status in being which phenomenological analysis cannot explore (see below, pp. 129-143). And the aesthetic value of the poem is not constituted by the aesthetic mode of apprehension, although the mind is not a mirror mind and has a role to play of a creative nature in the process of apprehension. But at the phenomenological level we need not explore these problems. All we need notice is that the definition of the experience—of any kind whatsoever—points to a relational complex which involves a subject related in a specific psychological manner to an object. Thus the phenomenological data given us by analysis is prior to the interpretation given it by ontology.

9 Many other terms may be used to refer to the same phenomenal data. The term "immanent meanings" may be employed as well as any other, so long as it is understood that it does not explain the manner in which these meanings came to be embodied in the object, but is taken to point only to the fact that they do.

10 Compare Vernon Lee, loc. cit., with Reid, op. cit., who denies this: "But consciousness of ourselves . . . can probably never disappear. It is a matter of degree and focus" (p. 80). Since a definition is an ideal or theoretical construct, whose purpose is to enable us to identify the aesthetic response and to distinguish it from other modes of experience, no one need have actually undergone this type of experience. All we need show is that some people under some circumstances approach more or less successfully the condition here referred to. The definition is an extrapolation from such data even if, as Reid claims, no one ever entirely loses consciousness of himself and if, therefore, no one is ever altogether free from emotion when attending upon an aesthetic object. Note however that Mr. Reid makes the statement on his own authority and does not offer us proof of the kind furnished by Vernon Lee.

11 Pratt, op. cit., p. 177.

12 Cf. William James, Principles of Psychology (London, 1901), Vol. II, Chapter XXI, pp. 287 ff. See a brief study of this question by the author under the title of "Reality in Art" in The University Review (The University of Kansas City), Vol. IV (1937), No. 1.

13 Cf. E. A. Shearer's criticism of Dewey's assertion of correspondence between perceiver and object in "Dewey's Esthetic Theory," The Journal of Philosophy, XXXII (1935), p. 651.

literature and knowledge

1 This paper is the result of preparation for two conferences I gave in Professors Redfield's and Singer's "Seminar On The Comparison of Cultures" in the University of Chicago, in the Fall of 1951. It was subsequently

worked up into an essay read at the Philosophical Association meeting, Western Division, at the University of Michigan in the Spring of 1952, and rewritten for publication.

[2] A. C. Bradley, "Poetry for Poetry's Sake," in *Oxford Lectures on Poetry* (London, 1914), pp. 3-34.

[3] I have in mind the claims made for the cognitive value of art by aestheticians like Croce and R. G. Collingwood. The latter tells us that art pursues "not a truth of relation," but "a truth of individual fact." In the context Collingwood makes clear what he means by truth of individual fact. *The Principles of Art* (Oxford, 1935).

[4] The documents which justify these observations are so numerous as to be overwhelming. See, among others, S. Alexander, *Beauty and Other Forms of Value* (London, 1933), Chapter IV; M. Anderson and others, *The Basis of Artistic Creation in the Arts* (New Brunswick, 1942); Phyllis Bartlett, *Poems in Process* (New York, 1951); Brand Blanshard, *The Nature of Thought* (London, 1939), Chapters XXI, XXII; Arthur R. Chandler, *Beauty and Human Nature* (New York, 1934), Chapter 16; Collingwood, *op. cit.*; Henri Delacroix, *Psychologie de l'art* (Paris, 1927), pp. 153-210; Liviu Rusu, *Essay sur la creation artistique* (Paris, 1935); below p. 145. Some of these works, especially Rusu's, contain valuable bibliographies on the subject of the creative activity.

[5] John Dewey, *Art as Experience* (New York, 1934), p. 288.

[6] I. A. Richards, *The Principles of Literary Criticism* (New York, 1925), p. 7.

[7] Collingwood, *op. cit.*, p. 295. That literature has at various times exercised profound cognitive influence, both revolutionary and conservative, is a matter of historical record and cannot be denied. For its influence on theology, during the period and area indicated by the title, see L. E. Elliott-Binns, *The Development of English Theology in the Later Nineteenth Century* (London, 1952), pp. 3-5. Theodor Reik confirms something we have known all along when he tells us that in his opinion "it is more useful for the student of psychology to read the great writers—Shakespeare, Dostoevski, Nietzsche, Tolstoy—than *The Psychoanalytic Quarterly*." And he adds, "Our students could learn more and better from such sources . . . than from psychiatric textbooks that muddy the waters with scientific terminology in an effort to make them appear deep." If this is what a psychologist finds in literature, why does not Richards find it? The answer is that empiricists are as given as others to cutting the legs of facts to make them fit into the beds of their theories. Were Richards to admit the fact that in some sense we can learn from literature, his aesthetics would collapse. *Listening with the Third Ear*, (Garden City, 1948), pp. 99-100. In view of the thesis developed in the

last section of this essay, it is interesting to note that Reik distinguishes between the job of the scientist and that of the artist; the artist "shapes" emotional processes of an unconscious kind while the scientist "investigates" them.

8 If the terms "espoused" and "recognized" are not self-explanatory, an account of how they are intended will be found in the writer's *The Moral Life and the Ethical Life* (Chicago, 1950), pp. 71, 190, 217.

9 The evidence for this statement is marshalled by Robert Redfield, *The Primitive World And Its Transformations* (Ithaca, N.Y., 1953), *passim*.

the object of the poem

1 This paper is a revised version of part of the second of two *Mahlon Powell Lectures*, given at Indiana University on 22 and 24 July 1952.

2 John Dewey, *Art as Experience* (New York, 1934), pp. 52 ff.

3 It would seem that all experience, whether outwardly or reflectively addressed, and whether moral, aesthetic, or religious, includes as one of its components a cognitive element, since it involves the more or less clear awareness or discrimination of an object proper to the interest that arouses in the responding mind its dynamic thrust. And it seems probable that all actual experience includes also a moral, an aesthetic, and even perhaps a religious component. We know from anthropology and from history that cultures display a tendency to subordinate and even to exclude the role played by some of these modes and to emphasize others. However, it seems that all experience involves a moral component, since it is purposive, except perhaps in those cases in which the subject loses control of himself and stands bewildered and baffled by what appear to him to be unpatterned events; and as purposive, experience is guided by operative values more or less clearly discernible prior to action, which give it a moral dimension. All experience, it would also appear, involves an aesthetic component, since the act of discrimination of an object or a situation is addressed, if the experience is to achieve completion, to a more or less intransitive apprehension of the object or situation of awareness as a self-sufficient object which is immanently significant. And I also believe that, whether we acknowledge it or not, all experience has a religious component, however recessive, since it discriminates objects which are never in fact unrelated to the total constellation of objects of experience, although in the aesthetic mode of apprehension they appear to be self-sufficient. Reflection, dramatic or technical, discloses the totality of experience to be worthy of a mode of response on

our part which is essentially religious. The internal dialectic of our wonder about the origin of the objects of experience and about the values which give experience substance, and the structures which inform it, pushes us, or, rather, pushes those of us who are bold and free from methodolatrous shackles, and who are concerned with the relation of man to culture, and of both to the universe, out beyond the rim of the positively knowable into areas which fall within the purview of metaphysics and theology.

4 See my "A Definition of the Aesthetic Experience," above, pp. 93-99 and "A Natural History of the Aesthetic Transaction," in *Naturalism and the Human Spirit*, ed. Y. H. Krikorian (New York, 1944), pp. 96-120. The definition of the aesthetic experience to be found in these papers is valid at the phenomenological level, although the metaphysic or, rather, lack of metaphysic, on which they are built is to be deplored.

5 The term "meanings" is used elliptically for "the meanings of a community," in the sense in which, as I take it, some anthropologists use this locution to refer to the structure of the institutionalized arrangements and processes of social life which embody such values as are operative in a community. It is these meanings and the values they sustain that the poet observes consciously or unconsciously and imports, in A. C. Bradley's term, as "subject," into the creative act. A society whose meanings and values are not grasped dramatically is lacking in the human dimension, is blind to the import of its destiny. It is these meanings and values that Robert Redfield, if I understand him, calls "social relations," which of course make possible, from a sociological point of view, the flourishing of a culture. Cf. *The Folk Culture of Yucatan* (Chicago, 1941), p. 13. As here employed the term "culture" refers to the interrelated constellation of activities of a social group, insofar as these activities, the social institutions through which they are carried on, and the physical instrumentalities that make them possible, embody values that enable the group to maintain itself as a purposive, distinctively human society; the meanings are the social structures as value carriers; the culture is the total pattern of values carried in the meanings. I hold that it is the poet's unique function to discover the meanings and values of a society through the act of creation.

6 L. A. Reid, A *Study in Aesthetics* (New York, 1931), p. 251.

7 "Reality in Art," *The University Review*, IV, No. 1 (1937), pp. 36-42. May I be permitted to call attention to the fact that I referred only to consciousness, and not to the whole mind? The mind has depths that consciousness knows not of. I do not deny these depths, and hence do not deny the connections between the object before consciousness and the universe of meaning required to make it a meaningful object.

8 I have argued it for moral values in *The Moral Life and The Ethical Life* (Chicago, 1950), and the arguments hold for aesthetic value; and I sum-

marize the argument in an essay entitled "The Nature of Aesthetics," in *The Return to Reason*, ed. by John Wild (Chicago, 1953), pp. 203-207.

9 The reader's attention is called to the fact that the appeal is not to the competence of the spectator or the sensibility of the critic, who decides on the basis of his idiosyncratic aptitudes or powers: the traits are in the object and if proof is required that they are there it is to the object that reference must be made. But not all readers are equally capable of discerning what is there. See "The Objective Basis of Criticism," below, pp. 191-206.

10 This prejudice is not as generally shared by European thinkers as it is by Americans. For instance, Herman Weyl in *Symmetry* (Princeton, 1952), pp. 6-8, tells us: "Did the artist discover the symmetry with which nature according to some inherent law has endowed its creatures, and then copied and perfected what nature presented but in imperfect realizations; or has the aesthetic value of symmetry an independent source? I am inclined to think with Plato that the mathematical idea is the common origin of both: the mathematical laws governing nature are the origin of symmetry in nature, the intuitive realization of the idea in the creative artist's mind its origin in art . . ." I am, however, going beyond Weyl and saying the creative mind discovers not only mathematical structure, but all kinds of structures and values.

11 The evidence for this assertion? It is to be gathered by anyone who chooses to look into the texture of our Western culture, as expressed in much of our poetry and painting, no less than in our philosophy, for our higher activities are instinct with self-hatred. It is to be found in Proust, in Joyce, in D. H. Lawrence, in Céline, in Paul Bowles, in Henry Miller, just as it can be found in the positivistic and analytic desire to debunk our belief in value and deny the objectivity of the structures which maintain culture. See Henry Miller, "The Universe of Death," in *The Cosmological Eye* (Norfolk, Conn., 1939), but note that the observations made by Miller about Proust and Joyce apply to Miller himself and to D. H. Lawrence, no less than they do to Proust, Joyce and many others of our contemporaries.

naturalism and creativity

1 *Naturalism and the Human Spirit*, edited by Yervant H. Krikorian (New York, 1944), p. 381. This volume will be referred to hereafter as *Naturalism*.

It is advisable to note "for the record" that the author of this note is one of the contributors to *Naturalism*. But if he once called himself a naturalist, the reader of his contribution to this book will notice, as one of the philosophers who reviewed it noticed, that even when he accepted the label, he was far from sharing the temper of the naturalist philosophy as represented by the majority of his fellow contributors.

[2] *Naturalism,* p. 252.

[3] Clark L. Hull, "Mind, Mechanism, and Adaptive Behavior," in *Psychological Review,* Vol. 44, No. I, p. 32 ff.

[4] R. W. Gerard, "The Biological Basis of Imagination," in *The Scientific Monthly,* Vol. LXII, June 1946, p. 487.

[5] *Naturalism,* p. 257.

[6] H. Poincaré, *The Foundations of Science.* Authorized translation by G. G. Halsted (New York, 1929), pp. 383 ff.

[7] John Dewey, *Art as Experience,* (New York, 1934), p. 70 and *passim.*

[8] *Naturalism,* p. 183.

criticism, intrinsic and extrinsic

[1] This paper is a revised version of part of the first of two *Mahlon Powell Lectures* given at Indiana University on 22 and 24 July 1952.

[2] "Archetype and Signature," *The Sewanee Review,* Spring 1952; see Mr. Brooks' reply in the Winter 1953 issue of *Sewanee.*

the objective correlative of T. S. Eliot

[1] John Crowe Ransom, *The New Criticism* (Norfolk, Conn., 1941), p. 145.

[2] T. S. Eliot, *Selected Essays* (New York, 1932), p. 124.

[3] *The Sacred Wood,* Essays on Poetry and Criticism (New York, 1930), pp. 47-59; and *Selected Essays,* pp. 3-12; The long passage quoted in the following paragraph is found on pp. 54 and 8 respectively, and is the same commented on by Ransom (*op. cit.* p. 153).

[4] This important distinction is frequently overlooked, though attention has often been called to it. See "A Definition of The Aesthetic Experience," above, pp. 93-99.

[5] As evidence I should like to cite only two eminent writers on aesthetics, representing different philosophic points of view. In his *The Aesthetic Judgment* (New York, 1929) D. W. Prall, a realist, argues, in section 5

of Chapter X and in the following chapters, that the arts express feelings and emotions precisely. But when he tries to tell us *how* the expression takes place, all I am able to find is his eloquent asseveration that the arts do express feelings and emotions. The same thing is true of Th. M. Greene, in whose idealistic treatise, *The Arts and The Art of Criticism* (Princeton, N. J., 1940) will be found an excellent discussion of our problem, in pp. 113-15, and in Chapters XV and XIX. But Mr. Greene does not tell us *by what means*, or *how*, does an art express feeling. This is what aesthe-ticians have not made clear.

6 *The Sacred Wood*, p. 14.

7 F. O. Matthiessen, *The Achievement of T. S. Eliot*; (New York, 1947) p. 57.

8 A translation of the "Llanto" by Lloyd Mallan appeared in *The Southern Review*, Winter, 1941.

9 Eliot, who in his criticism is anything but a systematic thinker, should have known this. See *The Use of Poetry and The Use of Criticism* (London, 1933), p. 138.

10 Susanne K. Langer, *Philosophy in a New Key* (Cambridge, Mass., 1942) Chapter VIII.

11 I. A. Richards, *Principles of Literary Criticism*, (London, 1925) Chapter XXII.

the objective basis of criticism

1 I have tried to elucidate the difficult problems involved in these claims in "The Nature of Aesthetics," in *The Return to Reason*, Ed. John Wild, (Chicago, 1953), 203-07, and for moral values, in *The Moral Life and The Ethical Life* (Chicago 1950) *passim.*

four notes on I. A. Richards' aesthetic theory

1 London, 1925. The epigraph is taken from p. 235 of this work.

2 See, as instance of the claims made for him by his followers, *The Week End Review* for December 24, 1932, p. 182. Not long ago the writer heard a Professor in a middle-western university assert with emphasis that Richards "had made the greatest contribution to aesthetics since Aristotle."

3 *Principles* 3, 274, and preceding note.

4 *Principles*, Chapter xi to xv, xxxi to xxxiii; *Science and Poetry* (New York, 1926) Chapters ii to iv; C. K. Ogden, I. A. Richards and James Wood, *The Foundations of Aesthetics* (New York, 1929), Chapter xiv.

5 *Principles* 244 ff.

6 See note 3.

7 *Principles* 250.

8 The number of times throughout his works that he uses this excuse to account for his failure to clarify some important point or other is legion; here only a few can be cited: *Principles* 50, 86, 89, 94, 95, 112, 113, 154, 170, 172, 173, 230, 248, 251; *Practical Criticism* (New York, 1929), 278, 322.

9 *Principles* 243. See also 61, 67, 109, 111, 132, 235, 249, 283.

10 *The Will to Power* (Edinburgh, 1910) II 245, 803. See also II 241, 799, 800.

11 *Principles* 234.

12 *Principles* 235. Also *Practical Criticism* 276.

13 *Principles* 235.

14 *Principles* 2, 23. *Practical Criticism*, Part III, Chap. viii.

15 *Principles* 202 ff., 230 ff.

16 *Ibid.* 21.

17 *Ibid.* 22.

18 *Ibid.* 21.

19 *Ibid.* 21.

20 *Foundations* 63.

21 *Principles* 135.

22 *Ibid.* 139.

23 *Ibid.* 150.

24 *Ibid.* Chapters viii, ix, x.

25 *Ibid.* 23.

26 *Practical Criticism*, especially Part III, Chapter iv; *Principles*, Chaps. xvii to xx, especially 139-145, 149-159, 165-167, 171-173; see also 212, 222, 224.

27 See also his constant use of objective categories of description in *Practical Criticism*, Chapter viii, and note how in Chapter iv (227) of the same book he is forced to redefine rhythm in objective terms, in a footnote, because the psychophysical terms in which he had previously defined it in the *Principles* are of no use at all when he wishes to discuss poetic form.

28 *Ibid.* 60, also 7, 32, 203, 231.

29 *Ibid.* Chaps. xvi and xxx, especially 114 and 224.

30 *Ibid.* 199.

31 *Ibid.* Chapters xxiv, xxvi, xxvii.

32 References to the competent reader or his various aliases are numerous throughout both *The Principles* and *Practical Criticism*. Here only a few are cited from the former: 10, 97, 156, 166, 178, 192, 224, and 252.

33 *Principles* Chap. xxx.

34 *Ibid.* 225.

35 *Ibid.* 225.

36 *Ibid.* 226.

37 *Ibid.* 227.

38 *Ibid.* 226.

39 *Practical Criticism* II.

40 *Principles* 23. See also Chap. vii, especially 47, 52.

41 *Ibid.* 46.

42 *Ibid.* 52.

43 *Principles*, *passim*, especially 47, 51, and *Science and Poetry* 42, wherein he tells us: "The more [a man] lives and the less he thwarts himself the better. That briefly is our answer as *psychologists*, as outside observers *abstractly describing* the state of affairs." (Italics not in the text.)

[44] Richards himself does not ignore this: He tells us (*Science and Poetry* 63): Science "can only tell us how so and so behaves. And it does not attempt to do more than this. Nor, indeed, can more than this be done." Yet see the preceding note.

a note on the emotion in Dewey's theory of art

[1] John Dewey, *Art as Experience* (New York, 1934). See Chs. I, III, XI, and XII, especially pp. 42, 67, 249, 254, 273-274. All page references following are from this book unless otherwise indicated.

[2] P. 69.

[3] P. 74. The following quotations and references will be found in pp. 76, 238 and 239 respectively. But see, also, 42, 70, 73, 76, 79, 86, 257.

[4] Pp. 67, 68, 79, 233, 237, 238, 257. There is still another view of the function of the emotion developed by Mr. Dewey. But since it refers to the creative act and not to the act of enjoyment, we may, for the purposes of this analysis, disregard it. Pp. 15, 42, 75, 257, where the emotion is said to be the moving and cementing force of the activity of the artist.

[5] Vernon Lee, *Music and its Lovers*, (New York, 1933) p. 28. The writer uses Vernon Lee's facts, which he considers of extreme importance, but would not always subscribe to her psychological interpretations.

[6] P. 83.

[7] P. 164.

[8] P. 174.

[9] Pp. 273 ff., also 242, "music is brutally organic."

[10] P. 249. See also p. 103 and Chs. I, III, VII, VIII, XI, and XII, especially pp. 246 ff.

[11] P. 15; also 42.

[12] "To limit aesthetic emotion to the pleasure attending the act of contemplation is to exclude all that is most characteristic of it," p. 257.

[13] "The Theory of Emotion." (II). "The Significance of Emotions." *The Psychological Review*, II (1895), 13-32.

Jordan's defense of poetry

[1] This study of *Essays in Criticism* (Chicago, 1952) was presented to The Metaphysical Society of America at its meeting 19 March 1952. In a severely compressed form it was published by *The Review of Metaphysics*, Vol. VIII, No. 1. Numbers between parentheses after direct quotations or after the treatment of Jordan's ideas refer to this book unless otherwise indicated.

[2] I read this statement as follows: poetry is literally the creator of and the legislator for the real world, the world of culture. As given us by Jordan it seems to me grammatically defective and that this is what he means can be inferred from numerous statements he makes, for instance: Words "are elementary constituents of the system of the nature of things" (16). They "are not signs" (34). Through words "the world itself has status, and it is they that are behind everything so far as reality is a cultural system" (44). "The poet is, with and because of his words, not only the legislator to mankind but also the maker for mankind of the world that makes Man" (53). "Nature is only real as art makes it so" (73). "Art is then the creator, the Demiurge" (79). "Art came into existence to create the real that actuality could only approximate" (258).

[3] The reader ought to be warned that Jordan rejects the language of this last paragraph, since the word "experience," which he did not hesitate to use in *The Aesthetic Object*, has been pressed into use, in his more recent work, to refer to the source of all evil—the subjective, the purely private, the idiotic. As here used it does not refer to the private, the idiotic. "Experience" may refer to the subjective aspect of perception or knowledge, and to its object, and also to the relational complex which includes the subject and the object; there is no need to degrade it or reduce it in meaning.

[4] A large number of passages could be cited to support this one. See for instance 30, 36, 46, 80, 110, 120. There are others.

[5] Let me confine myself to the ethnolinguistic evidence, of which I am less ignorant than the psychological. In the light of the hypothesis that has been suggested by students of language like Sapir, Whorf and Hoijer, we can pose the question whether language does not at least in part help to rear the world of culture in which man lives. Hoijer's formulation of the hypothesis which he credits Sapir and Whorf with cannot be dismissed as wholly idealistic speculation. As Hoijer puts it,

peoples speaking different languages may be said to live in different 'worlds of reality,' in the sense that the languages they speak affect to a considerable degree, both their sensory perceptions and their habitual modes of thought.

See Harry Hoijer, "The Relation of Language to Culture" in *Anthropology Today, an Encyclopedic Inventory*. Prepared under the chairmanship of A. L. Kroeber (Chicago, 1953), p. 558A.

aesthetics and theory of signs

[1] This essay is a revision and expansion of part of the second of two *Mahlon Powell Lectures* given at Indiana University on 22 and 24 of July, 1952.

[2] Among criticisms of Morris' theory, I have pre-eminently in mind Allen Tate's shrewd analysis, "Literature and Knowledge," in *On the Limits of Poetry* (New York, 1948). I have used only Morris' "Esthetics and the Theory of Signs," *The Journal of Unified Science*, VIII, Nos. 1-3 (1939), pp. 131-150. Page numbers between parentheses following quotations or statements about Morris' theory refer to this article. *The Kenyon Review* article (1939) is a popularized version of this one. And the material on aesthetics to be found in *Signs, Language and Behavior* (New York, 1946) is, for my purposes, of no use whatever. Whether it has value for the semiotician I do not know.

[3] That Morris is following Dewey we need not be told. It is obvious. But he acknowledges it freely. *Journal of Unified Science* article (Note 1, p. 132).

[4] Arthur W. Burks, "Icon, Index and Symbol," *Philosophy and Phenomenological Research*, Vol. IX, No. 4, p. 675.

[5] This is not to deny that a work of art can function as an imitation and as a work of art proper, or as a mixed affair, both as imitation and aesthetically. It is to assert, however, that what gives it its quality as work of art is not something we as perceivers project into it but that it possesses in itself. What it possesses is freshness and that kind of organization that can elicit the intransitive attention of the perceiver. Nor is this to assert that there is something inherently wrong in using a work of art for non-aesthetic purposes. It is merely to draw distinctions which are called for by the exigencies of our need to understand what is art and how it differs from other kinds of things we find in culture.

[6] Dewey, whose aesthetics Morris tells us he has transposed into the language of semiosis, does not make the mistake of assuming that the object of the poem exists independently of the linguistic medium. Dewey tells us that the meanings of art "present themselves as possession of the objects which are experienced . . . the meaning is as inherent in immediate experience as is that of a flower garden." *Art as Experience* (New York, 1934), p. 83. By means of the term "icon" Morris seems to follow Dewey on this point at

the explicit level. But in translating the aesthetic of Dewey into the language of semiotics, he re-introduces one of the basic errors against which contemporary aestheticians of the most diverse variety of affiliation have struggled more or less successfully—for it is not Dewey alone who repudiates the archaic theory of imitation.

[7] I hope I am not altogether ignorant of the fact that art historians are not all of one mind as regards the identity of the woman who posed for *La Maja Desnuda*. If it was not la Cayetana, it was some one else who posed, and it would be she who would provide the semiotician with a complete consummation. See Juan de la Encina, *Goya, su mundo histórico y poético* (Mexico, 1939), 91 ff.; Blanco Soler, Piga Pascual, Perez de Petinto, *La Duquesa de Alba y su tiempo* (Madrid, 1949), *passim*.

[8] *poetry*, Vol. 80, No. 3, pp. 153-58. There are a few instances in which the typographical arrangement of the poem is part of the revelatory vehicle, and we are all acquainted with the claims that have been made for the Chinese ideograph. Insofar as these factors are operative it may be argued that the poem is to some extent iconic. But the argument—in some of its possible forms at least—would then be open to the criticisms that are made of the iconic theory of painting. In any case, an adequate theory of poetry cannot be based on such relatively unimportant facts, although a minor movement was, not so long ago, if I understood its claims at all.

[9] Richard Rudner, "On Semiotic Aesthetics," *The Journal of Aesthetics and Art Criticism*, Vol. X, No. 1, p. 74.

Allen Tate as man of letters

[1] This piece confines itself to the ideas found in *The Forlorn Demon, Didactic and Critical Essays* (Chicago, 1953). For a more comprehensive study of Mr. Tate's views, see the essay of Mr. Monroe K. Spears, in *The Sewanee Review*, for Spring, 1949 entitled "The Criticism of Allen Tate."

index

Achievement of T. S. Eliot, The (Matthiessen), 293

Aesthetic experience, and attention, 95
and emotion, 93-95, 99, 225
as intransitive, 95-96, 131-133, 171
and the self, 234
as mediate and immediate, 264-265
varieties of, 94, 210, 211-212, 228

Aesthetic judgment, correction of, 196, 197, 199, 200, 205
and criticism, 193-194
kinds of (Richards), 213-214, 219
and objectivity, 192, 193-194, 200, 203

Aesthetic Judgment (Prall), 286, 292

Aesthetic object, and attention, 97
and iconic sign, 251, 254
presuppositions of, 114
purity of, 172
self-sufficiency of, 106, 116, 168, 236-237
structure of, 187
See also Object of art; Poem, object of

Aesthetic Object, The (Jordan), 229, 239, 240, 297

Aesthetics, and criticism, 162, 191-192, 205-206
field of, 90-91, 137, 231
and morality, 204-205
scientific, 210, 217
semiotic, 252

Alexander, Samuel, 288

Allegory, 33

Ambassadors, The (Henry James), 26

Anderson, Maxwell, 288

Antigone (Sophocles), 170

"Archetype and Signature" (Fiedler), 292

Arnold, Mathew, 231

Art, abstract (Morris), 255, 263

Apollonian and Dionysian, 212
autonomy of, 97, 162, 167-168, 235-236
and culture, 126-127, 232
and emotion, 180, 224-225
function of, 31-32, 74, 143, 210, 212-213, 231
and imagination, 237
and life, 122
as organic, 77
and reality, 133, 232
and religion, 108-109
and science, 120

semantic dimension of, 254-255
traits of, 214-217
and truth, 42
See also Aesthetic Object

Art as Experience (Dewey), 288, 292, 296, 298

Artist, experience of, 118
function of, 122
intention of, 163-165, 199
normality of, 218
problems of, 154
and society, 166-167
and tradition, 203-204

Arts and the Art of Criticism, The (Greene), 293

Attention, and aesthetic experience, 95, 97, 121, 172
and emotion, 96, 227-228
as intransitive, 133

Babbitt, Irving, 203

Basch, Victor, 231

Basis of Artistic Creation in the Arts, The (ed. Anderson), 288

Beach, J. W., 17

Beauty and Human Nature (Chandler), 286, 288

*Beauty and Other Forms
  of Value* (Alexander),
  288
Behaviorism, 146, 151,
  155
Berdyaev, N., 118
Bergson, Henri, 23, 120
Berkeley, G., 205
"Biological Basis of
  Imagination, The"
  (Gerard), 292
Blackmur, R. P., 231
Blanshard, Brand, 288
Boas, Franz, 244
Bowles, Paul, 291
Bradley, A. C., 77, 102,
  129, 288
Brod, Max, 30, 31, 33, 40
Brooks, Cleanth, 77, 162
Brooks, V. W., 122-123
Brothers Karamazov, The
  (Dostoevski), 170
Bullough, E., 225
Burks, A. W., 298

Cántico (St. John of the
  Cross), 259-260
Cassirer, E., 74, 82
Castle, The (Kafka), 35,
  36-38
Céline, L. F., 112-117,
  291
Chandler, A., 286, 288
Coleridge, S. T., 149
*Collected Essays and Re-
  views* (James), 285
Collingwood, R. G., 79,
  101, 288
Communication, 73, 80-
  81
Conception and expres-
  sion, 155
Consciousness, stream of,
  in W. & H. James,
  24-25
Content of poem, 185
  See also, Substance;
  Matter
Coplas (J. Manrique),
  168, 169
Cosmological Eye, The
  (Miller), 291
Craft of Fiction, The
  (Lubbock), 77
Creation, and behavior-
  ism, 151-155

and discovery, 90, 104,
  120, 123-124, 127,
  140, 143, 154, 188-
  189, 237-238
and emotion, 186, 224
and intention, 163
and language, 136-137
nature of, 104, 124
and transformation of
  forms, 102, 104, 151,
  262-263
Creativity, grounds for,
  106
and iconic theory, 262
and imitation, 156, 253
knowledge of, 108, 153
and poetry, 106, 112
and science, 104-105,
  147, 148, 157
Criticism, conservative,
  275
contemporary, 274
function of, 31, 34-35,
  114, 119, 191-193,
  216
intrinsic, 164
Marxist, 275
and psychoanalysis,
  115, 275
and value, 201, 217
"Criticism of Allen Tate,
  The" (Spears), 299
Croce, B., 79, 101, 155,
  288
Culture, and art, 126-127,
  139, 141, 244-245
and Jordan's aesthetics,
  231
philosophy of, 231
and values, 139

Data of Ethics (Spencer),
  22, 285
Delacroix, Henri, 288
Denotatum, 250-251
Designatum, 250-251
*Development of English
  Theology in the
  Later Nineteenth
  Century, The*
  (Elliott-Binns), 288
Dewey, John, and creativ-
  ity, 155-156
on empathy, 95
and Morris, 250
on reflexive meanings,
  171

on uniqueness of art,
  108, 263
on subject-object,
  226-228
Cited, 286, 288, 289,
  292, 296, 298
"Dewey's Esthetic The-
  ory" (Shearer), 287
Disbelief, suspension of,
  107
Discovery and creation,
  (*See* Creation)
Dostoevski, F., anti-rationalism of, 69-70
Berdyaev on, 118
conservatism of, 59
doubt of, 62
and Freud, 51, 54
on God, 49, 56
on human destiny,
  60-61
ideas in, 50-51, 118
and immortality, 65-66
and Kafka, 41, 48
on liberal, 52-58
as psychologist,
  48, 51, 58
and socialism, 60-61
and "type," 52
unconscious in, 55
Dreiser, Theodore, and
  contemporary
  naturalism, 4, 5
contradiction in, 9-10
individualism in, 5
on meaning of life,
  7-8, 12
moral theory of, 6
and value, 9
*Duquesa de Alba y su
  tiempo, La* (Soler,
  et al), 299

Einstein, Alfred, 105
Eliot, T. S., and auton-
  omy of poetry, 75-76
and emotion, 94
and Jordan, 230
on poet's task, 268
on Richards, 110
Cited, 286, 292
Elliott-Binns, L. E., 288
Emotion, and aesthetic
  experience, 93-94, 99
aroused by art, 180,
  224-225

and attention, 96,
    227-228
and creative activity,
    184-186
and expression, 223-224
and feeling, 96,
    177-178
and music, 85-86
and objective charac-
    ters, 225-226
and objective correla-
    tive, 175-176, 179
sui generis, aesthetic,
    215
Empathy theory, 94-95
*Essai sur la creation artis-
    tique* (Rusu), 288
Essays in Criticism
    (Jordan), 229, 297
*Essays in Radical Empiri-
    cism* (James), 27
"Esthetics and the Theory
    of Signs" (Morris),
    298
Ethics of Rhetoric, The
    (Weaver), 270
Existence, 79, 138, 141,
    238
Experience, and creativity,
    152, 186, 219
modes of, 120-121, 130,
    289-290
organization of, 117-
    120, 121-122
standard of, 219
and value, 146, 197-198,
    217-218
See also Aesthetic
    experience
Expression, and concep-
    tion, 155
and emotion, 223-224
in poetry, 188
theory, 188
"Ezra Pound and the
    Bollingen Prize"
    (Tate), 280

Fallacy, intentional,
    162-165
of projection, 215
Feeling, and emotion,
    96, 177-178
and language, 178-179
in Prall, 95
Feibleman, J. K., 126
Feidelson, Charles, 74, 75

Fiedler, Leslie, 161-162,
    167, 172
Fitness of language,
    135-136
Flores, Ángel, (ed.), 29,
    285
*Folk Culture of Yucatan,
    The* (Redfield), 290
Forlorn Demon, The
    (Tate), 280-281, 299
Form, and attention, 97-98
and creative activity,
    261, 262
Jordan on, 238-239
and matter, 102, 104
in poem, 131-132, 185
and substance, 103
Formalism, rejection of,
    137
*Foundations of Aesthetics,
    The* (Ogden et al),
    294
Freud, S., 30, 47, 48, 115,
    147

Garcia Lorca, 182-187
Gerard, R. W., 147-148,
    292
Giotto, .181
Golden Bowl, The
    (James), 16, 26
*Goya, su mundo histórico
    y poético* (de la
    Encina), 299
Grammar and rhetoric,
    270
Gray, Cecil, 102
Greene, T. M., 101. 202

Hamlet, 164, 176, 189
Hartshorne, Charles, 243
Hoijer, H., 81, 297, 298
Hull, C., 147-148, 292
Humanism, literary,
    203-204

Icon, and meaning, 107,
    171
semantical dimension,
    257
"Icon, Index and Symbol"
    (Burks), 298
Idealism, 236
Ideas and poetry (Jordan),
    244-247
Identity, analogical (Jor-
    dan), 238, 240-241

Idiot, The (Dostoevski),
    62
Image in constitutive
    process, 82
Imagination, active,
    149-150
and art, 233, 237,
    239-242
as cognitive, 239
and criticism, 242-243
Imagists, 83
Imitation, and art, 255-256
and creativity, 32, 85,
    110, 140, 156, 253
and expression, 79,
    123-124, 188-189
and literalness, 253
and object of poem,
    138-139
objections to, 103, 104,
    105, 137
and philosophic criti-
    cism, 32
and semiotic aesthetics,
    252
Impressionism, 25
Intelligence, task of, 280
Intention of artist,
    163-165, 261
Interest and value, 197
Intransitivity (*See*
    Aesthetic experience)

James, Henry, and his
    brother, 15, 16, 20,
    22, 27
on Dostoevski, 48
ethical neutrality in,
    17-18
"germs" of stories, 119
last phase, 165
Leavis on, 165
and morality, 17
Notebooks, 77, 117,
    124
Prefaces, 77
value of consciousness,
    16-17
James, William, on art
    and reality, 132
criticism of Henry, 16
moral Darwinism of, 21
will to believe, 44
Cited, 287
John of the Cross, St.,
    259-260

Jordan, E., central thesis
    of, 231-232
    difficulties in, 229-230
*Journey to the End of the
    Night* (Celine), 112-
    117, 123

Kafka, Franz, comedy in,
    43
    conception of existence
        in, 34, 40-46
    and contemporary nat-
        uralism, 45
    criticism of, 130-135
    empiricism in, 41
    failure of, 32-33
    mytho-poetic world of,
        33-34
    as psychologist, 48
    short stories of, 39-40
Kant, I., and Cassirer, 74
    on disinterested interest,
        121
    and mind as constitu-
        tive, 80
Kierkegaard, S., and Dos-
        toevski, 58, 69
    and Kafka, 32, 41, 43-44
Knowledge, in art, 103,
        108, 125-126
    and novelty, 108
Krieger, Murray, 91
Krikorian, Y. H., 146, 286,
        291
Kroeber, A. L., 298

la Encina, de, J., 299
Langer, S. K., 107, 171,
        185-186, 293
Language, as constitutive,
        81, 84, 136-137
    and culture, 233
    and experience, 168-169
    function of, 232, 236,
        264, 269-270
    as iconic, 260
    and its objects, 133-135
    as ostensive, 133, 262
    and poetry, 74-75, 80,
        131, 135, 167, 262
    reigning theory of, 75,
        78-79, 86
Lawrence, D. H., 164-165,
        291
Leavis, F. R., 165
Lee, Vernon, 94, 225, 286,
        287, 296

*Letters from the Under-
    world* (Dostoevski),
        69, 70
Lewis, C. I., 194
Life and art, 122
Linguistic analysis and
    poetry, 91
Listener, 226
*Listening with the Third
    Ear* (Reik), 288
Literature, (*See* Art;
    Poem; Poetry)
"Literature and Knowl-
    edge" (Tate), 298
"Llanto por Ignacio San-
    chez Mejias" (Garcia
    Lorca), 182-187, 293
Lorca (*See* Garcia Lorca)
Love in poetry (Jordan),
        245-246
Lubbock, Percy, 77

Mack, Robert, 241
Magny, C., 29, 34
Malraux, André, 118-119
"Man of Letters in the
    Modern World, The"
    (Tate), 268
Mann, Thomas, 230
Manrique, Jorge, 168, 169
Matter and form, 102, 104
Matthiessen, F. O., 180,
        293
McKeon, R., 103, 124
Meaning, in art, 107
    immanent, 95-96, 171-
        172, 287
    and language, 236
    See also Language
Meaning of Music, The
    (Pratt), 286
Meanings, and culture,
        139
    as possessions of objects,
        225-226
Metamorphosis (Kafka),
        40, 78, 126
Metaphor, 233, 239, 241
Mind, as constitutive, 80,
        82, 84, 88, 233-239
    our knowledge of, 148
    naturalistic theory of,
        145
    and object, 234
    of poet (Eliot), 177,
        179
    spontaneity of, 106

"Mind, Mechanism and
    Adaptive Behavior"
    (Hull), 292
*Moral Life and the Ethical
    Life, The* (Vivas),
        289, 290, 293
*Moral Philosopher and the
    Moral Life, The*
    (James), 21
Music, Dewey on, 226
    and emotion, 85-86
Music and Its Lovers
    (Lee), 286, 296
Myers, C. S., 225

"Natural History of the
    Aesthetic Transac-
    tion, A" (Vivas), 286
Naturalism, and Dostoev-
    ski, 58
    and Dreiser, 4
    and Kafka, 45
    and scientific method,
        146
*Naturalism and the Hu-
    man Spirit* (Kri-
    korian), 286, 291
"Nature of Aesthetics"
    (Vivas), 291, 293
Nature of Thought, The
    (Blanshard), 288
Neo-Aristotelians, 91
New Criticism, The (Ran-
    som), 175, 292
Nietzsche, F., and Kierke-
    gaard, 69
    and Richards, 211
Nims, J. F., 259-260
Notebooks (James), 77,
        117, 124
*Notes from the Under-
    ground* (Dostoevski),
        63
Novelty (*See* Creativity)

Object of art, how re-
    vealed, 80-83, 87-90,
        253, 254
    status of, 133-137, 238-
        239
Objective correlative and
    association, 181, 185-
        186
Objectivity, and criticism,
        191-192, 197-198
    meaning of, 194

of characters, 225-226
and poetry, 140
"Objectivity of Esthetic
    Value" (Pratt), 286
Objects and words, 236
Ogden, C. K., 294
On the Limits of Poetry
    (Tate), 298
Onomatopoeia, 135, 260,
    262
Organicism, 103
Organization of experi-
    ence, 117-118, 210,
    214, 218
"Ought," aesthetic, 126

Painting, object of, 254
Paraphrase, 134-135, 253
Parker, D. H., 77
Pascual, P., 299
Pepper, S. C., 194
Pei, Mario, 236
Peirce, C. S., 171, 250
"Perfect Critic, The"
    (Eliot), 180
Petinto, de, P., 299
Philosopher and poetry,
    244-245
Philosophy in a New Key
    (Langer), 293
Plato, and aesthetic knowl-
    edge, 103
    and dialectics, 201
    and existence, 139
    and Kafka, 40
Pluralistic Universe, The
    (James), 27
Poe, Edgar Allan, 104, 276
Poem, and artist's experi-
    ence, 219
    defined, 73, 90, 219
    and metaphor, 239
    object of, 78, 80, 87,
        134, 135, 262, 264
    and ontology, 172
    and poet, 90
    as self-sufficient, 76,
        106, 112, 132, 171
    See also Aesthetic
        object; Art; Object
        of art
Poems in Process (Bart-
    lett), 288
Poet, availability of his
    experience, 186
    and creative activity,
        261

function of, 87, 122-123
limitations of, 246-247
mind of (Eliot), 177
and philosopher, 246
Tate on, 268-271
See also Artist
Poetry, as autonomous,
    75, 168, 171
    and culture, 139, 141,
        232, 236, 244-245
    and emotion, 176,
        179-185
    and existence, 78, 141
    and ideas, 244-245
    and insistence, 138
    and language, 74-75, 80,
        131, 133, 167, 262
    as normative, 125, 126,
        140
    and objectivity, 140
    and subsistence,
        137-138
    and tradition, 203
    senses of, 243
    and values, 259
"Poetry for Poetry's Sake"
    (Bradley), 288
Poetics (Aristotle),
    123-124
Poincaré, Henri, 152, 292
Positivist, 79, 271, 272
Possessed, The (Dostoev-
    ski), 48, 49, 60, 61,
    174
Pound, Ezra, 230
Practical Criticism (Rich-
    ards), 220, 294, 295
Prall, D. W., 94, 95, 286,
    293
Pratt, C. C., 286
Primitive World and Its
    Transformations, The
    (Redfield), 289
Principles of Art, The
    (Collingwood), 288
Principles of Literary
    Criticism, The (Rich-
    ards), 109, 162-163,
    209, 288, 293
Principles of Psychology,
    The (W. James), 23,
    287
Problems of Aesthetics,
    The (ed. Vivas and
    Krieger), 91
Proto-image, 82-83
Proust, Marcel, 23, 291

Psychoanalysis (See
    Freud)
Psychologie de l'Art
    (Delacroix), 288
Psychology, and aesthetics,
    213-214, 217
    and value, 220-221

Qualities, objective, criti-
    cized, 215

Rahv, P., 35
Randall, J. H., 145, 271
Ransom, J. C., 175, 292
Reader, competent,
    218-219
    and historical scholar,
        170-171
    and poem, 136, 173
Realism, axiological, 141
    and language, 243
Reality, and art, 120, 132-
        133, 187-188, 232,
        239
    meanings of, 89, 120,
        141
"Reality in Art" (Vivas),
    287, 290
Reason, 63, 69-70,
    240-241
Redfield, Robert, 287,
    289, 290
Reichenbach, H., 271
Reid, L. A., 95, 132, 286,
    287, 290
Reik, T., 288
"Relation of Language to
    Culture, The"
    (Hoijer), 298
Relativism, objective, 111,
    225, 250
Religion, and art, 108-109
    and socialism (Dostoev-
        ski), 60, 65
Religious type, in Dostoev-
    ski, 54, 68
Representation
    (See Imitation)
Return to Reason, The
    (ed. Wild), 291, 293
Rhetoric, 269-270
Rhythm and emotion, 261
Richards, I. A., on
    aesthetic experience,
        162-163
    defense of poetry,
        108-109, 231

on Eliot, 110
and knowledge in art, 108-109
on poet's experience, 186
Cited, 288, 293, 294
Rudner, R., 264, 299
Rusu, L., 288

Sacred Fount, The (James), 17
Sacred Wood, The (Eliot), 286, 292, 293
Sailing to Byzantium (Yeats), 259, 263
Sapir, E., 83, 297
Schopenhauer, A., 69, 188
Schweitzer, A., 102
Science, and art, 120-121
and value, 221
Science and Poetry (Richards), 294, 295
Scientist, on man, 271-272
Tate on, 270-271
Selected Essays (Eliot), 292
Semiosis and creativity, 262
"Semiotic Aesthetics, On" (Rudner), 299
Shakespeare, 189, 230
Shearer, E. A., 287
Shelley, P., 230
Sign, iconic, 251
indexical, 254
defined, 250
and meaning, 107, 171, 257
and values, 255
"Significance of Emotions, The" (Dewey), 296
Signs, Language and Behavior (Morris), 298
Simmons, E. J., 59
Singer, Milton, 287
Society and artist, 122, 166-167
Soler, B., 299
Sophocles, 170
Spears, Monroe K., 299
Spencer, Herbert, 22, 285
Spoils of Poynton, The (James), 18-20, 119
Spontaneity (*See* Creativity)

Stein, Arnold, 77
Stein, Gertrude, 28, 230
Stimulus and image, 82
Structure and value, 195, 199
Study in Aesthetics, A (Reid), 286, 290
Style, Dreiser's, 3, 4
and psychological knowledge, 25-26
H. James', 26-27
Subject matter, and artist's experience, 118
of the poem, 129-130
See also Matter; Substance
Subjectivism in Richards, 219-220
Subsistence and poetry, 137-138
Substance, informed, 102, 103
of the poem, 129-130
Symbol, presentational, 107, 171
Symbolism and American Literature (Feidelson), 74
Symmetry (Weyl), 291
Synthesis, creative, 153

Taste, and aesthetic judgment, 202
correction of, 194
Tate, Allen, on Descartes, 278-280
on literature and knowledge, 101, 299
and new criticism, 273
on poet, 268
Cited, 298, 299
Tenor (Richards), 32
"Theory of Emotion, The" (Dewey), 296
"To Whom is the Poet Responsible?" (Tate), 273
"Tradition and the Individual Talent" (Eliot), 176, 203
Trial, The (Kafka), 35-36
Truth and art, 42, 256-257

Unamuno, M., 44
Uniqueness of art, 263

Universality, how achieved, 81
and love, 245-246
Universe of Death, The (Miller), 291
Use of Poetry and the Use of Criticism, The (Eliot), 293

Valuation, and *a priori*, 221
and private factors, 146, 203
Value, and aesthetic object, 195, 199, 251
and criticism, 201, 217
and culture, 139
and desire, 142-143, 220
espoused, 289
and interest, 81-82, 197
locus of, 195
and poetry, 259
recognized, 289
and signs, 255
Value theory, Richards', 220
Vehicle (Richards), 33
Vogt, V. O., 101

Waste Land, The (Eliot), 110-11
Weaver, Richard, 269-270
Weitz, Morris, 101-103
Wells, H. G., 17
Weyl, H., 291
Whitman, W., 122-123
Whorf, B. L., 81, 297
Wild, John, 291, 293
Wilde, Oscar, 122
Will to Believe, The (James), 285
Will to Power, The (Nietzsche), 294
Wings of the Dove, The (James), 16
Wood, J., 294
Woolf, Virginia, 28
Words and objects, 236
Wordsworth, W., 226, 230
Wright, Andrew, 77
Writer (*See* Artist, Poet)

Yeats, W. B., 230, 245

Zossima, 170